Real FAMILY VALUES

Real

FAMILY VALUES

Keeping the Faith in an Age of Cultural Chaos

ROBERT LEWIS WITH RICH CAMPBELL

VISION HOUSE™
PUBLISHING, INC.
Gresham, Oregon 97030

REAL FAMILY VALUES

© 1995 by Robert Lewis

Published by Vision House Publishing, Inc.
1217 NE Burnside, Suite 403
Gresham, Oregon 97030

Edited by Stephen T. Barclift

Printed in the United States of America

International Standard Book Number: 1-885305-22-2

95 96 97 98 99 00 01 02 03 04 — 10 9 8 7 6 5 4 3 2 1

To my children:

Sherard Elizabeth
Rebekah Helen
Robert Garrett
William Mason

Your mom and I pray that when you leave our home,
you will take with you deep roots,
strong wings, and GOD's heart.

CONTENTS

SECTION I
YOUR FAMILY AND THE BOLD NEW WORLD

SECTION II
YOUR FAMILY AND REAL FAMILY VALUES

SECTION III
YOUR FAMILY AND ONGOING
SOCIAL CONTROVERSIES

ACKNOWLEDGMENTS

To the following people I owe a special debt of gratitude:

Tracy Noble—My super secretary and administrative assistant who handles every assignment with a cheerful heart! Thank you. You make work fun and you perform it with excellence.

Nancy Deas—Thanks for the hours you spent proofreading the manuscript.

Craig and Judy Cheney; Jerry and Camille Richardson—Thanks for reviewing the manuscript and following through on your Family Values assignment. You are dear friends and special role models.

Dennis and Barbara Rainey—Your passion for the family has been a constant inspiration to me. My family is better because of you.

The elders of Fellowship Bible Church:
Mike Boschetti
Tom Hill
Norman Hoggard
Randy Mano
Tim McKenzie
Bill Parkinson
Jerry Richardson
Mike Robinson
Bill Wellons
John White
Dan Woods
—You are humble servants of the church and honorable men in your homes.

Toxic Culture. Sometime in our recent past, American culture went from being a friend of the family to an adversary. Somehow, clear lines of right and wrong—of understanding what "family values" means—were lost under the blanket of a "do your own thing" mentality. Community values that once aligned with, reinforced, and supported marriage and family have all but evaporated. If anything, today's community standards threaten the family. Evolving and ever changing, they allow our airwaves and movie theaters to be drenched with obscenities; justify and glorify all kinds of perversion; grant cheap, easy, no-fault divorce; reward out-of-wedlock pregnancies; promote "safe sex"; undermine parental authority; confuse sex roles; challenge any form of male leadership in the home. The tragic results of this new morality are reported daily. Does your family feel overwhelmed by it?

For children, the cultural chaos is crippling. Children don't grow well in the soil of moral contradiction, moral hypocrisy, and moral ambiguity. Though many parents are alarmed at what they see taking place, few seem willing to accept any responsibility for it. And yet, much of what is happening around us can be traced directly back to the values vacuum and values confusion that lurks at home. Yes, even in *our* homes.

Real Family Values has two objectives. *First, it is designed to help take the moral confusion out of the cultural chaos crashing around us.* Experts tell us our world is in the midst of a historic transition that seeks to redefine all of life. In the midst of all this change, people are growing morally numb. Toxic culture leads to toxic shock. People become blinded to the *real* forces at work behind the changes we are experiencing. Most of us are not aware of the evil values driving these forces, either.

We are confused today. Families drift along, unknowingly embracing values we would knowingly reject. And by the time we discover our folly, it's too late. Hopefully, throughout this book—but especially in Section I ("Your Family and the Bold New World") and Section III ("Your Family and Ongoing Social Controversies")—some of the confusion you are experiencing amidst overwhelming change will begin to clear.

Second, this book is designed to help take the moral confusion out of your home. As you will see in Section II ("Your Family and Real Family Values"), every parent and child is being sorely tested by today's Bold New World. Unmasking and making sense of what is happening, not just to our world but to *us,* is the goal of these seven chapters.

The high point of the book comes in chapter 11. There, you will be challenged to do more than just read a book. I will give you the opportunity to *define your values* and personally stand up to today's moral turbulence. I will ask you to establish in writing *your own real family values.* This could be one of the most important actions you will ever undertake for your family.

Most of us feel overwhelmed by today's world. Much of what we see, we don't like. It seems impossible to halt our headlong plunge into darkness.

Don't you believe it!

You *can* change your world; but not by addressing all of the problems you see. You can change the world by zeroing in on that small, precious part you love and treasure the most: your family. And at the heart of this process stands real family values.

If you're up to meeting the challenge of a toxic culture, rather than succumbing or numbing out to it, turn the page. We have a Bold New World to address!

YOUR FAMILY

and the Bold New World

CHAPTER ONE

WELCOME
to the Bold New World

"The strength of a nation lies in the homes of its people."
ABRAHAM LINCOLN

It all began with a rainstorm somewhere in the upper midwest. In places such as Rushford, Minnesota, and Packard, Iowa, townsfolk went about their usual business, giving little or no thought to the showers falling to earth. After all, this was spring. It always rains in the springtime.

But this year would be different. Very different.

The spring turned into summer. Yet throughout America's heartland, the rains continued to fall. Creek bottoms and gullies churned with soil-tinged water. Huge ponds formed in fields of waist-high corn. Like an advancing army, rivulets and brown tributaries pushed downstream, swelling the banks of rivers with names such as the Raccoon, the Red, and the Missouri. The ultimate objective of these gathering waters was the Mississippi River, an enormous drainage that collects forty percent of the water in the continental United States and dumps 100 trillion gallons annually into the Gulf of Mexico.

On July 8 in Independence, Iowa, more than three inches of rain fell on already water-logged fields. Three days later, another three inches tumbled to earth. By the second week in July, the Wapsipinicon River was at flood stage. City officials in Des Moines expected the Raccoon River to crest at twenty-two feet on July 10. It actually topped off at twenty-five. The Mississippi River rose to its highest level in several hundred years at Hannibal, Missouri—the birthplace of Mark Twain.

A Flood for the Record Books

Up and down America's great midwestern river systems, the normally placid days of summer took on an air of desperation. Night and day, weary residents bagged sand and did their best to strengthen sagging levees. But rain continued to fall.

For months, a stunned nation watched in horror as one-hundred-year-old family homesteads were destroyed. Teary-eyed residents mourned the loss of their homes, their farms, and in some cases, family members. Forty-year-old Jackie Meek of Lemay, Missouri, articulated the heartache of thousands. "I feel about sixty-five right now. I see my house on the news and I just cry."[1] A way of life was vanishing.

When the river waters finally receded, the extent of the damage was staggering: fifty people were dead; seventeen thousand square miles of rich farmland were under water; seventy thousand people were left homeless; property losses totaled eight billion dollars. In the pantheon of American floods, this one stands alone. The Great Flood of 1993 is considered to have been, not a fifty-year flood, nor even a one-hundred-year flood; the Army Corps of Engineers called it a *five-hundred-year flood*—one so unlikely that an event of its magnitude can be expected only once in five centuries.[2] Few in the Midwest ever expected to witness such a flood—but they did. Now tens of thousands of American families are struggling to put their lives back together.

Flood of Another Sort: Change

The Great Flood of 1993 is a fitting metaphor for families and family life at the twilight of the twentieth century. As humanity creeps toward the third millennium, a chorus of voices from every quarter—social analysts, historians, and theologians —proclaim one singular, powerful message: Our world is in the midst of great transition. Not a fifty-year transition, or a one-hundred-year transition, but a once-in-five-hundred-years transition. Alvin Toffler writes: "We live at a moment when the entire structure of power that held the world together is now disintegrating. A radically different structure of power is taking form. And this is happening at every level of human society."[3] John Naisbitt says simply, "We stand at the dawn of a new era."[4]

This new era will look and feel much different from today's world. For one thing, it will be a lot more crowded. At present, there are approximately 5.2 billion people on planet earth. But according to one moderate estimate, by the year 2025 the earth's population will swell to 8.5 billion people.[5] The face of America's ethnic and social composition will also change drastically. Two colors will become much more prevalent: gray and brown. In 1990 there were 31 million Americans aged sixty- five and older. By 2030 there will be twice that number—65.5 million.[6] Can you imagine an America with more elderly people than children? It's just a generation away. Day care centers may well be converted into nursing homes. Like no generation before it, this older population will wrestle with the issues of euthanasia and "quality of life."

A constant stream of immigrants from Mexico and Latin America will gradually transform America from a predominantly white nation to a brown one. Some demographers believe that Caucasians will be a minority by 2050.[7] Racial prejudice will continue to inflame the hearts of people as different cultures attempt to coexist with one another.

This new era will also arrive on a tidal wave of information. Words such as "interactive," "fiber optics," "virtual reality," and "CD-ROM" will soon become ordinary household terms. Fueling the information explosion is something called fiber-optic cable. Made of thin strands of pure glass, fiber optics are "the most perfect transmitters of information ever invented."[8] This marvel of science can transport 250,000 times as much data as standard copper wire. Telecommunication companies are now scrambling to replace their networks of antiquated copper cable with fiber optics. The day is coming when "channel surfers" will inebriate themselves with hundreds of TV selections. Cable subscribers will have access to "a plethora of random-access services—movies on demand, video telephony, expanded home shopping, scores of sports events, and interactive programming."[9]

A Bold New World

As social critic Neil Postman observes, this glut of information which assaults us even today, "has called into being a new world."[10] A Bold New World is breaking upon us. The information age has arrived. Our grandchildren may well look at their world, not as Americans, but as members of a new configuration of nations. They will sit at home and do all of their business on computers and fax machines that connect them with a worldwide network of services.

Theologian Leonard Sweet has stated emphatically that "the world as you and I know it has come to an end."[11] Sweet's analysis of historical periods lends credibility to his conclusion. There was a time, says Sweet, at about A.D. 400, when the ancient world collapsed: Its customs, institutions, and value systems were swallowed up by what we now know as a brutal and less civilized medieval world. This period lasted for a thousand years and was characterized by small feudal states; the absence of a coherent national system; knights and kings, peasants and serfs. By A.D. 1300, this age began to yield to the light of the Renaissance and the Reformation. And for the past five hundred years, mankind has toiled in the modern world these two lights produced: A world of books, scientific discoveries, industrial inventions, and expanding personal freedoms.

But if the experts are right, the rains of a monumental transition have started to fall. A flood is coming. A new world is being birthed—right now—a world which seeks to reinvent everything, including long-standing moral values and what we once called "family." The Bold New World is not the usual "spring rains of progress"; it's a flood of change sweeping aside the way of life we all once knew.

The 1890s: A Pivotal Decade

As we stand on the frontier of this Bold New World, it's difficult to imagine what the landscape will look like. But consider this: How could anyone living in the 1890s have imagined the world of the twentieth century? In the 1890s, Great Britain stood alone as the world's preeminent power. Englishmen boasted that "the sun never sets on the British Empire." The Queen's flag flew high over New Zealand, Canada, Australia, and India. But within only fifty years, "almighty" England would cower before the onslaught of Hitler's war machine, a shadow of its former self.

In the 1890s, America was largely a rural country. The majority of Americans who inhabited this land were Protestants, a great number of them evangelicals. Our country had been impacted by a number of revivals; people were profoundly moral. Seventy-five percent of the population in 1890 was of British or Irish descent.

But the seeds of change were already being planted in the soil of a vanishing culture.

A massive immigration of Europeans altered forever the ethnic constitution of our population. People began to move from the farm to the city. But a perhaps more important shift also was taking place—a shift away from biblical truth. In the 1890s, Charles Darwin's theories were becoming popular in intellectual circles and were being disseminated in the universities. As a result, biblical authority was undermined. Also in the 1890s, a young psychologist named Sigmund Freud was grappling with radical concepts about human sexuality. His ideas would soon "liberate" the twentieth century from the moral restraints imposed upon it by the Victorian age. And throughout the 1890s, a German philosopher named Friedrich Nietzsche declared that "God is dead." His philosophy would later be used to justify the slaughter of millions of Jews, Gypsies, and homosexuals in Hitler's "work camps." In addition, the ideas of Karl Marx were germinating in the minds of revolutionaries like Vladimir Nikolai Lenin. In the twentieth century, half of the world's population would languish under the brutal fist of communism.

Vast social changes were taking place in America in the 1890s. The women's movement, which was largely unorganized throughout the nineteenth century, began to speak with a more centralized, forceful voice. Attitudes about homosexuality changed as well during this time. As E. Anthony Rotundo notes in his book, *American Manhood,* "the late nineteenth century marked a watershed in the history of homosexuality in the United States."[12] He elaborates:

> The two major developments were: the growth of areas in major cities where those interested in sexual relations with members of their own sex could meet and develop a sense of community; and a distinct change in the way society viewed that sexual behavior and those people.[13]

At the dawn of the Bold New World, there are some eerie similarities between the 1890s and the 1990s. America in 1995 looks frighteningly like the British empire of 1895. Preeminent among the world's powerful nations, the United States now casts a weak shadow. We are a people with feet of clay. There are major cracks in our foundation—especially morally and domestically.

Historian James Lincoln Collier writes:

America was once more than simply a place, more than simply a nation. It was an idea—an idea so powerful that it inflamed the imaginations of men and women around the world, and led them everywhere to topple emperors and kings. The world no longer admires the United States. It envies our prosperity and our freedoms; but it does not admire us. Yes, immigrants continue to swarm in, but that is mainly for the abundance of things that we have. They do not come because of an idea. And liberty weeps to see what we have done with her gift.[14]

Hidden beneath the surface of America's prosperity, a discerning ear hears the sounds of weeping. Most of the cries emanate from the embattled institution known as the family. Another child is abandoned by career-driven parents. Another family buries a child gunned down on the violent streets of America's cities. Another legal divorce leaves lifelong wounds. Another friend mourns the death of a loved one who contracted AIDS. Another tearful child watches a father leave home, forever. Another personal "right" replaces a traditional family responsibility—and someone suffers for it.

The Seasons of America

Over two hundred years ago, the world's greatest-ever experiment in democracy began in Philadelphia, Pennsylvania. Fifty-six men affixed their names to a document that inaugurated the birth of a new land. This was the spring of our existence as a nation.

Then in the nineteenth and twentieth centuries, the child called America moved into adulthood. We fought a great Civil War. We defended liberty around the world in two world wars. This was the summer of America's existence. Much that was good characterized this period in America's history.

But more time has passed. The season has changed again. Across America today, it is now fall.

Our age can be compared to the month of October. There are still brilliant hues and resplendent colors all around us. If we didn't know any better, we might think that the world birthed the previous spring is just getting bolder, rather than approaching its end.

But we know the month of October is in reality an aging, reckless playboy having a last fling, determined to go out in a blaze of glory before a winter of death sets in. America is in the fall of its existence, both figuratively and literally. A new election, a new congress, or even a new president cannot change this sad reality.

The words of Livy, the Roman historian, capture the essence of our own moral and social collapse. Looking back upon the demise of his beloved Rome, Livy wrote:

> I invite the reader...to trace the process of our moral decline, to watch, first the sinking of the foundations of morality as the old teaching was allowed to lapse, then the rapidly increasing disintegration, then the final collapse of the whole edifice, and the dark dawning of our modern day when we can neither endure our vices nor face the remedies needed to cure them.[15]

This is America at the dawn of a Bold New World. We are a nation in crisis.

At the heart of this book lies a simple postulate which I believe is the central proposition of our time:

IF it is true that our world is in the midst of a great transition, and a new world fundamentally different from the one we have known is being birthed, *THEN* we can either surrender to the currents of change and let them take us wherever they will, or we can discern our times and set out courageously to reestablish a biblical way of life that will first redeem our families and then our nation.

Yes, we can reinstate a Bible-based culture in America. *But we must start with our families.*

Once again, the Great Flood of 1993 provides us with a gripping analogy. As the rains fell and the waters rose higher and higher, the people of the Midwest responded to the crisis in a variety of ways. Some simply surrendered their fate to the circumstances. They gathered up what they could and got out of town. Then there were others who, for a time, decided to fight. These people stood shoulder to shoulder with neighbors and struggled to preserve their way of life. But as the odds mounted against them and hope faded into despair, they too packed up and left.

Then there were those who refused to surrender. We watched them night after night on the evening news. We marveled at their courage and their fortitude. These were the people who believed there was something worth fighting for, something worth preserving, no matter what the odds. Day after day they struggled and refused to sacrifice what they'd worked all their lives to achieve.

We Need to Make a Choice

Like the victims of the Great Flood, you and I are confronted with a decision. The flood waters of change are sweeping over every social institution and every moral and family standard we've ever known. It's time to choose. We can either surrender to those swift currents or oppose them. Let's look at the wreckage of our culture these currents have deposited at our doorstep:

- Men who relinquish their biblical role of leading and providing for their families;
- The "supermom" myth;
- A trivialized view of the sacredness and permanency of marriage;
- "Safe sex" rather than Bible-ordained sex;
- No-fault divorce;
- New definitions of what constitutes a "family";
- The "make me feel good" premise that all families are equal in what they offer their children;
- The attitude that day care is an adequate replacement for an involved mom;
- The tragic myth that human life begins whenever we *say* it does;
- The misguided stance that homosexuality is a valid, acceptable behavioral lifestyle;
- The notion that women find their ultimate worth and value through their pursuit of careers;
- Sons who find their way to manhood through a maze of seductive printed and celluloid images, rather than under the tutelage of mature male mentors;
- Schools which are "values-neutral," rather than values-rich;
- The celebration, rather than shunning, of lewdness, perversion, and vulgarity;
- A government which takes more and more responsibility for our children.

The hour is late—too late for vague family rhetoric. We can go with the flow, or we can stand tall and fight. In the midst of the cultural chaos, it's time for courage.

Preserving Family Values

The year was 1942. On the island of Corregidor, across the bay from Manila, a small army of embattled American soldiers fought to preserve the freedom of the Philippines. Under the command of Lt. General Jonathan Wainwright, this courageous band of men stood tall in the face of a Japanese bombardment that was unparalleled in the history of warfare. Depleted of food and ammunition and cut off from reinforcements, the Americans refused to surrender. Wainwright had promised President Roosevelt that the American flag would continue to fly over Corregidor as long as his men were still alive. The general was determined to keep his word.

In April of 1942, the Japanese intensified their attack. One afternoon, an exploding shell severed the rope that hoisted the flag over Corregidor. From the top of the one hundred-foot-tall flagpole, the symbol of freedom began its descent toward the ground. "Slowly, terribly," Wainwright said, "the flag began to descend down the pole as if drawn by some ghostly and prophetic hand, and most of those crouching in their batteries and holes looked at it as if it were the very sign of our doom."[16]

Then it happened. Seconds before the flag reached the ground, Captain Arthur Huff and three enlisted men raced from their positions and grabbed the coveted piece of cloth. They repaired the rope and hoisted the flag to the top of the pole while artillery shells exploded around them. For their courage, the four men were awarded the Silver Star.

My friend, the flag of our culture is slowly descending under the bombardment of cultural immorality and social insanity. The casualties are paraded daily in the pages of America's newspapers and on the nightly news.

Did we not promise God, our Commander in Chief, that we would keep His Word? If so, let's get out of our bunkers and run to the pole of timeless family values the Bible so clearly provides.

We have a flag to raise but it will take the new rope of our faith—a courageous faith.

Welcome to the Bold New World!

Notes

[1]"Troubled Waters," *Newsweek,* 26 July 1993, 24.

[2]Ibid., 21.

[3]Alvin Toffler, *Powershift (*New York: Bantam, 1990), 3.

[4]John Naisbitt and Patricia Aburdene, *Megatrends 2000* (New York: Avon, 1990), xvii.

[5]Paul Kennedy, *Preparing for the Twenty-First Century* (New York: Vintage, 1993), 23.

[6]Ibid., 311.

[7]Ibid., 312.

[8]"Electronic Superhighway," *Time,* 12 April 1993, 53.

[9]"Eyes on the Future," *Newsweek,* 31 May 1993, 46.

[10]Neil Postman, *Technopoly* (New York: Vintage, 1992), 70.

[11]Leonard Sweet, *Maps, Models, Muses: Christ as Medium and Message, The Church in the 21st Century* (Palm Desert, Calif.: Convention Cassettes Unlimited, 1993).

[12]E. Anthony Rotundo, *American Manhood: Transformations in Masculinity from the Revolution to the Modern Era* (New York: Basic Books, 1993), 274.

[13]Ibid., 274.

[14]James Lincoln Collier, *The Rise of Selfishness in America* (New York: Oxford University Press, 1991), 264.

[15]Livy, *The Early History of Rome* (New York: Penguin, 1960), 34.

[16]Duane Schultz, *The Hero of Bataan* (New York: St. Martin's Press, 1981), 265.

CHAPTER TWO

LOST
in the Bold New World

*"Indeed, the safest road to Hell is the gradual one—the gentle slope,
soft underfoot, without sudden turnings, without milestones, without signposts."*
C. S. LEWIS, *The Screwtape Letters*

Are you old enough to remember 1972? Let me describe the period for you. Richard Nixon occupied the White House. Women wore skimpy outfits called miniskirts. A young man named Bobby Fischer became chess champion of the world. Elvis Presley sightings were common (and verifiable!).

In 1972, the American public was transfixed by events that would shape the character of a generation.

Vietnam.

Nixon in China.

The Paris peace talks.

Watergate.

I still remember this convulsive time in our nation's history. The old order was being dismantled. As historian William Manchester has noted, "To Americans over the age of thirty the change was mind-boggling."[1] The unthinkable was creeping ever closer to the mainstream. Homosexuals marched in New York City. Adult bookstores and their X-rated poison began to expand beyond the seedy sections of our major cities and into mainstream America. Stay-at-home moms were quickly becoming an anachronism. Forty percent of married women were employed; twelve million of them had children at home under the age of eighteen.[2]

At this time something called "sex education" was infiltrating the public school system. The new curriculum represented a desperate attempt to arrest a burgeoning permissiveness among the young. A study of sexual mores by Arthur Vener and Cyrus Steward spotlighted the changes taking place: "The findings underscore our initial impression that substantial change has occurred in the social climate of the school system between 1970 and 1973."[3]

Marriage and family were in a state of flux, too. Unmarried couples were living together in ever-increasing numbers. "What had been a rare, even scandalous, lifestyle in 1960 was by the 1970s commonplace."[4] Divorce was sky-rocketing and gaining ever-increasing social acceptance. In some quarters, it was even being touted as "good for children."

The changes were occurring so quickly that social scientists were at a loss to make sense of the new world order. Alvin Toffler attempted to do just that in 1970. The title of his best-selling book captured the sentiments of most Americans. He called it, simply, *Future Shock*.

A Shocking New World

If these changes were a shock to those who lived through them, imagine the reaction of someone who had been removed from the cultural landscape for thirty years. The scenario is an intriguing one. What if a person had spent nearly three decades in isolation, only to reemerge in 1972?

Hypothetical? No. It actually happened in February 1972.

On the tiny island of Guam, deep in the heart of the Pacific Ocean, two fishermen captured a small, shriveled old man, and turned him over to police. We can only imagine the captors' surprise when they discovered their prisoner, Shoichi Yokoi, was a sergeant in the 38th Infantry Regiment of the old Japanese Imperial Army. The fifty-six-year-old man had been hiding in the jungles of Guam since the end of the war in 1945. For twenty-seven years Shoichi subsisted on a diet of mangoes, nuts, prawns, snails, rats, and wild pigs. He lived in a cave and made clothes from tree bark. The soldier's first question illustrates the length of his isolation. He asked: "Tell me one thing, quick. Is Roosevelt dead?"[5]

The world that greeted Shoichi was radically different from the one he remembered. In his absence, mankind had entered the atomic age. Jet aircraft now darted across the sky at supersonic speeds. The shadow of communism had descended over eastern Europe. Spaceships circled the earth. Three years before Shoichi returned to civilization, a man had even walked on the moon.

Time magazine summarized the dilemma of waking up in a Bold New World:

All in all, Yokoi may find modern life as much of an ordeal as existence in the jungle. "It's all like a dream, and I'm afraid of waking up from it," he said. "Once back home, I want to climb a tall mountain and meditate there alone for a long, long time."[6]

The arrival of a Bold New World precipitates feelings of bewilderment, doubt, and fear for anyone who takes the time to contemplate what has actually occurred in less than a generation. It shakes foundations and assaults beliefs. Like electric shock administered to a helpless patient, this strange experience is brutal and unrelenting. The piercing sensation of pain gives way to the hollow ache of numbness.

Trauma and confusion are the twin emotions of a person thrust into a Bold New World. This was true for Shoichi in 1972; it's equally true for many Christian families at the close of the twentieth century.

Christians in the Bold New World

For the majority of believers today, modern life has become an ordeal. The experience is very similar to walking out of a jungle after twenty-seven years in isolation. In every venue of life, be it our schools, our churches, our government, or in our marriages and families, our day is one of transition, flux, and overhaul. It's a Bold New World.

Everywhere the contemporary Christian turns, he discovers the old landmarks have disappeared, swept away by a sea of relativism. Mainline denominations ordain homosexuals for ministry and affirm that homosexuality is God-ordained, regardless of what the Scriptures say. Television infects our homes with information so vile and images so obscene they would have been considered illegal only a generation ago. Fetal tissue research receives presidential approval, and a charmed public stands by and applauds. Before she was fired, Surgeon General Joycelyn Elders attacked cigarette usage by the young and then postured for the legalization of harmful drugs. But these kinds of mixed moral signals are now an everyday affair.

The Christian family looks on while people in authority make decisions that contradict everything they've known to be true. The moral dissonance is perplexing. The believer begins to ask the same question Pilate put to Jesus in John 18:38, "What is truth?" The experience is not unlike taking a road trip with your family. Before you leave Little Rock for Denver, you sit down and map out your journey. With the map squarely in front of you, it becomes clear that you need to go west on I-40, then north on I-135, and west on I-70. Along the way, you pick up a hitchhiker. This man informs you that he's an expert with maps—an authority. He promptly turns your map upside down and begins to articulate a new route to Denver.

At this point, you have one of two choices. If you are a sensible person, you will conclude the man is a fool and chase him from your car. But if somehow you believe his bravado, you will travel along the highway trying to make sense of a map that has now become useless. In our world today, the so-called "authorities" have turned all the maps upside down. The tragedy is that too many Christian families are going along for the ride. Consider the following example from March 1993:

> Beverly Bradley, health director for San Francisco public schools, reported that just 612 (3.2%) of the parents of the district's 19,000 students withheld permission for their children's participation in a plan to give away condoms to high school students.'

This is a disturbing survey. It raises some serious questions. For starters, why is the percentage of dissenters so low? Does the decision by the majority reflect a deep-seated conviction for the necessity of condoms or, worse, a callous indifference? And how many of the 96.8 percent were Christians who mindlessly surrendered to the dictates of a secular school board? Examples of this kind could be multiplied *ad infinitum*. Speeding along with a culture that is headed toward destruction, believers seem to have lost their everyday moral compass. North is now south. Up is down. Wrong is right. The currents of the Bold New World move that swiftly!

In the face of massive change, it's imperative we recognize a sobering truth. The transformations that are occurring are not just *out there*—they are *in us* as well. What the Christian fails to realize is the enormous impact these changes are inflicting upon *him*. This dynamic is illustrated magnificently in the Old Testament book of Hosea.

The prophet Hosea lived in the midst of a religious society that had lost its moral compass. Less than three hundred years after the righteous reign of King David, the nation of Israel was adrift, wallowing in a vast ocean of moral ambivalence and cultural chaos. Hosea's description of Israel in 710 B.C. is a haunting anticipation of America in the 1990s.

In Hosea's day, worship celebrations abounded (Hosea 3:11), but worship was devoid of sincerity (7:14). Two pillars of a fair and just society, truth and loyalty, were in short supply (4:1). It was a time of great prosperity but people grew complacent in their wealth (13:6). Violence stalked the land: murder and bloodshed claimed the lives of innocent victims (4:2). Illegitimate births skyrocketed (5:7). Families were shattered by adultery (4:2). Of this time in Israel's history, Alfred Edersheim writes: "A more terrible picture of religious degeneracy and public and private wickedness could scarcely be imagined than that painted by the prophets in this the most prosperous period of Jewish history."[8] Hosea sums up the depth of the moral decay with one overpowering statement: "They have gone deep in depravity as in the days of Gibeah" (9:9).[9]

Do these statements resemble the America we know in the 1990s?

Incredibly, while society was crumbling around them, the nation of Israel was oblivious to the greatest change of all—the one taking place inside the hearts of the people. Hosea says as much in Hosea 7:9, "Strangers devour his strength, yet he does not know it; gray hairs also are sprinkled on him, yet he does not know it." In other words, while the moral foundation eroded and decayed, people were impervious to the way those changes impacted them. The explanation is obvious. The transformation that occurred was not instantaneous, but piecemeal. Unheralded, unannounced, it arrived on little cats' feet. The subtlety is illustrated by the imagery of the "gray hair." Few of us realize we're gray until we look in the mirror one day and discover, to our complete surprise, that white is now a competing color.

Culture, in other words, transforms us subtly, not directly. "Contemporary man is remarkably blind, irrational, and highly susceptible to the conditioning of his culture."[10]

Culture, of course, has this same impact upon the family. As Os Guinness has noted, society is not something we can lay our hands on—instead, it is an abstraction.[11] The family doesn't stand *outside* the culture, enabling it to objectively evaluate the changing landscape. Instead, the family is a *part* of and wedded with the culture. For this reason, we are all subject to "the climate of opinion, and network of ideas and values which form the social environment within which each individual lives his life."[12]

Unfortunately, few of us have ever stopped to discern the enormous impact of culture on our own lives or the lives of our family members. This oversight invites disaster. Consider just one example. In 1952, the highest rated show on television was "I Love Lucy." In April of that year, 10.6 million households were tuning in weekly to witness the madcap antics of Ricky and Lucy. But by December, CBS, the network airing the show, was confronted with a dilemma: Lucy was pregnant—in real life. Neither the network nor Phillip Morris, the chief sponsor of the show, liked the idea of a pregnant woman on television. As David Halberstam wrote, "A pregnant woman seemed in especially bad taste."[13] The decision was made to go ahead with a pregnant Lucy but the writers were instructed not to use the word *pregnancy*—it was thought too shocking for the American public. Therefore, to protect the cultural integrity of the show, "CBS lined up a priest, a minister, and a rabbi to review all pregnancy scripts to be sure that they were in good taste."[14]

Does this strike you as ludicrous? Can you think of anything more benign than using the word "pregnancy" on television? Probably not. But forty years ago, such language was considered offensive and *avant-garde*. It represented a radical departure from the social norms of the day.

From our "enlightened" point of view, the "I Love Lucy" fiasco seems innocuous, even archaic. Why? In part because of the subtle, pervasive influence of television. Over the past forty-plus years, television has slowly eroded the Christian's standard of decency. We have been bombarded with four letter words (now common in many shows), depictions of extramarital affairs, and violent deaths. Exposed to new and startling images, our response is always the same: first SHOCK, then ACCEPTANCE, followed by INDIFFERENCE.

Madonna understands this principle all too well. In an interview in *The Advocate*, a gay publication, the queen of shock rock assessed the impact homosexual imagery in music videos is having upon "straight" America:

> They [the American public] digest it on a lot of different levels. Some people will see it and be disgusted by it, but maybe they'll be unconsciously aroused by it…people keep seeing it and seeing it and seeing it, eventually it's not going to be such a strange thing.[15]

The gay producer of a homosexual cable show said their goal is to "desensitize the audience so that people will realize we're just like everybody else."[16] Shock. Acceptance. Indifference. The sad truth is, we tolerate indecencies that would have horrified the previous generation of Christians. Can you imagine the reaction of a 1950s Christian who is somehow suddenly transported in front of a television set in the 1990s? If the word "pregnancy" would have startled him, everything else we routinely tolerate would cause a massive coronary.

Anesthetized by a corrupt culture, many families have lost the ability to discern between good and evil. Our moral edge has become dull. Our children sit next to us on the sofa at night soaking up the opinions, values, and images of a godless society. Our silence and passivity is lethal to them. And then we have the audacity to marvel at their lack of spiritual passion and their propensity for moral compromise! A contemporary version of

Hosea 7:9 might read: "They tolerate immorality, and don't even know it. They are indifferent to godless philosophies, and don't even know it."

And television is just one of many cultural influences shaping the minds of Christian families in the Bold New World. A distinctively secular educational system is another. As Paul Blanshard wrote in *The Humanist*,

> I think the most important factor moving us toward a secular society has been the educational factor. Our schools may not teach Johnny to read properly, but the fact that Johnny is in school until he is sixteen tends toward the elimination of religious superstition.[17]

On multiple fronts, the contemporary Christian family is being conformed to the opinions and values of this world. When the people of God are "taken unaware," they can even find themselves endorsing that which God despises.

In this century, the most tragic example of this occurred in Nazi Germany.

During the summer of 1993, my family traveled to Poland. Our church supports a seminary in Wroclaw—we spent the month of July encouraging the staff and touring the Polish countryside.

One of the places we visited was Auschwitz, the Nazi concentration camp in southern Poland. I had been to Auschwitz once before, in the dead of winter; it is an equally chilling place in the heat of summer. The Lewis family walked slowly through the grounds, like aliens in a strange land. We stared at the barbwire and the ovens; we looked in horror at the graphic photographs. We stood in the showers and imagined what it was like to die such agonizing deaths. Again and again, we thought of the children: boys and girls just like mine whose fates were sealed the minute they stepped from the cattle cars.

How Could Christians Let It Happen?

Throughout our visit to hell, one question throbbed painfully in my mind. I couldn't escape it. I asked myself over and over again, *How could evangelical Christians have let this happen?*

Prior to World War II, the evangelical community in Germany was prosperous and strong. Families were in church. Husbands and wives gathered together for Bible studies and seminars. There were prayer meetings and outreach events. As is still true in America today, the Bible was the country's best-selling book.

But the Christians in Germany were just that—Christians in Germany. As such, they were subject to the opinions and ideas which formed their social, political, and domestic outlook. Like their non-Christian countrymen, evangelicals struggled in the midst of a tumultuous economy. In 1931, unemployment rose to 33.7 percent. The following year, it reached an unthinkable 43.7 percent.[18] Inflation became oppressive; the German mark wasn't worth the paper it was printed on. Desperate for change, the nation elected a new chancellor on January 30, 1933. Adolf Hitler came to power with the enthusiastic endorsement of the evangelical community. The German churches even signed a proclamation in 1934, extolling Hitler's rise to power.

> We are full of thanks to God that He, as Lord of history, has given us Adolf Hitler, our leader and savior from our difficult lot. We acknowledge that we, with body and soul, are bound and dedicated to the German state and to its Fuhrer. This bondage and duty contains for us, as evangelical Christians, its deepest and most holy significance in its obedience to the command of God.[19]

They should have known better. Back in 1925 and 1926, Hitler had published the two volumes of *Mein Kampf,* a frank, bloodcurdling book which outlined his plan for the resuscitation of Germany. It reads like a Stephen King novel. According to Konrad Heiden, sales of *Mein Kampf* began to rise three years before Hitler came to power. After his ascension, they rose exponentially. "Everybody was forced to buy it. It was presented as a gift to newlywed couples.... *Mein Kampf* made Hitler rich. It became a bestseller second only to the Bible."[20]

In the book, Hitler declared that the chief cause of Germany's demise was the Jew. "If we pass all the causes of the German collapse in review, the ultimate and most decisive remains the failure to recognize the racial problem and especially the Jewish menace."[21] The Jewish people were identified as parasites and offal (dung). The Jew had tainted the purity of German blood and destroyed the German economy. With Hitler's election, steps were taken immediately to deal with the "Jewish menace."

> On Wednesday, March 22, 1933, the first concentration camp will be opened near Dachau. It will accommodate 5,000 prisoners. Planning on such a scale, we refuse to be influenced by any petty objection, since we are convinced this will reassure all those who have regard for the nation and serve their interests. Heinrich Himmler Acting Police-President of the City of Munich.[22]

In *Mein Kampf*, Hitler had trumpeted the use of terror as a legitimate tool of government. "Terror at the place of employment, in the factory, in the meeting hall, and on the occasion of mass demonstrations will always be successful unless opposed by equal terror."[23]

Anti-Semitism became more violent in 1938:

> The Interior Ministry produced the "name decree," obliging all Jews to adopt Israel or Sarah as a middle name. This was followed by the terrifying violence of the Kristallnacht on Nov. 9, 1938, incited by Goebbels.[24]

Mein Kampf also delineated a program for ethnic cleansing. "It [the state] must declare unfit for propagation all who are in any way visibly sick or who have inherited a disease and can therefore pass it on, and put this into actual practice."[25]

On September 1, 1939, Hitler sent a note to Philip Bouhler, head of his Chancellery, ordering the extermination of the chronically insane and incurable. The work was done by SS doctors, who thus acquired experience of selecting and gassing large numbers.[26]

Before the program was discontinued in 1941, seventy thousand Germans had been murdered.

That's how the story goes. In case after case, the idea was father to the crime. It had all been laid out so clearly in black and white. When the final curtain fell, six million Jews, Gypsies, invalids, and homosexuals were dead.

Still, the question remains: How could evangelical Christians have let this happen?

The answer is forged in iron.

The entrance to Auschwitz is shaded by a big iron sign. It was there from the very beginning. In rusty letters, the sign reads simply: "Arbeit macht frei" (Work brings freedom). Obviously it was a propaganda statement. It led people to believe they were entering a work camp. *Work hard and you'll go free.* Across Germany, there were thousands and thousands of evangelical Christians who thought, "It's just a work camp."

I remember standing at the gate and asking myself, *Didn't anybody ask, early on, "What goes on in a work camp?" "What happens to people in a work camp?"* When I asked these questions, my heart shouted back: *These Christians probably lived with the same collective coping techniques we use when we hear the words, "fetal tissue research."*

Do you know what goes on in fetal tissue research? Do you know what it takes to gather and harvest fetal material—the freshest and the best? Isn't it troubling that our president stood in the Rose Garden, amid a jubilant crowd, and signed the Fetal Tissue Research Bill—and most of us went into collective denial? We cannot bring ourselves to think that fetal research feeds on child sacrifice.

Work Camp. Fetal tissue research. *It could never happen here, we tell ourselves.*

Lacking discernment, we surrender ourselves unconditionally to the Bold New World. Hosea's judgment is timeless in its application: "THE PEOPLE WITHOUT UNDERSTANDING ARE RUINED" (Hosea 4:14).

So, what's a family to do? Today's landscape can look and feel so threatening and intimidating!

First, we need to expose the elements of corruption which feed the cultural chaos in which we are now drowning. We must step into the light! A people without understanding may be ruined, but, conversely, a people with understanding at least have a fighting chance! Just by seeing and understanding these cultural muggers who are stealing the future from us and our children, we gain the strength to respond. As Proverbs 24:5 declares, "A man of knowledge increases power." Exposing the muggers will be our journey through chapter 3.

Then, in chapter 4, we will reach for a rock. A Rock which can hold us securely in the swift currents of the Bold New World. A Rock upon which, in the chapters that remain, we will seek to construct real family values.

It's a terrible thing to be lost. But, oh, the exhilaration of finding your way to safety!

Notes

[1]William Manchester, *The Glory and the Dream* (New York: Bantam Books, 1974), 1193.

[2]Ibid., 1196.

[3]Arthur M. Vener and Cyrus S. Steward, "Adolescent Sexual Behavior in Middle America Revisited: 1970-73," *Journal of Marriage and the Family,* 36 (November 1974), 734.

[4]James Lincoln Collier, *The Rise of Selfishness in America* (New York: Oxford University Press, 1991), 226.

[5]"The Last Soldier," *Time,* 7 February 1972, 41-42.

[6] Ibid., 42.

[7]*Arkansas Democrat,* 21 March 1993, 1.

[8]Alfred Edersheim, *Bible History: Old Testament, VII* (Grand Rapids, Mich.: Eerdman's, 1986), 64.

[9]The reference to the depravity of Gibeah speaks volumes about Israel's degeneration. It was at Gibeah that the men of the city clamored for homosexual sex with a visiting Levitical priest. Instead, the Levite's concubine was offered to the deviants, who then raped the woman to death. In response, the Levite hewed his concubine into twelve pieces to protest the moral corruption of the nation (Judges 19). This event represents the nadir of Israel's spiritual and moral collapse.

[10]Jim Peterson, *Living Proof* (Colorado Springs, Colo.: NavPress, 1991), 39.

[11]Os Guinness, *The American Hour* (New York: The Free Press, 1993), 71.

[12]H. D. McDonald, "Theology and Culture," in *Toward a Theology for the Future,* ed. David F. Wells and Clark H. Pinnock (Carol Stream, Ill.: Creation, 1971), 239-241.

[13]David Halberstam, *The Fifties* (New York: Villard Books, 1993), 200.

[14]Ibid.

[15]"The Gospel According to St. Madonna," *The Advocate,* 21 May 1991, 49.

[16]"New Varieties of Soap," *Newsweek,* 26 February 1990, 60.

[17]Paul Blanshard, "Three Cheers for Our Secular State," *The Humanist,* March/April 1976, 17-25.

[18]Paul Johnson, *Modern Times* (New York: Harper and Row, 1983), 280.

[19]Millard Erickson, *Christian Theology,* 1 (Grand Rapids, Mich.: Baker, 1983), 404.

[20]Adolf Hitler, *Mein Kampf* (Boston: Houghton Mifflin, 1971), xix.

[21]Ibid., 327.

[22]Paul Johnson, *Modern Times,* 288.

[23]Adolf Hitler, *Mein Kampf,* 44.

[24]Paul Johnson, *Modern Times,* 293.

[25]Adolf Hitler, *Mein Kampf,* 404.

[26]Paul Johnson, *Modern Times,* 413.

CHAPTER THREE

THE FORCES BEHIND THE ISSUES

in the Bold New World

*"A civilization unable to differentiate between illusion and reality
is usually believed to be at the tail end of its existence."*
JOHN RALSTON SAUL

There is a perilous stretch of water on the Deschutes River in central Oregon known as Dillon Falls. Located a few miles from the Inn of the Seventh Mountain, Dillon Falls is rated a class 6 rapid. Through a rugged gorge of jagged rock the river descends steeply for a hundred yards; here, the seductive Deschutes becomes a boiling cauldron of raging fury. Even the most experienced rafters refuse to navigate this menacing section of the river.

Dillon Falls is the last place you would expect to find people floating on rafts. Tragically, though, two men and three young boys did attempt to do this, on July 6, 1993.

The outing was a celebration of sorts—a family reunion. Ben Lockhart had traveled from Homer, Alaska, to visit his mother, Evelyn VonPoederoyen. Evelyn lived in Bend, a few miles downstream from Dillon Falls. Ben brought his three sons along with him: seven-year-old Kelly, four-year-old

Jeremy, and three-year-old Jesse. Ben's brother, Steven Sheldon, who was living with Evelyn, suggested the family float the Deschutes.

After stopping at a local store to purchase flotation cushions, the ill-fated party headed for the river. Oblivious to the danger, they launched their rafts between Benham Falls and Dillon Falls. Evelyn drove downstream to Big Eddy and waited for her sons and grandsons to arrive. According to an account carried in an Oregon newspaper:

> The first thing she saw was four-year-old Jeremy, floating along in the water. Thinking the men had allowed the children to float free of the boats, the grandmother felt anger. Then, to her horror, she saw that her grandson was clutching the body of Sheldon.[1]

With the help of bystanders, the frantic woman retrieved her grandson and the body of her son. He did not respond to CPR. A jet boat hurried upriver to search for the rest of the family. Miraculously, the three young boys survived the ordeal. Evelyn's sons, Steven and Ben, both died.

The tragedy easily could have been averted. All that was lacking was a little common sense: a respect for the river, a willingness to question basic assumptions, the capacity to think critically. The men who died simply didn't know what they were getting into.

People without Understanding Are Ruined

Caught in the current of a Bold New World, the contemporary Christian also finds himself being swept along by powerful forces that portend disaster. We should observe that the river hasn't been treacherous everywhere. At the beginning of our journey the drift was placid and predictable. Life moved along pretty much as it always had. Like giant boulders, our Judeo-Christian heritage dotted the river, slowing the current and stabilizing society. Criminals were deemed responsible for their crimes. Parents took responsibility for their children. Marriage was a sacred, lifetime commitment. Morality was based on transcendent values, not personal preference. Our culture reinforced the values taught in the home.

But with the arrival of the tumultuous 1960s, all of this began to change. Slowly, at first imperceptibly, the boulders that held the current in check began to disappear. Now, America is like a rubber raft, thrashing about in the midst of a Class 6 rapid. Lives are being destroyed on the jagged rocks of exaggerated personal rights, divorce, reckless careerism, "safe sex," child abuse, family abandonment, and violence. Social scientists document the carnage, but few Americans ever stop to discern the forces *behind* these issues. Just how did we get here in the first place? A number of significant questions remain unanswered. For example, what have we assumed, either correctly or incorrectly, about the nature of man? Is man basically good? Is a just society possible without absolute values? Without religion? What should be the goal of education? What is a family? When does life begin? If we are born with certain propensities, does that make them right?

There is much discussion today about the ills plaguing America. But who is plumbing the depths of our demise and bringing to the surface the real forces *behind* the issues? How ironic that we are inundated with information but are unable (or unwilling) to explore the more subtle movements that shape our society and our families.

Without question, one of the characteristics of our Bold New World is a disdain for critical thought. Douglas Wilson, in his book *Recovering the Lost Tools of Learning*, states the problem this way: "In modern America, the fast-food mentality has penetrated the realm of the mind. The modern student has a mind full of McThoughts."[2] As Malcolm tells Ellie in *Jurassic Park*, "Isn't it amazing, in the information society, nobody thinks. We expected to banish paper, but we actually banished thought."[3] Both inside and outside the church, critical thinking is on the critical list. Sound bites have replaced persuasive argumentation. George Will has said that if Abraham Lincoln were to give the Emancipation Proclamation today, he would probably say: "Read my lips. No more slavery."[4]

This absence of critical thought becomes readily apparent when the sacred and secular collide. Complex issues are often reduced to clichés. Dialogue between Christians and non-Christians quickly deteriorates into accusation and invective. All of which brings us back to our original proposition:

> *IF* it is true that our world is in the midst of a great transition, and a new world fundamentally different from the one we have known is being birthed, *THEN* we can either surrender to the currents of change and let them take us wherever they will, or we can discern our times and set out courageously to reestablish a biblical way of life that will first redeem our families and then our nation.

Once again, note that it all starts with family...and discernment.

The Role of Discernment

Discernment is the ability to look below the surface; to see things as they are, not as they appear at first blush. When the discerning Christian looks below the surface of culture, below popular rhetoric, opinion polls, and public policies that claim to speak for the majority of Americans, he or she discovers the real forces moving and shaping our society. We tend to think of drugs, crime, promiscuity, abortion, pornography, violence, homosexuality, and so on, as the issues of greatest import to us today. They aren't. They simply represent *points of engagement between two groups*—those who seek to reinvent our culture with a new set of "moralities," and those (many of whom are Christians) who seek to reestablish our society upon the timeless values history has affirmed in each and every generation. This struggle is the real issue behind our Bold New World. Russell Kirk poses this struggle as a question in the preface of his book, *The Roots of American Order*. He writes:

> Will the moral and social order that Americans have known for two centuries and more endure throughout the twenty-first century? That may depend upon whether enough men and women in these United States, informed by study of the institutions and convictions that have developed over three-thousand years, make up their mind to stand by the *permanent things* [italics are mine].[5]

Permanent things. What are they? God, faith, family, a healthy sexuality, a clear understanding of right and wrong, a belief in the sacredness of human life and when it begins…and all of them are being threatened and redefined in the Bold New World. Let me repeat: The real struggle of our time is between those demanding a new world with "updated" moralities and those seeking a better world stabilized by timeless truths. Permanent things. The discerning Christian understands this deeper struggle as the critical mass lying below the surface of most of our social controversies.

The discerning Christian also will unmask the specific *forces* that energize proponents of the New Morality—forces that empower the New Morality's efforts to remake our culture. Like feeder streams rushing into a larger body of water, these forces create a potent, destructive current for those seeking to hold on to permanent things. We will not be able to address all of these forces here. But we will examine, for a moment, four of the more powerful ones. These are the real power players behind the issues of the Bold New World.

1. The Stranglehold on Power and Influence Possessed by a Highly Liberal, Well-Positioned Elite Class Which Shapes Our Nation's Values and Course

Few will ever forget the explosive speech former Vice President Dan Quayle gave to the Commonwealth Club in San Francisco. He spoke on the then virgin topic of family values. (Yes, there was a time in America when politicians *didn't* talk about family values!) Quayle lamented the absence of fathers in the home; he showed the direct correlation between single-parent households and the rise of violent crime and poverty. The vice president's speech contained only one brief allusion to the television show "Murphy Brown":

> It doesn't help matters when prime-time TV has Murphy Brown—a character who supposedly epitomizes today's intelligent, highly paid professional woman— mocking the importance of fathers by bearing a child alone, and calling it just another "lifestyle choice."[6]

That's it, one compound sentence. The result was a firestorm of rage. For months, the media and Hollywood cast Quayle as an antiquated, idealistic, fundamentalist buffoon.

Why?

The vice president's remarks were greeted with scorn for one simple reason: He had exposed a vital force which is shaping the moral and cultural climate of America—a highly liberal, well-positioned Elite Class.

Quayle's speech continued:

> I know it is not fashionable to talk about moral values, but we need to do it. Even though our cultural leaders in Hollywood, network TV, the national newspapers routinely jeer at them, I think that most of us in this room know that some things are good and other things are wrong. Now it's time to make the discussion public.[7]

The discussion did become public. Like a junkyard dog surprised by an intruder, this elite class brutalized its challenger. In doing so, they demonstrated their immense power to shape any issue to their liking.

Who are these elitists?

They are the academicians who teach at our universities; the editors of newspapers and magazines who control what we read; the network executives who determine what we watch on television; the Hollywood movie moguls and media giants; even judges, whose questionable decisions sometimes rest more on a personal social bias than on our nation's Constitution.[8] Elitists are men and women in positions of power who set the moral agenda for a nation. They can easily suppress information and promulgate their own values upon a naive, susceptible society. They are the trendsetters of our day, the opinion-makers and architects of the Bold New World. And their influence is enormous, primarily because it is so dominant and visible.

Columnist Joe Sobran has witnessed the ascension of liberal elitists in the news media. He says, "The deepest challenge in journalism during my lifetime has been the subtle erosion of the old standard of nonpartisan, even noncommittal, reporting. The old journalist had a sense of duty; the new ones have a sense of mission. There's a big difference."[9] With refreshing candor, Margaret Carlson, a writer for *Time* magazine, confesses to a predisposition to slant the truth in favor of her liberal heroes. Of Hillary Clinton, she writes, "Something inside you roots for her. You're rooting for your team. I try to get that bias out, but, for many of us, it's there."[10]

The implications for you and me are alarming: Every time we reach for a newspaper or turn on the evening news, we are being handed information that has been filtered, shaped, and packaged by hidden values that interpret the facts with a specific end in mind.

If you want to know what some of these hidden values are, listen to Robert Novack, a nationally syndicated columnist and host of the television program, "The Capitol Gang":

Am I exaggerating the impact of this liberal ideology? Of the five hundred or so reporters and editors I know, I am aware of only two who are well-known, admitted conservatives. Nationwide, there are only about ten editorial pages in America that could properly be called "conservative."… At the very least, this striking imbalance speaks volumes about the potential for liberal ideology to dominate the news.[11]

Novack then goes on to list some views championed "almost universally by the members of the national media." The media believe that:

- Americans are undertaxed. Our taxes are well below those imposed in Europe and the federal government should, therefore, raise taxes, especially for those who earn more, save more, and invest more.
- Being pro-choice is not enough; there should be absolutely no interference with the reproductive rights of a woman.
- Term limits are dangerous and are also undemocratic.
- The "religious right" is a serious menace to the future of American society.
- Conservatism is a narrow philosophy; liberalism, by contrast, is more broad, unprejudiced, and compassionate.[12]

Whether you know it or not, a subtle twisting of truth is clouding our perception of the very society in which we live:

Our reality is dominated by elites who have spent much of the last two centuries, indeed of the last four, organizing society around answers and around structures designed to produce answers.… Never have people so adept at manipulating the word held the levers of power. Western culture, as a result, has become less and less a critical reflection of its own society.[13]

And, what about those twin pillars of American entertainment—television and movies? If you think what you see on the tube and the silver screen is representative of your values, think again. Over one hundred television writers and executives were asked to state their positions on moral and religious issues. To the question, "Do you believe adultery is wrong?"—only 49 percent said yes. By contrast, 85 percent of the American public believes adultery is wrong. "Do you believe homosexual acts are wrong?" Only 20 percent of those surveyed answered yes (as opposed to 76 percent of Americans). And to the question, "Do you believe in a woman's right to an abortion?"—97 percent of Hollywood's movers and shakers said yes! A much smaller number, 59 percent, of the general population agrees with them.[14]

The people in positions of power and influence possess a radically different set of values than the rest of us. And this elite class isn't content to lay aside their values for the sake of objectivity. Does anyone now question where Hollywood and the national media stand on abortion, homosexuality, feminism, premarital sex, and a number of other issues? Do you? Most disturbingly, through the suppression, exaggeration, and celebration of different bits of information, their positions become grossly apparent through their highly influential mediums.

The elite class's favorite whipping boy is the evangelical Christian. Columnist Molly Ivins labels evangelicals "Shiite Baptists," and media mogul Ted Turner has called Christianity "a religion for losers."[15] The resentment is deafening.

The pro-life movement is often portrayed as a terrorist organization because of the regrettable acts of a few fringe lunatics who betray the movement's commitment to the sacredness of human life.

I was shocked when our local newspaper allowed Planned Parenthood to run a large advertisement shortly after David

Gunn, the abortion doctor, was murdered in Pensacola, Florida. The banner headline was spread across the top of the page. It read, "They Shot Him!" *They?* Wasn't this the act of one deranged man? Never mind the fact that every pro-life organization, nationwide, condemned the act as murder. "They Shot Him!" The fact that this slander was allowed in print is an outrage.

Some of the propaganda is overt; most of it is subtle. Why is it you've never seen an aborted fetus on television? The networks won't allow it to happen. When pro-life groups attempt to get this on the airwaves, the response by the networks is always the same: "It's offensive."

When a television network says this, I want to laugh. Offensive! They must be kidding! Isn't "NYPD Blue" offensive? What about the mangled bodies of American soldiers paraded through the streets of Somalia or the shredded remains of Bosnian children? Isn't this offensive? Or how about the violence portrayed so graphically each night during prime time? What about the X-rated sex that's crammed into a thirty-second commercial for an upcoming movie release? I can't even find the channel changer before my family has been violated by this obscenity. I call this offensive and a majority of Americans agree. An aborted fetus? Yes, it is offensive. But the reason you'll never see one on network television is not because it's offensive but because it's convincing! Anyone who looks closely at an aborted baby knows beyond a doubt that he or she is looking at human life. The first time I saw the picture of an aborted child, I turned away in shame. Everything within me shouted, "This is wrong!"

Why is it you never see a Mapplethorpe picture in a news story on the arts? Why do we get sanitized versions of a gay parade, like the one held not long ago in Washington, D.C.? Why do the decisions of our courts correspond to liberal positions with suspicious consistency? Because this elite class *is* liberal.

Highly liberal. And they press their agenda every chance they get with their well-positioned stranglehold on power and influence.

According to the media, evangelical Christians are trying to cram their biblical ethics down everyone else's throat. But I have to ask, who is imposing their values on whom? Who has redefined when life begins? Who has changed the way we think about premarital sex, or what is decent and what is not, or what is normal and what is not, or who lives and who dies, or where you can pray and where you can't?

The discerning Christian knows.

2. The Emergence of a Powerful Philosophical Pluralism

From our inception as a nation, America has been guided and heavily influenced by Judeo-Christian values. For over 180 years, until we fell into the convulsive 1960s, America was essentially a monoculture. Our founding fathers began with one basic assumption: They believed a transcendent being governed this world. They also believed this divine ruler had communicated to mankind through the Scriptures. The Bible became the basis for our moral and social constitution. Our Christian heritage is woven throughout our political past—we find it in the Constitution and the Bill of Rights; it is printed on our coins and our paper money.

Americans have not always obeyed the transcendent commands they found in Scripture; nevertheless, they affirmed their existence and leaned heavily upon these values as the sole foundation for a fair and just society. For 180 years a biblical ethic prevailed over American cultural life. Few Americans, Christian and non-Christian alike, questioned the validity of the Ten Commandments. We never doubted the permanency of marriage or the existence of one true God. The phrase that is stamped on our one cent coin is witness to our cultural unity; it reads "*e pluribus unum*"—"from the many, one." This oneness found its identity in common values and common truths derived from our Judeo-Christian heritage.

But in the Bold New World, this moral and cultural unity is gone, or, at best, fading quickly.

We live today in the midst of an ever more complex polyculture, and, as Christians, we feel the tension at every turn. Our coin should now read, "*e pluribus pluris*" —"from the many, many." The fashionable term "multiculturalism" is descriptive of things in the present and a harbinger of things to come. America is moving, not toward oneness, but toward diversity. We are becoming a multicultural society. A tribal state. The real danger in this transformation is not ethnic or racial, but philosophical. America has lost its philosophical unity. In the ongoing debates regarding abortion, feminism, and family values, this force *behind* the issues is one of philosophy.

A number of philosophies are vying for the intellectual assent of Americans in the 1990s. They are competing for supremacy in the marketplace of ideas. Each philosophy comes complete with a host of spokesmen and a band of faithful followers. Let me mention four of the more prominent ones.

Humanism

Probably the most pervasive philosophy in America today is that of Humanism. (I've capitalized the word because it is more than just a philosophy; to many, Humanism is tantamount to a religious belief.) As an idea, Humanism has been around for centuries. It wasn't until 1933, however, that it inched ever closer to religious status. It was then that a group of intellectuals—John Dewey, Julian Huxley, and B. F. Skinner among them—signed their names to a document called The Humanist Manifesto. In doing so, these "progressive" thinkers consummated a process that had begun two centuries earlier during the period known as the Enlightenment. The Manifesto affirmed many of the tenets of Enlightenment philosophy: the basic goodness of man, the notion of a self-caused universe, the relativism of truth, the exaltation of reason.

The Manifesto proclaims:

Religious humanists regard the universe as self-existing and not created. Humanism asserts that the nature of the universe depicted by modern science makes unacceptable any supernatural or cosmic guarantee of human values.[16]

The moorings that secured America to its Judeo-Christian heritage were being severed.

The Supreme Court formally recognized Humanism as a religion in 1961. In the case of *Torcaso v. Watkins,* the Court defined secular humanism as "a religion equivalent to theistic and other non-theistic religions."[17]

In April 1993, the *New York Times* ran a large advertisement entitled, "What on Earth Is Humanism?" It provides us with a contemporary definition of this pervasive ideology. The advertisement read in part:

Humanism is a joyous life-affirming philosophy that relies on science, reason and democracy; it believes in an ethic of morality that grounds all human values in this one earthly experience, and holds as its greatest goal the happiness, freedom, and progress of all humanity in this one and only life.[18]

At a casual glance, Humanism sounds appealing. After all, who is against "the happiness, freedom, and progress of all humanity"? These are values that all Americans hold dearly. But on a deeper level, when placed under the searching light of a Christian world view, Humanism is fraught with problems. As a philosophy, Humanism collides with Christianity at two significant points. First, Humanism affirms what the Bible radically denies—the basic goodness of man. Second, Humanism denies what the Bible radically affirms, that there are absolute values in this world. This two-fold affirmation—of human goodness and relative truth—has spawned a bevy of mindless social and educational policies that continue to erode American society.

The Humanist philosophy is responsible for the "Values Clarification" model of decision-making that is now regularly taught in our public schools. Emphasizing feelings and a non-judgmental attitude, Values Clarification moves children away from absolute standards of right and wrong and allows them to "make up their own minds." Introduced in 1966 with the publication of *Values and Teaching* by Raths, Harmin, and Simon, we now have a generation of adults who have been weaned on this deleterious ideology. Humanist philosophy has given us sex education manuals such as *Changing Bodies, Changing Lives,* a Planned Parenthood production that infiltrated the public schools in the late seventies. Trumpeting a relativistic approach to morality, *Changing Bodies* is filled with egregious advice. One statement is representative: "If you feel your parents are overprotective...or if they don't want you to be sexual at all until some distant time, you may feel you have to tune out their voice entirely."[19] Such instruction is an affront to the concept of absolute values and undermines the protective nature of parental authority.

Humanist philosophy has created an entire generation of "victims." How could it be otherwise? If man is basically good, then his problems are somebody else's fault. Charles Sykes states, "Something extraordinary is happening in American society. Crisscrossed by invisible trip wires of emotional, racial, sexual, and psychological grievance, American life is increasingly characterized by the plaintive insistence, *I am a victim.*"[20] We have become a people who are forever looking for someone else to "fix" us—the government, the schools, the therapist. Since many, if not most, of our national leaders adhere to humanistic ideology, we see government officials throwing dollar after dollar at problems that have been misdiagnosed due to philosophical error.

There is a cancer in the land. It cannot be cured by clean needles, condoms, and self-esteem training. The problem is philosophical.

Man is not basically good. Truth is not relative.

The Humanist's great god—reason—has proven to be a weak, emasculated impostor. This charlatan is the mastermind behind the bloodiest century in human history. John Ralston Saul writes:

> The twentieth century, which has seen the final victory of pure reason in power, has also seen unprecedented unleashings of violence and of power deformed. It is hard, for example, to avoid noticing that the murder of six million Jews was a perfectly rational act.[21]

Professing to be wise, we have become fools. This is the legacy of Humanism.[22]

New Age Polytheism

There is a second philosophy impacting our society today—New Age polytheism. While it borrows from some of the basic tenets of Humanism (that is, man is good, truth is relative, the universe is a closed system), New Age polytheism is much broader in its philosophical reach. It is essentially an eclectic system, and draws upon a wide array of religious and philosophical traditions, such as pantheism, animism, and materialism. At the heart of New Age polytheism lies the conviction that humanity is in the process of a great transformation. In this sense, it is highly utopian. We are poised to usher in a new millennium. In the words of Jean Houston, "It's almost as if the species [humanity] were taking a quantum leap into a whole new way of being."[23] The only obstacle standing in our way is ignorance. Mankind doesn't need regeneration but enlightenment. Higher consciousness thinking frees man from his own inherent limitations. Hence the emphasis upon visualization, transcendental meditation, and positive thinking. We can actually determine our own destiny.

For the New Age polytheist, ultimate reality is not God, but SELF. We are prime reality. We become God. Answers to all the riddles and mysteries of life (its purpose and meaning) lie within us. It's up to each individual to unlock this untapped reservoir of wisdom and knowledge.

Driven by an intense desire for authentic spiritual experience, New Age devotees dabble in a wide variety of religious interests. For example, take the case of Rita McClain.

Rita McClain's spiritual journey began in Iowa, where she grew up in the fundamentalist world of the Pentecostal Church. What she remembers most about that time are tent meetings and an overwhelming feeling of guilt. In her twenties, she tried less doctrinaire Protestantism. That, too, proved unsatisfying. By the age of twenty-seven, McClain had rejected all organized religion. "I really felt like a pretty wounded Christian," she says. For the next eighteen years, she sought inner peace only in nature, through rock climbing in the mountains or hiking in the desert. That seemed enough.

Then, six years ago, in the aftermath of an emotionally draining divorce, McClain's spiritual life blossomed. Just as she had once explored mountains, she began scouting the inner landscape. She started with Unity, a metaphysical church near her Marin County, California home. It was a revelation, light-years away from the "Old Testament kind of thing I knew very well from my childhood." The next stop was Native American spiritual practices. Then it was Buddhism at Marin County's Spirit Rock Meditation Center, where she has attended a number of retreats, including one that required eight days of silence.

These disparate rituals melded into a personal religion, which McClain, a fifty-year-old nurse, celebrates at an ever-changing altar in her home. Right now the altar consists of an angel statue, a small bottle of "sacred water" blessed at a women's vigil, a crystal ball, a pyramid, a small brass image of Buddha sitting on a brass leaf, a votive candle, a Hebrew prayer, a tiny Native American basket from the 1850s, and a picture of her "most sacred place," a mandrone tree near her home.[24]

From crystals to channeling to the occult, these people seek a genuine spiritual encounter. One has to wonder, though, just how much the church has contributed to this burgeoning religious movement. After all, when people walk into dead churches and suffer through dry, lifeless sermons that stultify the Spirit, it's difficult to blame them for seeking more lively surroundings. For all of its faults, New Age polytheism is motivated by a deep need for an authentic spiritual encounter.

Hedonism

A third contemporary philosophy shaping America is that of hedonism. If the truth be told, hedonism impacts the Christian more than we are willing to admit. This philosophy defines good and evil, not in terms of right and wrong, but in terms of pleasure and pain. The hedonist's perpetual goal is to pursue those things which increase pleasure and decrease pain.

The chief proponent of this philosophy in our generation has been Hugh Hefner, the founder of *Playboy*. When the editors of the magazine were asked to define the concept of the "playboy," they responded with the following definition:

What is a playboy?... Is he simply a wastrel, a ne'er-do-well, a fashionable bum? Far from it: he can be a sharp-minded business executive, a worker in the arts, a university professor, an architect or engineer. He can be anything, provided he possesses a certain point of view. He must see life not as a vale of tears, but as a happy time; he must take joy in his work, without regarding it as the end and all of living; he must be an alert man, an aware man, a man of taste, a man sensitive to pleasure, a man who...can live life to the hilt. This is the sort of man we mean when we use the word "playboy."[25]

While this hedonistic "playboy" philosophy permeates our society, it is most readily apparent in youth culture. MTV promulgates the message of hedonism: "Live for the moment!" "Pursue pleasure, regardless of the consequences." Madison Avenue captures the hearts of television viewers at an early age and sows seeds of desire that bloom in adulthood. One of the great ironies of our generation is that we affirm this philosophy but fail to make the logical connection between the philosophy itself and the problems it breeds. A generation of kids are given drug counseling, sex education, and alcohol rehabilitation, while those in authority remain strangely silent about the cause—a live-for-the-moment philosophy that leads, ultimately, to despair.

No one epitomizes this contradiction better than Joycelyn Elders, the former surgeon general of the United States. Speaking in *The Advocate,* a gay publication, Elders outlined her agenda for a "sexually progressive" America. One of our biggest problems, as she sees it, is the fact that

> society wants to keep all sexuality in the closet. We have to be more open about sex, and we need to speak out to tell people that sex is good, sex is wonderful. It's a normal part and healthy part of our being, whether it is homosexual or heterosexual.[26]

Her vision for sexual reform includes sex education for children beginning in kindergarten, condom distribution throughout the public school system, and abortion on demand. The American taxpayer is responsible to pick up the tab for all sexual irresponsibility. But what is the real force lying silently behind all this political rhetoric? Clearly, it is a philosophy of life with a growing public acceptance. It is the wanton, indiscriminate pursuit of pleasure. It is hedonism.

Majorityism

A fourth philosophy is what I've termed majorityism. The electronic age has created this powerful, influential force. With majorityism, the public is asked to give their opinion on a wide variety of subjects. Pollsters reduce complex issues to "yes" and "no" questions. Americans give answers off the top of their heads, and the results are published for all to see. Here's how the process works.

The Pope comes to Denver and discovers that 55 percent of Catholics believe priests should have the right to marry; 76 percent want the church to permit divorce; 70 percent prefer the ordination of women. Even before John Paul steps from the plane, the battle lines have been drawn. The overwhelming sense is, "The Pope is wrong! We have proof—just look at the figures!"

Never mind that the questions are often manipulated to guarantee specific responses. The majority rules! This is the new philosophy today. Americans look at the latest USA *Today* poll and measure themselves against the results. We change our views to stay in line with the cultural consensus.

But this whole process begs a question: Since when did morality become a popularity contest?

In moral and spiritual matters, the majority does not determine what is right. What's right is RIGHT, whether the majority believes it or not. Jesus was quite clear on this point. In Matthew 7, Jesus said,

> Enter by the narrow gate; for the gate is wide, and the way is broad that leads to destruction, and many are those who enter by it [the majority]. For the gate is small, and the way is narrow that leads to life, and few are those who find it [the minority] (Matthew 7:13-14).

The rise of these philosophies (Humanism, polytheism, hedonism, majorityism) signal the arrival of a Bold New World.

The harsh truth is that America has now entered a new age—paganism. You and I live in the midst of a pagan culture, and we need to recognize and respect this powerful new force which attacks real family values at every turn.

3. A Soul-Numbing Prosperity

On a number of occasions, I have had the privilege of hearing Peter Drucker, a man famous not only for his many outstanding books on business and management, but a man who many consider to be a true Renaissance thinker. Few men have a better grasp of history, world events, organizations, and social structures. Few men can summarize the complexities of our age the way he can. In fact, one of the things I have come to admire about Mr. Drucker is the way he often begins a lecture with a simple observation. From there, he proceeds to weave that simple, singular thought through a myriad of historical circumstances involving people, problems, organizations, and events. Then, at the end, he draws you back again to this simple statement that has now taken on a profound, almost genius-like sense to it.

One morning as I listened to Mr. Drucker, he began this way: "As I look over human history, I would have to conclude that prosperity has not been good for humanity." Though he proceeded to masterfully state why, the veracity of this opening statement needed very little support. I can provide much support from my own life, and so can you. The fact is, prosperity and the incessant pursuit of more, has a way of clouding the mind, causing us to devalue that which is real and important, while exalting that which is unreal and unimportant. There are too many options, too many opportunities, too many choices. Confusion gives way to compromise. In the end, prosperity makes mincemeat of priorities. And the priority of family is often the first to fall.

In our more lucid moments, we all long to have a strong family that possesses time for love and encouragement; a family which is rich with personal interaction and cherished experiences. Unfortunately, surrounded by comfort, wealth, and too many things, these holier desires quickly fade away. We chase fantasies, idols, and heresies, and are consumed by them. For the undiscerning, prolonged prosperity is lethal.

Throughout Scripture, there is the constant reminder of the soul-numbing power of wealth that steals our hearts away from God and family in pursuit of lesser things:

> Beware lest you forget the LORD your God by not keeping His commandments and His ordinances and His statutes which I am commanding you today; lest, when you have eaten and are satisfied, and have built good houses and lived in them, and when your herds and your flocks multiply, and your silver and gold multiply, and all that you have multiplies, then your heart becomes proud and you forget the LORD your God.... And it shall come about if you ever forget the LORD your God, and go after other gods and serve them and worship them, I testify against you today that you shall surely perish (Moses, in Deuteronomy 8:11-14,19-20).

> As they had their pasture, they became satisfied, and being satisfied, their heart became proud; therefore, they forgot Me (Hosea, in Hosea 13:6).

> "And the one on whom seed was sown among the thorns, this is the man who hears the word, and the worry of the world, and the deceitfulness of riches choke the word, and it becomes unfruitful" (Jesus, in Matthew 13:22).

> "It is easier for a camel to go through the eye of a needle than for a rich man to enter the kingdom of God" (Jesus, in Mark 10:25).

But those who want to get rich fall into temptation and a snare and many foolish and harmful desires which plunge men into ruin and destruction (Paul, in 1 Timothy 6:9).

Prosperity has never been good for humanity, nor to any other species for that matter. Dr. James Dobson writes:

Biologists have long recognized this...in the world of plants and animals, habitual well-being is not advantageous to a species. An existence without challenge takes its toll on virtually every living thing. Just look at the flabby animals in a zoo, for example. Food is delivered to them every day, and they need do nothing but lie around and yawn. Or consider a tree planted in a rain forest. Because water is readily available, it does not extend its root system more than a few feet below the surface. Consequently, it is often poorly anchored and can be toppled by a minor windstorm.[27]

Prosperity has not been kind to the American family, either. It breeds short, shallow roots. Fragile anchors. It's not that prosperity and wealth are inherently evil. They aren't. But their presence constantly tempts us to believe we are secure without God and that money can be an adequate substitute for real family values. Dad's money can make up for Dad's absence. Things can replace time spent together. Cash can replace convictions. Wealth can pay for irresponsibility and buy out mistakes. A big house can substitute for a sense of home.

Don't believe it. *These statements aren't true!*

Dealing with soul-numbing prosperity is one of the most formidable challenges facing today's family, and minimizing this insidious infection requires great discernment. Even families that fall well short of being wealthy are corrupted by the consuming pursuit of "more." And what are the fruits of the unending pursuit of material possessions? Dr. Dobson explains:

Easy living and abundance often produce a certain indulging weakness. With due respect for my countrymen here in the United States, I believe we have been made soft and vulnerable by materialism and ease. Prolonged prosperity, at least as compared to the rest of the world, has given us a seductive love of comfort.... Alcoholism, immorality, drug abuse, family disintegration, child molestation, pornography, delinquency, homosexuality, and gambling are more pervasive than ever.... It would appear, indeed, that prosperity is a greater test of character than is adversity.[28]

Behind the declining morality and deteriorating family values of our land is the seductive power of ease and comfort. Beware of soul-numbing prosperity.

4. The Rise of the P.C. Bible

One of the forces fueling the new morality is, of all things, the Bible. Not the Bible you and I have come to know. And certainly not the Bible the apostle Paul speaks of when he says, "Hold fast the faithful word" (Titus 1:9). No, this is a *new* Bible.

The P.C. BIBLE.

"P.C." are the "call letters" for the reinvention of Scripture, both personally and politically. P.C. allows for sin and Scripture to coexist as friends in a perverse kind of harmony. P.C. speaks specifically to two kinds of heresies.

First, it addresses the *personally compatible Bible*. As a pastor overseeing a sizable congregation, I have had first-hand experience with this form of the P.C. Bible. Wayward members quote from it often.

Recently, a good friend of mine invited me to breakfast. What expectations I had of a friendly get-together soon vanished when John announced he was leaving his wife. He had been considering this for some time, and after considerable prayer he had come to believe God was in this.

"You're not serious," I said in stunned amazement. John was well-versed when it came to Scripture. He and I had even been part of an intense discipleship group several years earlier. "I'm quite serious," he replied. "Barbara is pleading for me to stay and join her in counseling, but I'm leaving."

"What are your grounds in this divorce?" I asked. John knew the Bible allowed divorce only for a spouse's adultery. But even in that, he also knew our church would strongly encourage forgiveness and reconciliation. "I have no grounds based on *your interpretation,*" he said. "What do you mean, my interpretation?" I replied. John then began to give me a rather lengthy, disjointed explanation of how the Bible allows for divorce in his case. He even reinterpreted Jesus' comments on divorce in Matthew as "for the Jews and not applicable to us today." In the world of the personally compatible Bible, all interpretations are considered equal.

Forget Christian orthodoxy.

Forget two-thousand years of church history that reaffirms the sacred permanency of marriage and its stand against frivolous divorce.

Forget that no Bible-believing church John knew of held to such an interpretation.

"Barbara and I are just wrong for each other. Our differences have created an irreparable breach in our relationship. I trust God and I believe the Bible gives me the freedom to leave. Robert, it's your interpretation versus mine."

It's your interpretation versus mine. This is the rallying cry of those possessing a personally compatible Bible. I have heard it used to justify homosexuality, marriage role reversals, abortion, alcohol abuse, greed; all too often it's used to justify divorce. It is every pastor's worst nightmare.

With the personally compatible Bible, *sinfulness actually becomes a new spirituality*. This P.C. has become a significant threat to establishing real family values.

There is a second P.C. Bible that concerns us. Its force is more public than personal. It is also more formal than informal.

This P.C. is the *politically correct Bible*.

Consider the response that Harvard professor John D. Levinson received when he inquired about the fundamental beliefs of a prominent denominational seminary. To the question, "Are students and faculty required to believe a specific statement of faith?" a member of the faculty said, "No." The only exception to this blanket statement was the requirement that students use inclusive language. Levinson discovered that students being trained for Christian ministry were free to believe whatever they wanted about the cardinal doctrines of Christianity. They were under no obligation to affirm the deity of Christ, the inerrancy of Scripture, or the doctrine of the Trinity. But they could be expelled from school for referring to God as "Father." To do so would only perpetuate the myth of patriarchal authority and lead to the further oppression of women.

> Feminists complain that the Bible is hopelessly immersed in a patriarchal culture that relegates women to an inferior status. In order to make the message of the Bible credible to the new world-consciousness we must therefore proceed to desex and depatriarchalize the language of the Bible.[29]

In the Bold New World of the politically correct Bible, Sunday school curricula are being altered; hymnals have been rephrased in the name of "cultural sensitivity." Certain passages of Scripture have been changed or jettisoned altogether. God is no longer "Father." Instead, He is the "Holy Other," or "our Person," or "the Womb of Being."

Hard topics such as feminism and homosexuality are deliberately ignored in many church pulpits. If these subjects are preached, biblical passages are often reinterpreted or diluted to appease an "enlightened" audience. Much of what passes for "Christian theology" today is nothing more than cultural pablum coated with a thin scriptural veneer. Our Bibles are being stripped of all the difficult texts; they are becoming narrower, more and more inclusive. If Americans will not alter their lifestyles, the growing Christian response seems to be, "Let's alter the *prohibitions*—we don't want to give offense." Because of our passionate embrace of tolerance, the church has lost its moral voice. It reminds me of a powerful statement made by Jamie Buckingham. Reminiscing about the first-century church, a church characterized by bold proclamation that often ended in martyrdom, Buckingham says, "The problem with Christians today is that no one wants to kill them anymore."

Today's world of the politically correct Bible is a world of questionable hermeneutics, textual revisionism, and "red-letter" theology.

Liberal elitists, philosophical pluralism, soul-numbing prosperity, P.C. Bibles. These are just four of the powerful forces behind the issues rocking our culture today.

For the Christian, they have created cultural and spiritual white water. They jar us, shake us, and leave us grasping for a lifeline. At times, we feel like the psalmist who said, "I have come into deep waters, and a flood overflows me" (Psalm 69:2).

Wherein lies our salvation?

When their rafts plunged into Dillon Falls, Steven, Ben, and Ben's three boys were thrown into the raging current. Pushed helplessly downstream, each person struggled to survive. The river meted out death to the strongest members of the party; the weakest escaped by grasping on to the nearest objects they could find. Four-year-old Jeremy rode the rapids on the back of his dead uncle. Seven-year-old Kelly managed to make it to shore. Three-year-old Jesse survived by clinging to something that had lined the river for ages. It was an obstruction in the water—a granite formation that had stood the test of time. Impervious to change, this immovable object was fixed and secure. For two hours, the young boy clung tenaciously to that which would eventually save his life.

A rock.

Notes

[1] *The Oregonian,* 8 July 1993, 1.

[2] Douglas Wilson, *Recovering the Lost Tools of Learning* (Wheaton, Ill.: Crossway, 1991), 91.

[3] Michael Crichton, *Jurassic Park* (New York: Ballantine, 1990), 72.

[4] George Will in Anthony Pratkanis and Elliot Aronson, *Age of Propaganda* (New York: W. H. Freeman and Co., 1991), 12.

[5] Russell Kirk, *The Roots of American Order* (Washington, D.C.: Regnery Gateway), XIX.

[6] "Prepared Remarks by the Vice President at the Commonwealth Club," San Francisco, 19 May 1992, 6.

[7] Ibid., 6.

[8] An excellent book in this regard is Robert Bork, *The Tempting of America* (Simon & Schuster, Inc., 1990).

[9] Joe Sobran, "The Media as the Mission," *Arkansas Democrat-Gazette,* 4 February 1993, 8B.

[10] Suzanne Fields, "Hillary Swims in the Whirlpool of Whitewater," *The Conservative Chronicle,* 23 March 1994, 15.

[11] Robert Novack, *Imprimis* (A Monthly Journal of Hillsdale College), December 1994, 3.

[12] Ibid.

[13] John Ralston Saul, *Voltaire's Bastards: The Dictatorship of Reason in the West* (New York: Free Press, 1992), 16.

[14] "The Elite and How to Avoid It," *Newsweek,* 20 July 1992, 55.

[15] Don Feder, *A Jewish Conservative Looks at Pagan America* (Lafayette, La: Huntington House, 1993), 134.

[16]Quoted in Francis Schaeffer, *A Christian Manifesto* (Wheaton, Ill.: Crossway, 1981), 53.

[17]Ibid., 54.

[18]Don Feder, *A Jewish Conservative Looks at Pagan America*, 75-76.

[19]Ruth Bell, *Changing Bodies, Changing Lives* (New York: Random House, 1980), 90.

[20]Charles Sykes, *A Nation of Victims* (New York: St. Marten's Press, 1992), 11.

[21]John Ralston Saul, *Voltaire's Bastards,*16.

[22]For all of its exaltation of reason, Humanism is, nevertheless, a philosophy built upon faith. Proponents of Humanism often resort to faith statements to explain the unexplainable. In doing so, they deny one of the very premises upon which their philosophy is built. One example will suffice. In his book, *A History of the Mind,* Nicholas Humphrey spends over two hundred pages trying to explain the concept of "mind." Beginning with an evolutionary schema, Humphrey attempts to explain the appearance of mind. How is it that man possesses subjective feelings? How did we develop the capacity of self-consciousness? Is Humphrey's answer scientific? No, it's a faith statement. To explain the appearance of mind, the author says simply: "A seeming miracle? No, as close to a real miracle as anything that ever happened" (p. 228). So much for the irrationality of faith!

[23]Jean Houston in James Sire, *The Universe Next Door* (Downer's Grove, Ill.: InterVarsity Press, 1988), 159-160.

[24]"In Search of the Sacred," *Newsweek,* 28 November 1994, 53.

[25]*Representative Men: Cult Heroes of Our Time,* ed. Theodore L. Gross (New York: Free Press, 1970), 508.

[26]"The Condom Queen Reigns," *The Advocate,* 22 March 1994, 35.

[27]Dr. James Dobson, *When God Doesn't Make Sense* (Wheaton, Ill.: Tyndale House, 1993), 147.

[28]Ibid., 150-151.

[29]Donald Bloesch, *A Theology of Word and Spirit* (Downer's Grove, Ill.: InterVarsity Press, 1992), 85. Bloesch goes on to explicate the logical connection between language of accommodation and spiritual destruction. To illustrate his point, Bloesch makes reference to the Christians in Nazi Germany. "The German Christians, that segment within the church who felt led to accommodate the faith to the ideology of National Socialism in the 1930s, also

sought a new language for divinity. They objected to the Judaic character of the Bible and were determined to de-Judaize the language of faith." Instead of the "people of Israel," the Jews were referred to as the "people of God." "The liturgy and hymnody of the church were purged of Judaic expressions like 'Amen' and 'Hallelujah.'... God, they said, must not be restricted to biblical history but must now be seen as revealing Himself in universal history" (p. 86). A politically correct Bible is a prelude to disaster.

CHAPTER FOUR

The ROCK
in the Bold New World

"Nor is there any rock like our God."
1 SAMUEL 2:2

He is one of the most influential moral philosophers of the nineteenth and twentieth centuries. Surprisingly, most Americans can't even pronounce his name, let alone articulate what he taught. Yet the philosophical seeds this man planted are reaping a harvest of immorality and violence in the Bold New World.

There are two things you need to know about Friedrich Nietzsche (pronounced freed-rick nee-chuh). First, Nietzsche declared God dead. By this he meant the rational grounds for a belief in God's existence had become untenable. Second, Nietzsche went insane. As we will discover momentarily, the latter was (and is) a logical consequence of the former.

Friedrich Nietzsche was born on October 15, 1844 in Prussia. His father was a German pastor. A master student of both theology and philology, Nietzsche studied at Bonn and later transferred to Leipzig. In 1869, at the young age of twenty-five, he became a full professor of classical philology at the

University of Basel, where he taught for the next nine years. It was during this period of time that Nietzsche began to formulate the ideas that would turn the western world of the twentieth century upside down.

"God Is Dead"

The centerpiece of the philosopher's ideology is the much repeated phrase, "God is dead." In Nietzsche's mind, modern man had entered a new age—one which was no longer constrained by, in his view, the pervasive, debilitating influences of Christianity. This new reality was a cause for celebration and presented mankind with untold opportunities for moral and spiritual advancement:

> The most important of more recent events—that "god is dead," that the belief in the Christian God has become unworthy of belief—already begins to cast its first shadows over Europe.... In fact, we philosophers and "free spirits" feel ourselves irradiated as by a new dawn by the report that the "old God is dead"; our hearts overflow with gratitude, astonishment, presentiment and expectation.[1]

According to Nietzsche, humanity had toiled for eighteen hundred years under the crushing weight of "mankind's greatest misfortune"—Christianity.[2] He despised the faith because he maintained it represented a turning away from life. Confronted with the terrors of human existence, mankind found solace in a series of myths that were supposed to bring freedom but actually resulted in slavery. In *The Will to Power*, Nietzsche identified the "myths" that have imperiled humanity. He called them, collectively, the "holy lie." At the center of this holy lie was: 1) a God who punishes and rewards; 2) belief in the immortality of the soul; 3) conscience; 4) morality; and 5) truth as revelation.[3]

In combination, these "lies" prevent a person from becoming what Nietzsche prized above all else—an individual:

> The virtuous man is a lower species because he is not a "person" but acquires his value by conforming to a pattern of man that is fixed once and for all. He does not possess his value apart; he can be compared, he has his equals, he must not be an individual.[4]

Ignorant of the false assumptions that define his existence, Nietzsche claimed, the Christian becomes a "herd animal"—a person who conforms to and perpetuates the values of lesser men. "To accommodate oneself, to live as the 'common man' lives.... This is to submit to the herd instinct."[5]

In the face of this intolerable situation, the only hope for mankind was the complete overthrow of Christianity. The key factor in the equation was God. Nietzsche realized that if God was dethroned, or emasculated, then the rest of the building would crumble to dust. So, beginning with naturalistic presuppositions, Nietzsche posited the death of God. He writes poetically about God's demise in *The Joyful Wisdom*. "The holiest and mightiest being in the world bled to death under our knives.... No greater deed was ever done, and whoever is born after us will, thanks to this deed, live in a higher history than there has ever been."[6]

It should be noted that Nietzsche was not the first thinker to postulate God's death. The Romance-era poet Jean Paul (1762-1825) had written a work entitled, "Discourse of the dead Christ from atop the cosmos: there is not God." Hegel had also used the phrase "God is dead" prior to Nietzsche. But Nietzsche was unique in one respect: Like no one before him, the philosopher understood the *implications* of the idea "God is dead." As Ronald Hayman observes, "human illogicality was rare in the nineteenth century, and it was this, above all, that enabled him [Nietzsche] to exert such an enormous influence on the twentieth [century]..."[7] Many of his secular contemporaries wanted to deny God's existence and, at the same time, retain Christian morality. Nietzsche would have none of it. To employ a fashionable phrase, Nietzsche was an atheist with an attitude. If God was dead, Christian morality ceased to exist.

> Christianity is a system, a consistently thought out and complete view of things. If one breaks out of it the fundamental idea, the belief in God, one thereby breaks the whole thing to pieces: one has nothing of any consequence left in one's hands.... Christian morality is a command; its origin is transcendental;...it stands or falls with the belief in God.[8]

The logic was incontrovertible—the tree of Christian morality grew out of the root of divine transcendence. Destroy the root and the tree would fall.

For one hundred years now, the tree for many has been severed from the root. With the death of God and the eclipse of absolute values, modern man stepped into the void and created his own values. The eternal, immutable, transcendent God of the Bible—purged of His authority—has become a museum piece in the Bold New World. He still exists in the minds of many Americans. After all, the vast majority of us believe in God's existence. But in truth, He has become irrelevant. This God no longer has the right to make moral demands upon His creatures. Like a pet dog, He is nice to have around primarily because He makes few, if any, demands upon our personal lives.

The death of God was supposed to inaugurate a sweeping transformation of society. Nietzsche looked forward to the future with great expectation. Man was now free to shape his own existence. But the results have been catastrophic. Nietzsche's ideas have resulted in moral chaos. In a world without God, his philosophy has spawned massive confusion. The situation is strikingly similar to the final outcome of his own life. Our society is plagued by the same condition to which Nietzsche succumbed—insanity.

Nietzsche's Insanity

Symptoms began to appear in his middle age: delusions of grandeur, megalomania, euphoria, and fits of depression. Nietzsche went crazy. Some scholars have argued that Nietzsche's insanity was caused by cerebral syphilis, supposedly contracted in the 1860s. This conclusion is speculative at best. According to biographer Ronald Hayman, "It is improbable that the delusions of grandeur before the breakdown (in 1889) or the madness after it had anything to do with syphilis."[9] Hayman's analysis is much more thought-provoking. The author posits a direct correlation between Nietzsche's philosophy and the madness of his latter years. Writing in *Beyond Good and Evil,* Nietzsche himself recognized the relationship between a man's philosophy and his private life:

> I have gradually come to understand what every great philosophy until now has been: the confession of its author and a kind of involuntary, unconscious memoir.... Nothing at all about the philosopher is impersonal; above all his morality provides decided and decisive evidence about who he is.[10]

If it is true that the man shapes the philosophy, it is equally true that the philosophy shapes the man. Hayman is intrigued by the connection. He cites a friend of Nietzsche's who suggested that "he [Nietzsche] had lived his way toward madness."[11]

Like no one before him, Nietzsche lived out the consequences of a universe without God. The result was madness.

Hayman went on to pose a question that reverberates with relevance for us today. He asks: "Is it possible to reject as much of our moral and linguistic tradition as Nietzsche did without following him down the road to insanity?"[12] The answer is categorical: NO, this is not possible. A world devoid of transcendent, absolute truth inevitably reduces to *insanity.*

This one word—insanity—describes America's moral condition in the Bold New World.

Insanity is former Supreme Court Justice Harry Blackmun declaring he will no longer uphold the death penalty—for any reason whatsoever—because he finds it personally offensive. This is the same justice whose legacy will turn on a 1973 decision (Roe v. Wade) that paved the way for the murder of millions of unborn children. Insanity is the knowledge that condoms work effectively only 87 percent of the time but distributing them anyway, as a "safe" alternative to abstinence. Insanity is an American public that reacts with outrage at the abandonment of week-old infants but remains unmoved by the slaughter of thousands of seven- and eight-month preborns who could exist outside the womb. Insanity is a judicial system that increasingly makes the perpetrator of a crime the "victim," and refuses to exact justice for those who have been violated.

A world devoid of absolute truth inevitably reduces to INSANITY.

Just ask the residents of Dale, Indiana. This small midwestern town (population 18,000) is unique for one very special reason: Dale is halved by two different time zones. The eastern side of town is in the eastern time zone; the western half is in the central time zone. Time is probably an absolute where you live; everyone sets his clock by one fixed standard. Not so for the residents of Dale. Four o'clock in the eastern half of Dale is three o'clock in the western half, and so forth. To compound matters, many of the townspeople live in one sector but work in the other. A lunch appointment with someone across town must be carefully orchestrated. Watches must be synchronized: "Is that 11:30 your time or mine?" When asked what life was like in Dale, a woman at the chamber of commerce responded by saying, "Not very much fun." She went on to describe the confusion that attends a place where the absolute of time no longer exists.

Insanity and relativism are kissing cousins. Without an absolute standard to which all can look for guidance (moral and otherwise), confusion abounds. Historian Paul Johnson writes: "All forms of moral relativism have an innate tendency to generate moral collapse since they eliminate any fixed anchorage and launch the ship of state on an ocean where there are no bearings at all."[13] Senator Daniel Patrick Moynihan has witnessed the gradual erosion that occurs when relativism reigns. He calls the process "defining deviancy downward." Perverse behavior once considered deviant is redefined as normal. Over time it is embraced as the norm.

The Bold New World is mired in absurdity because the tree has been severed from the root. God is dead, or, at best, irrelevant.

There is good reason for America's moral morass.

A Firm Foundation

At the conclusion of the previous chapter, I posed a question: Wherein lies our salvation? How is the Christian to make sense of the moral chaos that pervades the Bold New World? Who is able to part the current and rescue the drowning swimmer?

The Rock.

It is time for the church to rediscover the eternal, immutable, transcendent God of the Bible. For too long we have taken our cues from society. "Since the eighteenth century, humanity rather than God has been the focal point of theology and philosophy."[14] To borrow from C. S. Lewis's imagery of a British courtroom, man has been on the bench and God has been in the dock (the place where the defendant stands during a trial).[15]

Divine revelation has been made to cower shamefully before the bar of human reason. Without even realizing it, the

Christian has supplanted God's authority. Influenced by opinion polls, political agendas, and media hype, we have relegated biblical truth to a subordinate or (at best) complementary status. To the present generation of believers, Scripture no longer speaks with a clarion voice. It is more like a muffled groan. In the face of confrontation, we hesitate and hedge our positions. We just aren't sure whether homosexuality is really a sin or abortion is the taking of human life. The Reformation advanced on Luther's audacious cry: "Here I stand, I can do no other. God help me!" When a courageous Christian does something equally bold in our day, he is often branded as a radical and viewed with disdain—sometimes by the members of his own church!

Our ambivalence is causative. The sad truth is, we doubt the character of God and the authority of Scripture. On the other hand, resolute conviction is the product of a sturdy faith. And a sturdy faith always begins with the person of God.

So, who is this ROCK?

The firm foundation upon which we stand is the God who called the world into being (Genesis 1—2). This God created man in His own image (Genesis 2:7), and imprinted within our breast the faculties of reason, morality, beauty, and spirituality. From the beginning, our existence was defined in relation to the God of the universe. Though time would witness the corruption of humanity, the Rock would remain impervious to change. He is transcendent (Isaiah 55:8-9) and self-existent (Exodus 3:14-15), wholly unique in His person and nature. He is immutable (Numbers 23:19), the same today as He was ages past. This God is truth (John 17:3), the fountainhead of wisdom and knowledge. He is sovereign (Psalm 103:19) and just (Job 36:6), a moral lawgiver (Exodus 20:1-17) who one day will call each individual to give an account for the deeds he has done (Revelation 20:11-15). And though His glory is shrouded momentarily by the wickedness of men, this God is ever-present, ever-holy, ever-loving, waiting patiently for fallen man to come to repentance through His Son, Jesus Christ.

He is the Rock who speaks to us, boldly and authoritatively, through the pages of Scripture. The Bible's words are His words. For this reason, we don't have to guess or speculate about the moral issues that confront us in the Bold New World. If we will but take the time to read and listen, the Rock has answers. Graciously given by His character, the Bible stands as the living expression of absolute truth. Donald Bloesch has stated that Scripture is "an infallible standard transcending and governing history... [it is] an anchor in the transcendent."[16] To the drowning Christian, the Word of God is the lifeline amid the white water of relativism.

In the Bold New World, husbands, wives, and children need something to help them navigate the currents of change. Listen! Only God's Word can accomplish this monumental task. Tossed about by the torrents of cultural transformation, we have an anchor: one that is dependable, certain, incontrovertible. The solutions found in the Bible will sound harsh to the person steeped in modernity. But don't discount them for this reason. Truth is indeed a hard master, but a faithful one.

We have reached the top of the falls. Danger lurks below. Fortunately, this is not an amateur float trip. We have a Guide in our raft. The Lord God is going to take us safely through the waters. So take courage! Along the way, if you feel yourself being jarred and jostled, don't jump overboard; just secure your grip on the Guide and hold on.

Throughout the rest of this book we will allow the Word of God to chart our course over perilous waters. Our goal is to discern these difficult times with biblical knowledge of what a Christian family should do and believe and pass on. Real Family Values.

Notes

[1]Colin Brown, *Philosophy and the Christian Faith* (Downer's Grove, Ill.: InterVarsity Press, 1968), 139.

[2]Friedrich Nietzsche, *Twilight of the Idols* (New York: Penguin, 1968), 101.

[3]Friedrich Nietzsche, *The Will to Power,* ed. Walter Kaufman (New York: Vintage, 1968), 90-91.

[4]Ibid., 176.

[5]Ibid., 252.

[6]Ronald Hayman, *Nietzsche: A Critical Life* (New York: Oxford University Press, 1980), 238-239).

[7]Ibid., 2.

[8]Friedrich Nietzsche, *Twilight of the Idols,* 69-70.

[9]Ronald Hayman, *Nietzsche: A Critical Life,* 11.

[10]Ibid., vii.

[11]Ibid., 11.

[12]Ibid., 3.

[13]Paul Johnson, *Modern Times* (New York: Harper and Row, 1983), 403.

[14]Donald Bloesch, *A Theology of Word and Spirit* (Downer's Grove, Ill.: InterVarsity Press, 1992), 25.

[15]C. S. Lewis, *God in the Dock* (Grand Rapids, Mich.: Eerdman's, 1970), 244.

[16]Donald Bloesch, *A Theology of Word and Spirit,* 123.

YOUR FAMILY
and Real Family Values

CHAPTER FIVE

All FAMILIES Are Not EQUAL

"The family is the finest humanitarian organization we know because it alone responds to the needs of its members on a voluntary unpaid basis throughout life. These contributions are a distinct form of social reproduction, too long ignored."
WILLIAM GAIRDNER

I traveled to my hometown of Ruston, Louisiana, a number of times during the spring and summer of 1992. The circumstances were less than desirable. My mother was dying of cancer, and I wanted to be near her side for the last few months of her life. On one trip I awoke early in the morning and went for a jog. I decided to visit some of the memorable haunts from my childhood. I jogged to Eastland Elementary School, the place where I first learned my ABCs. I gazed at the playground and thought about touch football games, kickball contests, and endless hours of irresponsibility and fun. I ran down the path leading to my old house, past the homes of childhood friends, past vacant lots where I threw rocks and hung out with the boys. The jog became less of a workout and was quickly transformed into a stroll down memory lane.

My only remaining anchor to the past—my mother—lay dying, and the fond memories of childhood flooded my soul and choked my heart. Hoping to relive the joys of my childhood, I headed toward the old Lewis homestead. But when I came upon my old street and glanced at the place where our house should have been, I was devastated to discover it no longer existed. A bank had purchased the property, leveled the Lewis "estate," and was turning this treasured icon into a parking lot. The glorious oak trees that shaded our front yard were gone; the pecan trees that had supplied the filling for many of mom's delectable pecan pies were no more. I stood motionless, in a state of disbelief, overwhelmed by the disappearance of my childhood home. Images of mom and dad, games of hide and seek with my brothers, backyard basketball, and pleasant meals around the dinner table—all of these timeless memories were tied to a white brick house with gray shutters on South Bonner Street. But that house was now gone.

I felt as if my childhood had disappeared, too.

My old house was anything but extraordinary. It was constructed of brick and mortar, glass and cement—just like many other homes in America. But this old house was special to me because it was invested with memories of *family*. It was impossible for me to think of this place without recalling laughter and tears, heartache and happiness—the stuff of childhood. The thought of *home* released in me powerful memories. Even as an adult, I still find myself daydreaming about this place from my childhood, recounting the pleasurable experiences of my youth that are now gone. In this matter of the heart I have a soul mate. When Abraham Lincoln was thirty-seven years old, he penned a poem, *Memories,* which says in part:

> My childhood home I see again,
> And saddened with the view.
> And still, as memory crowds my brain,
> There's pleasure in it, too.

Where many things were, but few remain
Of old familiar things.
But seeing them to mind again,
The lost and absent brings.[1]

The Power of Family Memories

Memories of FAMILY are a powerful and ever-present force; they sculpt and shape our lives in a thousand different ways. This is why *It's a Wonderful Life*, the classic movie starring Jimmy Stewart, retains such an emotional hold over us. In his book *The War Against the Family*, William Gairdner captures the mystical power of memories in the life of each individual.

Part of the joy—and the sadness—of growing older is the experience of memory of the primal home. Almost regardless of its material comforts, the intimacy of the home and, for many, the memory of the land on which one first became aware of life lingers forever—often as a basic mood or condition we attempt ever afterward to retrieve, or to duplicate. When we return years later to the scene of intimate childhood life, we are likely to be shocked by the humdrum nature of a place or a mood that in our minds had assumed an almost transcendent quality or permanence. If by chance the primal dwelling is now gone [these words were written for my benefit] the wound of disbelief is palpable.[2]

The memories of family exert a remarkable influence over our lives; this influence remains with us until the day of our death. Great writers have given testimony to the power of family and the influence of childhood. For some, the experiences are too painful to recall, though even in heartache the memories are impossible to forget. With his own troubled childhood animating his work, Charles Dickens would write of David Copperfield, "The remembrance of that life is fraught with so much pain to me, with so much mental suffering and want of hope, that I have never had the courage even to examine how long I was doomed to lead it."[3]

Dickens's novel, *Bleak House,* an appropriate title for the author's own life, has as its major theme the painful experiences of childhood. The haunting works of Franz Kakfa, most notably *The Metamorphosis,* are expressions of a disjointed, often tumultuous, childhood. Later in life, Ernest Hemingway recounted the times when he had grown angry with his father. It is reported that he "had sometimes sat in the open door of the shed [out back] with his shotgun, drawing a bead on his father's head."[4] The memories of family and youth are potent forces in the life of an adult. Destinies are shaped in childhood—often for the good. For example, at the age of thirteen, Douglas MacArthur overheard his father say to his mother: "I think there is the material of a soldier in that boy."[5] William Manchester notes that "the son swore never to forget it—and never did."[6] Corrie ten Boom's father used to place his hand on her head every night at bedtime and pray for her. His last words were always, "Corrie, I love you." When she found herself in the concentration camp at Ravensbruck, Corrie would fall asleep at night imagining her heavenly Father's hand on her head.

Memories of family. Some are good, some bad. All are powerful. Someone has said that "family is culture." How true this is. In every home across our land today, tomorrow's culture is incubating. Right now. Each experiment has the potential for good or for evil. In the hands of responsible parents, children become responsible citizens. When parents define standards of morality and model those same standards for their kids, children can be expected to practice honesty, integrity, and chastity. When parents give love and kindness, their children do the same. Family is culture.

Assault upon the Family

But for the last thirty years, America has entered into an experiment that bodes ominously for our culture. At the heart of this experiment lies the family. Like a cadaver donated to the university, the family is being dissected and analyzed by pragmatic politicians and simple-minded sociologists. Theories abound as to how the corpse can be revived, but the reality is that much of our public policy—from crushing taxation to no-fault divorce—has sucked the life out of this priceless institution. Increasingly, homosexual partners are being allowed to adopt children, and the legal system, in state after state, recognizes this as "normal." Divorce is now as simple as one or two court appearances. Condoms are dispensed without the consent of parents. A teenager needs permission to receive Tylenol at school but can get an abortion without her mom or dad's consent—assuming the "patient" can pay for the procedure.

Over the last thirty years we have been conducting what is tantamount to a massive national experiment. Commenting upon this radical agenda, and specifically upon the exodus of fathers from the home and the feminization of American culture, Sociologist Marion J. Levy writes:

> Most of us have not even noticed this change, nor do we have any realization of its radicality. We certainly do not have any systematic body of speculation on what the significance of so radical a change are or could be. To put the matter as dramatically as possible, we do not even know whether viable human beings can over a long period of time be reared in such a fashion. After all, this has never held true of any substantial portion of any population for even one generation in the history of the world until the last fifty years.[7]

American culture is convulsing. But how could it be otherwise when we have suffocated, strangled, and drained the lifeblood from the very heart of culture—the family? Clearly,

all is not lost. There have been recent developments that portend hope. As I write this chapter, there is a renewed national
interest in fatherhood. *Newsweek* designated 1994 as the "Year
of the Father." Thousands of men are jamming stadiums across
the country to attend seminars sponsored by Promise Keepers,
a ministry for men and their families. A National Summit on
Fatherhood was held in Dallas, Texas, in the fall of 1994.

A Generation at Risk

Slowly, the family is coming back into favor. It can't happen
too soon. For too long the Rousseauian vision of "the state as
family" has permeated our social landscape. More and more
parental rights have been rescinded; government policy, in the
areas of education, welfare, and abortion, have engendered
wanton dependence upon the state. Growing numbers of
mothers—single and married—now farm out their children to
daycare centers. Our indifference to the needs of children and
the primacy of the family have placed a generation at risk. In a
haunting book entitled *High Risk: Children without a
Conscience,* Dr. Ken Magid and Carole A. McKelvey track the
rise of psychopaths in our culture and identify the source of
this frightening new development. We shouldn't be surprised
to learn that the culprit is the fractured family.

> What happens, right or wrong, in the critical first two
> years of a baby's life will imprint that child as an adult.
> A complex set of events must occur in infancy to assure
> a future of trust and love. If the proper bonding and
> subsequent attachment does not occur—usually
> between the child and the mother—the child will
> develop mistrust and a deep-seated rage. He becomes a
> child without a conscience.[8]

Like a prophet of doom, novelist William Golding foresaw
the present crisis and detailed its consequences in his powerful
story *Lord of the Flies.* The book is about a group of English

boys who are marooned on a tropical island following a plane crash. The setting is a perfect version of Rousseau's idealized state: abundant food and water, the camaraderie of children, and unbridled freedom. But as you know if you've read the story, an idyllic paradise quickly turns into a tortured, violent hell. Unrestrained by parental authority, these "noble savages" degenerate into vicious predators. *Lord of the Flies* is a graphic condemnation of modern America, filled as it is with absent, irresponsible parents and kids killing kids. As Golding writes in his notes on the book, "The moral [of the story] is that the shape of a society must depend on the ethical nature of the individual and not on any political system however apparently logical or respectable."[9]

Lord of the Flies was written in 1954 but its plot elements appear nightly on the local news. Teen violence, drug abuse, and exploding birth rates among unwed mothers have their genesis in the breakdown of the one institution that is best suited to constrain and retrain "the ethical nature of the individual"—the family.

"Family": What Is It Really?

Two blatant lies permeate our politically correct culture with respect to the family.

The first lie is that all families are equal. They are not. No arrangement even comes close to the natural family. In the words of William Gairdner, the natural family, composed of a father, mother, and children, "is the most basic universal fact of our existence."[10] Every other arrangement—whether it be single parents with children, homosexual couples, monogamous live-in relationships, blended families, or grandparents caring for grandchildren—remains something *less* than a natural family.

It's difficult to discuss the inequities between families. It is an unpopular subject and one that strikes at the core of our society. My intention is not to hurt anyone or to heap guilt upon those who find themselves, for no fault of their own, in a difficult family situation. But the family is where culture is won or lost. And behind every family masquerading as "natural," there are lives being shattered and children being scarred. I'm not naive enough to believe this doesn't occur in natural families as well. I'm only making the point that the ideal has been breached in the name of "normality."

All families are not equal. But you would never know this by what is reported in the media. Just recently I read an article supporting the outlandish notion that single parents make better parents than couples. The reasoning: Single parents, because they are "unencumbered" by marital relationships, have more time to devote to their children. This strikes me as odd. Most of the single parents I know are always exhausted; they struggle to fulfill their career and family obligations.

Family diversity in the form of single-parent families, step-parents, and live-in relationships does not strengthen the fabric of society. Instead, this diversity weakens it. Such arrangements place ever-increasing burdens upon our schools, our courts, our prisons, and our welfare system. These new families are not an improvement upon the nuclear family. In fact, far from advancing social progress, family changes in America have resulted in social regression. This is a hard truth but it is undeniable. Some family structures are better than others. And the structure most advantageous for children is the one God designed and reproduced on the opening pages of the Bible— the natural family of one man, one woman, committed to each other and their children, for life. No one has been able to improve upon this radical arrangement.

The second lie is that children are quick to recover from divorce and other family crises. They aren't. (Because I have devoted an entire chapter to this myth—chapter 10—we will touch upon it briefly here.) In the 1970s, a best-selling book by Mel Krantzer propagated the notion that divorce had little negative effect upon children. *Creative Divorce* became a Bible for thousands of parents who were bailing out of marital commitments. Krantzer argued that children were resilient, and that the consequences of divorce upon children were minimal at worst.

Time and experience have combined to refute the folly of Krantzer's ideals. A number of social scientists have tracked children of divorce over ten- to fifteen-year periods; they've discovered that children are not resilient.[11] Far from it! The wounds of parental desertion and rejection linger for a lifetime. Anyone who has ever tried to roll a snowball knows the center must be solid. If it isn't, if there are flaws or cracks in the core, no matter how many layers of snow cover them, these cracks will inevitably surface with disastrous consequences. Childhood is like that. Childhood is the core of life. It, too, must begin solidly, for we never really leave childhood. Instead, we layer experiences and time over it. If the core is wounded or damaged, these flaws inevitably surface in adulthood with equally distressing consequences. The wounds of divorce last a lifetime.

All families are *not* equal. Children are *not* resilient. The nuclear family, with all of its room for imperfection, still remains the best and most desirable arrangement for children. Americans in large numbers seem to recognize, or at least yearn for, this primal family structure.

A 1987 survey carried out for *Rolling Stone* magazine, based on a national sample of eighteen- to forty-four-year-olds, asked its respondents to list the television shows with values they wanted their children to learn; they named "Father Knows Best" and "Leave It to Beaver," along with their counterparts from the 1980s, "The Cosby Show" and "Family Ties."[12]

The Primacy of the Family

Family is culture. The natural family, which anthropologist Margaret Mead called "a commitment of permanence to the community," is the lifeblood of society. But why? What is it about the family that makes it indispensable to cultural health and vitality? Consider these four essential components.

1. Like no other institution, the family is singularly committed to children. No organization or institution—not the state, not the public schools, not the welfare system—is as passionately committed to children as are loving, responsible parents. "The essential fact of and fundamental reason for the existence of the natural family," writes Gairdner, "is that it is *the only entity in human history that has ever been dedicated, with utter partiality, to the nurturing and protection of children*" [author's emphasis].[13] Lacking this protective cocoon, children are thrown back on the arbitrary benevolence of others. This creates insecurity; children in this predicament often become angry and resentful.

2. The family functions as an emotional safety net. The passage from childhood to adulthood is like a minefield laden with emotional trauma. Do you recall the confusion you experienced as you muddled your way through puberty? Or the disabling agony of unrequited love during adolescence? I do. When the storms of life swirl violently in a child's life, the family softens the pain and disappointment. Seared emotions can be healed; fears can be allayed with love.

3. The family is the premier training ground for virtue. Someone has said that "virtue is the result of training, not education." You don't become honest and compassionate by merely learning about these qualities; instead, these character traits are born and bred in the closeness of intimate relationships. And there is no relationship more intimate than the family.

4. The family is a source of powerful, unforgettable memories. As discussed earlier, the experiences of childhood comprise a timeless wealth of resources which we draw upon throughout the course of our lives.

Family is culture. But there are many in our day, simpleminded sociologists among them, who want to do away with the family because it is prone to failure. G. K. Chesterton had this group in mind when he wrote, "[The family] is like the church and like the republic, now chiefly assailed by those who have never known it, or by those who have failed to fulfill it."[14]

The primacy of the family is established by personal experience; it is also substantiated by the testimony of history. In a truly remarkable book, *Family and Civilization,* Carle Zimmerman proves beyond question the role of the family in guiding and sustaining human societies.[15] Zimmerman studied the correlation between family and the life span of civilizations. His research covered not only the Greek and Roman Empires, but also the democracies of western Europe—France and Germany—as well as the United States. The author discovered that every civilization in human history began with a particular, and predictable, type of family structure. Zimmerman calls this primary family the "trustee family."

The trustee family was distinctively authoritarian. It possessed a shared set of core values and called forth a radical selflessness on the part of its members. The trustee family became the foundation of each civilization. But then, as a nation solidified, a different family structure was birthed. Zimmerman called the next stage the "domestic family." The domestic family was still patriarchical in nature but exhibited less leadership from the top and was more cooperative. The family became more of a team than a monarchy. Within the domestic family, both parents shared domestic responsibilities, often at the expense of personal ambitions. At this stage, Zimmerman notes, an empire or nation attained the pinnacle of greatness. The existence of the domestic family paralleled periods of national prosperity.

But as it often does, great prosperity leads inevitably to decay. A corruption of values led to the demise of the domestic family and ushered in the final stage, what Zimmerman calls the "atomistic family." People began to view themselves as autonomous, no longer interconnected with others. Personal rights took precedent over personal responsibility and self-sacrifice. Over time, the atomistic family disintegrated, as did the civilizations in which it existed. Zimmerman's conclusion is that family and culture, family and the life span of a civilization, go hand-in-hand.

Characteristics of an Atomistic Society

Incredibly, Carle Zimmerman penned this book in 1947. His work stands outside the purview of modern American history, though his conclusions are prophetic for us today. Consider the following characteristics of an atomistic society, as defined by Zimmerman, and listen for the resounding echo of modern America. When the atomistic family arrives on the cultural scene, eight characteristics follow in its wake.

- Marriage loses its sacredness and is frequently broken by divorce.
- The traditional meaning of the marriage ceremony is lost. Alternate forms of marriage arise and individual marriage contracts supplant traditional agreements.
- Feminist movements abound. Women lose their inclination for childbearing and childrearing; birth rates decrease.
- There is a growing disrespect for parental authority, for parenthood, and for authority in general.
- There is an increase in juvenile delinquency, promiscuity, and rebellion.
- Members of traditional marriages refuse to accept family responsibilities.
- There is an increasing desire for, and acceptance of, adultery.
- There is greater tolerance for perversions of all kinds, especially homosexuality. According to Zimmerman, this final stage signals the demise of culture.

I liken these statements to the warning sirens that sound during violent storms here in the South. Weathermen appear on television and alert us that conditions are right for a tornado. But not until the sirens blare does the danger become real. Only then does the need to seek shelter become imminent. So it is with the characteristics of the atomistic family. The temptation in our day is to seek shelter, to barricade ourselves against the storm and pray for salvation. Our only hope in this convergence of violent and destructive forces is to cover ourselves with the wisdom of God's Word.

The Family Ideal

To help you visualize the wide array of family "options" that permeate our society, I'd like you to study the diagram on the next page. At the top of the page you will find the family ideal. This model derives from Genesis 2 and consists of one man and one woman, committed to one another and their children for life. The members of this family are submissive to God and His Word and to others. The closer a family gets to the ideal, the more they cooperate with one another, honor one another, support one another, and communicate with one another. Couples who pursue this model produce children who are "healthy" and "wealthy"—they step into the world as adults and make a radical difference. This is the ideal. But you notice the word "sin" in the diagram. This is the reality of life in a fallen world. Every person who enters marriage brings with him or her some type of dysfunction. All dysfunction is debilitating, but the godly man or woman seeks to conquer the liabilities of the past. They can learn to become "functional," or they can choose to remain "dysfunctional."

Notice also that Christian families come in all shapes and sizes. They are found throughout the diagram—near both the top and the bottom. Some non-Christian couples even come closer to the ideal than certain Christian couples. Why is this?

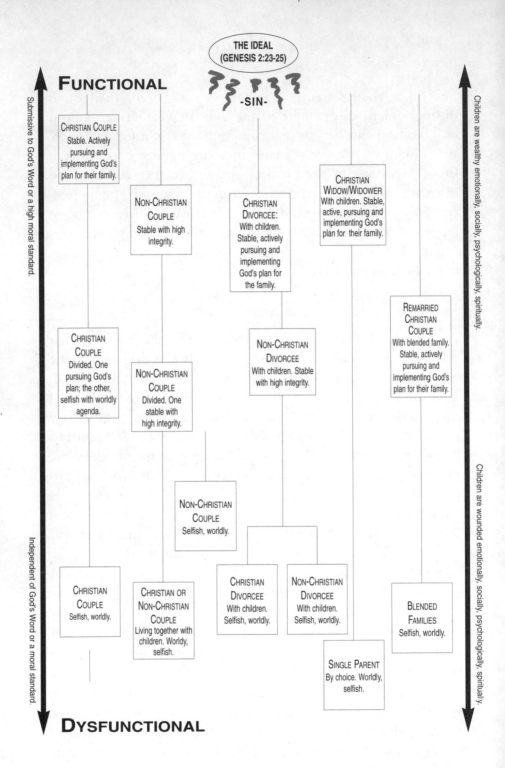

FUNCTIONAL

THE IDEAL
(GENESIS 2:23-25)

-SIN-

CHRISTIAN COUPLE
Stable. Actively pursuing and implementing God's plan for their family.

NON-CHRISTIAN COUPLE
Stable with high integrity.

CHRISTIAN DIVORCEE:
With children. Stable, actively pursuing and implementing God's plan for the family.

CHRISTIAN WIDOW/WIDOWER
With children. Stable, active, pursuing and implementing God's plan for their family.

CHRISTIAN COUPLE
Divided. One pursuing God's plan; the other, selfish with worldly agenda.

NON-CHRISTIAN COUPLE
Divided. One stable with high integrity.

NON-CHRISTIAN DIVORCEE
With children. Stable with high integrity.

REMARRIED CHRISTIAN COUPLE
With blended family. Stable, actively pursuing and implementing God's plan for their family.

NON-CHRISTIAN COUPLE
Selfish, worldly.

CHRISTIAN COUPLE
Selfish, worldly.

CHRISTIAN OR NON-CHRISTIAN COUPLE
Living together with children. Worldy, selfish.

CHRISTIAN DIVORCEE
With children. Selfish, worldly.

NON-CHRISTIAN DIVORCEE
With children. Selfish, worldly.

BLENDED FAMILIES
Selfish, worldly.

SINGLE PARENT
By choice. Worldly, selfish.

DYSFUNCTIONAL

Submissive to God's Word or a high moral standard.

Independent of God's Word or a moral standard.

Children are wealthy emotionally, socially, psychologically, spiritually.

Children are wounded emotionally, socially, psychologically, spiritually.

Well, the answer is found in the genius of the family. A stable non-Christian couple might not contribute spiritually to the lives of their children but they still have a lot to offer. For example, they can provide a stable home, emotional security, character formation, and precious memories. Even lacking the spiritual dimension, this couple is producing healthier children than the "Christian" couple characterized by moral hypocrisy and spiritual compromise.

If you follow the vertical line on the left to the bottom of the page, you will see the polar opposite of the ideal family. Chief among this group is the "Single parent by choice," the Murphy Brown individual. For this group, childrearing is a hobby, entered into for the express purpose of fulfilling one's self, not for the welfare of the child. Will Durant discovered this group in his study of ancient Rome; he said of these women that they "saw children as a toy."[16] The members of this bottom group are "Independent of God, His Word, and others." Autonomy and selfishness are the hallmarks of this household. Children reared in families near the bottom of the diagram enter adulthood with deep wounds and scars.

The Healthy Family

What are the characteristics of a healthy family? Surprisingly, they are fairly easy to define. Whether you study Christian or non-Christian sources, the answer to this question, with some exceptions, is essentially the same.[17] The fact that there is so much overlap between Christian and secular sources only serves to buttress the point. Healthy families are easy to define; they are a lot harder to create. You may be tempted to skip over the list below. Please resist the temptation. Every principle is a pivotal component in the life of a healthy, vibrant family.

1. Healthy families are characterized by strong, supportive, honest communication. They talk to one another—about everything. They turn off the television set during dinner and ask questions. Healthy families are committed to Ephesians 4:29, which reads: "Let no unwholesome word proceed from your mouth, but only such a word as is good for edification according to the need of the moment."

2. Healthy families spend a large quantity of time together. Please dispel from your mind the mistaken idea that quality time is an adequate replacement for quantity time. It isn't. There is no substitute for large blocks of time spent together as a family—talking, playing, laughing, praying.

3. Healthy families share a common faith and practice. This is why the apostle Paul writes in 2 Corinthians 6:14, "Do not be bound together with unbelievers." Intimacy is the backbone of family life, and the most intimate relationship of all is one's relationship with God. A common faith enables a couple to develop oneness in marriage and work through the inevitable conflicts that arise within the family.

4. Healthy families agree on key values. The prophet Amos asked a question that illustrates this point. In Amos 3:3, he says, "Do two men walk together unless they have made an appointment [agreement to do so]?" The implied answer is "no." There must be agreement on a variety of issues, such as disciplining the children, financial expenditures, moral standards, and career decisions.

5. Healthy families practice love and mutual appreciation. Peter voiced this truth when he wrote: "Husbands likewise, live with your wives in an understanding way...and grant her honor as a fellow heir of the grace of life" (1 Peter 3:7).

6. Healthy families have common goals and interests. Writing to the "family" of believers in Philippi, Paul says, "Make my joy complete by being of the same mind, maintaining the same love, united in spirit, intent on one purpose" (Philippians 2:2). Common goals and interests become an incentive to spend time together.

7. Healthy families are able to negotiate solutions to crises. They have formulated clearly defined parameters for such things as conflict resolution, family squabbles, and disagreements. These standards limit the use of strong language or offensive accusations. And when rules are broken, the members of healthy families are quick to ask for forgiveness and make restitution. "And be kind to one another, tender-hearted, forgiving each other, just as God in Christ also has forgiven you" (Ephesians 4:32).

8. Couples in healthy families have regular sexual intercourse with one another. Paul articulates this principle in 1 Corinthians 7:4-5, "The wife does not have authority over her own body, but the husband does; and likewise also the husband does not have authority over his own body, but the wife does. Stop depriving one another, except by agreement for a time that you may devote yourselves to prayer, and come together again lest Satan tempt you because of your lack of self-control."

9. Healthy families make sacrifices for the good of the family. The truest measure of health in a family is the amount of self-sacrifice by each of its members. "Do nothing from selfishness or empty conceit," writes Paul, "but with humility of mind let each of you regard one another as more important than himself" (Philippians 2:3).

10. Healthy families exhibit trust among family members. Trust is the glue that holds a family together. It is said of the "excellent wife" of Proverbs 31, "The heart of her husband trusts in her, and he will have no lack of gain" (Proverbs 31:11). When trust is nurtured and protected, the family develops a priceless sense of safety and security.

Growing a Healthy "Family Tree"

How can you apply the principles we've enumerated above? Let's apply them to three distinct but overlapping areas: personal, church, and society. First, in the arena of the personal, *fight for your family*. No matter how old you get—whether you are twenty-five, forty-five, or sixty-five—you can never stop fighting for your family. Every season of life brings new opportunities and new temptations. Marriage is one of the greatest challenges each of us will face. I love the words of G. K. Chesterton:

> If Americans can be divorced for "incompatibility of temper," I cannot conceive why they are not all divorced. I have known many happy marriages, but never a compatible one. The whole aim of marriage is to fight through and survive the instant when incompatibility becomes unquestionable.[18]

Fight for your family. Fight for your marriage. A great place to start would be for you and your spouse to spend an hour or two discussing the ten principles listed above. On a scale of one to ten, rate your relationship in each of the categories. Measure your family against the ideal family. When you are finished, add up your aggregate score. If your total falls within the 0 to 50 range, get some help. Make an appointment with your pastor or a counselor and begin to work through the tough issues. If your total is 50 to 75, make yourselves accountable to another couple. Make them aware of the tensions in your marriage and covenant to work harder. And if your total falls into the 75 to 100 range, thank God for His grace and set out to fine-tune your relationship even more. But regardless of your score, fight for your family.

Second, in the arena of church, I encourage you to *invest down*. If you are an older couple with years of wisdom to impart to the younger generation, I plead with you: *Don't retire!* Look for opportunities to mentor struggling couples. Get involved! Encourage and teach the younger generation about real life! Share your experiences—your failures and successes—with those who need hope, wisdom, and practical insight. You have so much to give! Invest down.

Third, with regard to society, *become an activist for the family.* Support legislation that strengthens parental rights. Speak out against frivolous divorce. Be willing to exert pressure on friends who are tempted to walk away from their spouses and children. Make it clear that God's ideal is being breached and that the decision to divorce will alter forever the relationship you have with this individual. Divorce is a lethal drug that is poisoning our society, yet too many Christians sit idly by while brothers and sisters in Christ desert their families and destroy their children. This is a blatant violation of Christian responsibility—not just by faithless spouses but also by fearful Christians. Support ministries, financially and with prayer, that are committed to the family. Ask your pastor to preach on the family and to hold high this Christian ideal.

Family is culture. Tomorrow's culture is incubating in your home—and in every other American home—right now. The blueprints for the next generation are being drawn up, the foundation is being laid, the walls are being constructed. Family is one of our few links with the future. When we are gone, all that will remain of our efforts will be our children.

Throughout the remainder of this section we will examine four issues that empower or imperil the family: the making of real men (chapter 6), the choices of women (chapters 7 and 8), the rearing of children (chapter 9), and the subject of personal morality (chapter 10). What happens in each of these areas will shape the destiny of your family, the destiny of our country, and the destiny of the evangelical church.

So build wisely!

Notes

[1]Abraham Lincoln, "Memories," *The Best Loved Poems of the American People,* Selected by Hazel Felleman (New York: Garden City Publishing, 1936), 540-541.

[2]William Gairdner, *The War Against the Family* (Toronto, Canada: Stoddart, 1992), 69.

[3]Charles Dickens, *David Copperfield* (New York: Signet, 1962), 221.

[4]Carlos Baker, *Ernest Hemingway: A Life Story* (New York: Avon Books, 1969), 45.

[5]William Manchester, *American Caesar* (New York: Dell, 1978), 58.

[6]Ibid.

[7]Marion J. Levy, quoted in Stephen B. Clark, *Man and Woman in Christ* (Ann Arbor, Mich.: Servant Books, 1980), 637.

[8]Dr. Ken Magid and Carole A. McKelvey, *High Risk: Children without a Conscience* (New York: Bantam, 1987), 3.

[9]"Notes on Lord of the Flies," William Golding, *Lord of the Flies* (New York: Paragon, 1954), 189.

[10]William Gairdner, *The War Against the Family,* 55.

[11]See Judith Wallerstein and Sandra Blakesly, *Second Chances: Men, Women, and Children: A Decade After Divorce* (New York, New York: Ticknor & Fields, 1989). This is an excellent, well-researched study; a must-read for anyone wanting to know the truth about the effects of divorce on children.

[12]Arlene Skolnick, *Embattled Paradise: The American Family in an Age of Uncertainty* (New York: BasicBooks, 1991), 49-50.

[13]William Gairdner, *War Against the Family,* 55.

[14]G. K. Chesterton, *What's Wrong with the World* (San Francisco, Calif.: Ignatius Press, 1994), 41.

[15]Carle Zimmerman, *Family and Civilization* (New York: Harper and Row, 1947).

[16]Will Durant, *Story of Civilization—Caesar & Christ,* 3 (New York: Simon & Schuster, 1994), 222.

[17]Sources for the list come from George Berna, *The Future of the American Family* (Chicago, Ill.: Moody, 1993).

[18]G. K. Chesterton, *What's Wrong,* 46.

CHAPTER SIX

BOYZ II MEN

"I see many men walking around in mid-life with a sense of yearning for things they can't get from their wives and can't get from their jobs and can't pull from inside themselves. Having listened to thousands of stories in workshops around the world, I'm convinced that what men are missing is a sense of their own identity; a very primitive and very deep sense of validation that passes from father to son"

KEN DRUCK

I've discovered that kids are intrigued by manhole covers. They are fascinated by the imaginary dangers that lurk below. Recently my six-year-old son, Mason, and I were speeding across town in the family van. The Lewis-mobile drove over a manhole cover and, out of the blue, my young "Ninja Turtle" devotee asked a question that had probably been troubling him for some time. "Dad," he asked, sincerity streaming from every pore in his body, "do turtles really live in there?"

Children are intrigued by the sheer invulnerability of manhole covers. They wonder what evil, or good, lurks in the darkness. These steel plates are strong and virtually impenetrable. They are built to withstand harsh temperatures, extreme conditions, and crushing weight. Manhole covers accomplish one other task as well—they prevent intrusion by outsiders into a subterranean environment that remains foreign and mysterious.

Manhole covers are an appropriate symbol for the American male in our generation. The typical male is tough on the outside, and even tougher to pry open. And lurking below the surface of his life is a subterranean cavern filled with mystery and intrigue. Some time ago, the following statement was sent to me. Though the source of these words is unknown, the description it gives of modern manhood is amazingly accurate:

> Within each man there is a dark castle with a fiery dragon to guard the gate. The castle contains a lonely self, a self most men have suppressed, a self they are afraid to show. Instead, they present an armored knight. No one is invited inside the castle. The dragon symbolizes the fears and fantasies of masculinity, the leftover stuff of childhood.

Men today feel confused and incomplete. They are afraid to let others look below the surface of their lives, and equally afraid to dredge up "the fears and fantasies of masculinity, the leftover stuff of childhood." Stirring the waters of confusion is a central question that remains unanswered, and that is, *How does a boy become a man?* Does the journey through puberty make a boy into a man? How about when he kills his first deer or beds his first sexual conquest? Is manhood conferred upon a boy when he graduates from high school or goes off to college? Or how about when he gets married? Is this the seal of manhood?

No one captures the desperate plight of the American male more humorously than columnist Bob Haltom. In a tongue-in-cheek article entitled "Demise of 'Real Men' Has Guys Wandering in the Woods," Haltom ponders the confused state of the male psyche.

> Frankly, I'm concerned about the future of my gender. Let's face it. These are tough times for guys. The problem is that these days, we men aren't quite sure what it means to be a man. When I was a child, America had

three basic role models: John Wayne, Clark Gable, and the Marlboro Man. These were strong, tough, self-assured men who rode horses, smoked cigarettes, ate red meat and never worried about their cholesterol. Did you ever see John Wayne sitting on horseback eating an oat bran muffin? Of course not. But Duke Wayne and Rhett Butler and the Marlboro Man—they're all gone now. In their place are new sensitive males, such as Alan Alda and Phil Donohue. In fact, one could make the argument that the only real men in America today are General Norman Schwartzkoff and Nancy Reagan.

Remember the Aqua Velva man? He proudly stated the simple truth that a man wants to smell like a man. Well, he's gone now and in his place is a fellow named Calvin Klein. He's obsessed with something, but I'm not sure what it is. The problem is that we males no longer have a clear vision of what a real man is. We've been told that real men don't eat quiche—but what do real men do?[1]

The answer to Haltom's final question is, "No one knows."

Ironically, for much of the past generation definitions of manhood have come primarily from women. Masculine images of manhood have been replaced by feminized ones. In the absence of a compelling vision of manhood, society has been altered. Soft, sensitive males now populate the American landscape. Robert Bly, the founder of the Men's Movement and author of *Iron John,* writes this about today's young men. "They are lovely, valuable people. I like them…. But many of these men are not happy. You quickly notice the lack of energy in them. They are life-preserving, but not life-giving."[2]

The result is a generation of men who are nice to be around—they are fun and lovable and sensitive—but they have cast aside the mantle of leadership. Stephen B. Clark has contributed a great deal to the study of human beings. In his compelling treatise, *Man and Woman in Christ*, Clark characterizes this vast group of men who, though heterosexual, are nonetheless feminized in the social arena.

> Compared to men who have not been feminized, he [the feminized male] will place a much higher emphasis and attention on how he feels and how other people feel. He will be much more gentle and handle situations in a "soft" way. He will be much more subject to the approval of the group, especially emotionally expressed approval (that is, how others feel about him and what he is doing, how others react to him). He will sometimes tend to relate by preference to women and other feminized or effeminate men, and will sometimes have a difficult time with an all-male group.[3]

Both American society and the American family have suffered drastically as a result of male feminization. In the absence of male role models and fathers in the home, the present generation of men find themselves lacking the courage and confidence necessary for leadership. We have been confused by our culture and intimidated by our female counterparts. And our increasingly feminized society only exacerbates our frustration.

The Passages to Manhood

How does a boy become a man? Or, how can a feminized man get beyond his limitations and take up the mantle of leadership, otherwise known as manhood? How does a real man lead his family and gain the admiration of his wife and children? It will help to know, first of all, that there are three major passages to manhood. Each passage is fraught with problems and snares, but each one must be traversed if a boy is to become a man.

Passage #1: From Mother to Father

The first passage is from mother to father. There is a natural tendency during childhood for a boy to identify with his mother. This is good. Mothers provide a nurturing environment that is essential to a child's emotional stability. Without this, a child experiences an emotional deficit and often enters adulthood in search of something—anything—that will fill this void.

It is natural for a boy to bond with his mother. It's also natural for a boy to *remain* bonded with his mother. But this is detrimental. At some point in his adolescence, the emotional bond with mom must be severed if a boy is to traverse the path to manhood. This is where a father comes in. Gordon Dalbey writes:

> Given the biological and emotional intensity of the mother-son bond, only someone whose intrinsic identification with a boy exceeds that of a mother can draw him away into individuality and manhood. Clearly, only the father meets such a requirement.[4]

Only a father can break this bond between mother and son and shape it in a positive way. Lacking this transition, a man will overly identify with mom throughout the course of his life and, in the process, wound his masculine soul.

A recent episode of "20/20" illustrates the over-identification taking place today between mothers and sons. The segment was entitled, "Single and Still Living with Mom." According to a study cited by the producers of the show, one-third of all single men from twenty-five to thirty-five are still living at home with mom. Their mothers cook their meals and clean their clothes, while the sons toil in the workplace. We could call this modern-day phenomenon "the Peter Pan Syndrome." It represents a generation of men who have yet to grow up.

Though we tend to sneer at some of the primitive societies of the past, they can teach us a thing or two about this passage from mother to father. In a number of ancient cultures, the break with mom was orchestrated with timely precision. When the boy reached a certain age, the men of the community would enter a family's home, take the boy from his mother's arms—often amidst tears and protest—and induct him into the community of men. This bold act symbolized the emotional and psychological break taking place between mother and son. It caused a young man to look to the male community, instead of his mother, for guidance and affirmation.

How does a young man, or a feminized man, traverse this first masculine passage? What can he do, especially if mom doesn't understand and dad isn't there to call him out into the arena of manhood? Three images from the life of Christ will shed light on these crucial questions.

The first image is found in Luke 2. We learn at the outset of this story that Jesus is twelve years old—the time when most boys enter puberty. Our Lord's family has traveled to Jerusalem to celebrate the Passover. When their time of worship is over, Jesus' family packs up the caravan and begins the return trip to Nazareth. But unknown to mom and dad, Jesus is still in Jerusalem. Frantically the family retraces its steps and searches for the missing boy. Three days later, He is found—in the temple. Exasperated, the mother of our Lord voices her concern. "Son, why have You treated us this way? Behold, Your father and I have been anxiously looking for You" (Luke 2:48).

Jesus' response strikes us as callous and insensitive: "Why is it that you were looking for Me? Did you not know that I had to be in My Father's house?" (Luke 2:49). What is the significance of Christ's response? Simply this: Even at this young age, Jesus Christ is starting to move away from His mother. He is beginning to break the emotional ties with mom and is fixing His eyes upon His heavenly Father, with whom He will identify from this day forward. This is a powerful moment. It represents a break with the emotional bonds of Mary.

A second image occurs in John 2. Jesus is thirty years old now. Even though Christ is well into adulthood, His mother is still finding it difficult to let go. Like many mothers, Mary still wants to control her son's life. Mother and son are at a wedding when a minor crisis ensues—the host runs out of wine. Jesus' mother jumps into the breach and commands her boy to fix the problem. John 2:3 relates, "And when the wine gave out, the mother of Jesus said to Him, 'They have no wine.' " Do you hear the message imbedded in that statement? It's, "Son, they're out of wine. Do something about it." (I know a number of thirty-something men who still live slavishly ensnared to mom's wishes.)

Once again, Jesus' response is far from subtle. "Woman, what do I have to do with you? My hour has not yet come" (John 2:4). This is the essence of Christ's response: "Mom, this is not a boy you're speaking to; I'm a man now. Don't try to lead me." Jesus is making it clear that mom is no longer in control. He is not speaking derogatorily; instead, He is defining the parameters of their relationship.

The third and final image is found in Matthew 12. Jesus is in a house speaking to the multitudes. Mary and her other sons arrive on the scene and Christ is told by an informant, "Behold, Your mother and Your brothers are standing outside seeking to speak to You" (Matthew 12:47). For some reason, every time I read this story I picture the scene outside a college football locker room following a big game. The parents of the players congregate in the hallway, waiting to honor, and identify with, their sons. At the pinnacle of Jesus' success in ministry, you can picture Mary wanting to do the very same thing—to identify with Christ.

In this particular case, I've often wondered who initiated the message for Jesus. Did someone in the crowd recognize Mary and report her presence to Christ? I don't think so. Instead, I can imagine Mary sending a bystander into the house with the not-so-subtle message, "Your mother and brothers are outside; don't dare ignore us." But what is Jesus' response?

> But He [Jesus] answered the one who was telling Him and said, "Who is My mother and who are My brothers?" And stretching out His hand toward His disciples, He said, "Behold, My mother and My brothers! For whoever does the will of My father who is in heaven, he is My brother and sister and mother" (Matthew 12:48-50).

In another bold statement, Jesus Christ redefines His relationship with His mother. He is a man now, with a clearly defined mission. Jesus has identified, totally, with His heavenly Father.

The passage from mother to father may well be the most difficult of the three passages to manhood, primarily because it is charged with so much emotion. But it is an essential step along a man's journey. For when a mother's influence and control predominates in a man's life, he will tend to look to mom, and other women, to complete his development. Instead of the natural progression from mother to father, this individual moves from mother to wife. King Ahab is a prime example of one who turned to his wife—Jezebel—for nurturing and protection. Ahab's crisis over Naboth's vineyard in 1 Kings 21, and Jezebel's subsequent intervention, is a graphic portrait of stunted manhood—and the need for a mother-wife.

> So Ahab came into his house sullen and vexed because of the word which Naboth the Jezreelite had spoken to him; for he said, "I will not give you the inheritance of my fathers." And, he lay down on his bed and turned away his face and ate no food. But Jezebel his [Ahab's] wife came to him and said to him, "How is it that your spirit is so sullen that you are not eating food?" So he said to her, "Because I spoke to Naboth the Jezreelite, and said to him, 'Give me your vineyard for money; or else, if it

pleases you, I will give you a vineyard in its place.' But he said, 'I will not give you my vineyard.' "And Jezebel his wife said to him, "Do you now reign over Israel? Arise, eat bread, and let your heart be joyful; I will give you the vineyard of Naboth the Jezreelite." So she wrote letters in Ahab's name and sealed them with his seal, and sent letters to the elders and to the nobles who were living with Naboth in his city (1 Kings 21:4-8).

We could write over this passage, "Mama, take care of your little boy!" That's right, *boy!* We see here a king who never grew up. A boy who, in a king's body, needed a mother-wife to lead him.

A woman can never initiate a man into manhood.

In a moving article in *Parade* magazine, Burt Reynolds describes the incompleteness he experienced at the hands of a father who failed to initiate his passage from mother to father.

My dad was the chief of police, and when he came into a room all the light and the air went out of it. There's a saying in the South that "no man is a man until his father tells him he is." It means that some day, when you're thirty or forty, grown up, this man whom you respect and love and want to love you, puts his arms around you and says, "You know, you're a man now. And you don't have to do all those crazy things and get into fist fights and all that to defend the honor of men. You're a man and I love you." But we never hugged and we never cried. We never said, "I love you."

...So what happened later was, I was desperately looking for someone who'd say, "You're grown up, and I approve and I love you, and you don't have to do these things anymore." But I was lost inside. I couldn't connect. I was incomplete. I didn't know then what I needed to know.[5]

The passage from mother to father is a critical step in the journey to manhood.

Passage #2: From Father to Male Mentors

The second passage is from father to male mentors. This occurs when a man makes a personal decision to separate himself from his father and looks to other men who will help craft and shape his life in a positive way. A father, significant as his contribution is, can only take a son so far. Like his wife before him, a father must pass the baton at some point and let his son go.

The value of mentoring is extolled repeatedly throughout the pages of Scripture. Proverbs 27:17 says, "Iron sharpens iron, so one man sharpens another." Examples of mentor-protégé relationships abound in the Bible: Moses was mentored by his father-in-law, Jethro; Joshua was mentored by Moses, Elisha by Elijah, and Paul by Barnabas. The list goes on and on. Each of these men made a practical contribution to another's life, a contribution that bore great fruit for the kingdom of God.

Our word "mentor" derives from Homer's classic, *The Odyssey.* In the story, Ulysses asks a wise man named Mentor to instruct his son, Telemachus. A mentor is a coach, a teacher, a cheerleader, and a confidante. He imparts critical skills that are vital to spiritual, social, and career success.

I'm convinced much of my own masculine health is the direct result of the mentoring I received from other men throughout my life. Because I grew up with an alcoholic father, I entered adolescence with an emotional deficit. This deficit may well have continued in to the present, if not for strong mentors who shared their lives with me and challenged and motivated me to a higher level of maturity. One such individual in my pantheon of heroes is a man named L. J. ("Hoss") Garrett.

Hoss Garrett was the football coach at my high school in Ruston, Louisiana. Coach Garrett had been at Ruston High for twenty-five years when I came along; when he retired five years later, he was one of the most successful high school coaches in Louisiana history. For some unexplained reason, Coach Garrett took a liking to me, and even gave me a nickname. He called me "Sister." Isn't that manly? But from Hoss's lips, the title "sister" was anything but derogatory; instead, it was both a term of endearment and a challenge to push my athletic abilities (which he believed in) to an even higher level. Coach Garrett would speak my nickname and, as he did so, his face would light up. He realized I knew he was knighting me as a man. His man. I reveled in our relationship and in Coach Garrett's continuous affirmation of me as a person.

At the sports banquet during my senior year, the coaches presented awards for Most Valuable Back and Most Valuable Lineman. Because I had been selected Most Valuable Lineman the year before, I fully expected to win it again. But the presenter called out someone else's name. I was deeply surprised. Then something happened that had a profound impact upon my life. Coach Garrett announced that a new award had been created called the "Coaches' Award." Hoss Garrett walked to the podium and presented this award—to me. I still have the picture of Coach Garrett and me—I'm standing tall, with a broad-as-a-barn-door smile on my face—next to my mentor. I can't tell you the importance of that moment in my life. At a crucial time in my life, with all the turmoil of youth, I received the affirmation I desperately longed for.

A male mentor is one who cares for your soul. Fathers can help their sons begin the journey to manhood but other men must shape it and affirm it. Quoting George Gilder, William Gairdner makes this powerful observation:

> Men and women, he [George Gilder] argues,…are from birth very, very different from each other. But men become radically different from women around puberty, with the onset of male androgenic hormones, and from that point onward a man's body is full only of

undefined energies—*and all these energies need the guid-ance of culture* [emphasis mine].[6]

And the one aspect of culture that is crucial to a man's development is the community of other men.

Passage #3: From Male Mentors to the Lord Jesus Christ

From mother to father; then father to male mentors; and finally, from male mentors to the Lord Jesus Christ. The final path to manhood is internal, and is consummated when a man develops an authentic personal relationship with Jesus Christ. At some point in his life—whether it's at thirteen, twenty-two, thirty-four, forty-five, or fifty-seven years of age—a man must enter into a relationship with the living God. He must begin to take his cues, formulate his decisions, and accept his responsi-bilities from this eternal power source. In doing so, such a man becomes uniquely masculine.

The third passage to manhood is intensely spiritual. It is a place of complete and utter dependence upon Jesus Christ for one's identity, as well as one's emotional and psychological well-being. In Ephesians 3, Paul articulates the essence of this revolutionary experience. His goal for the Ephesian Christians is the holy ground that all men—all real men—must ascend.

> For this reason, I bow my knees before the Father, from whom every family in heaven and on earth derives its name, that He would grant you, according to the riches of His glory, to be strengthened with power through His Spirit in the inner man; so that Christ may dwell in your hearts through faith; and that you, being rooted and grounded in love, may be able to comprehend with all the saints what is the breadth and length and height and depth, and to know the love of Christ which surpasses knowledge, that you may be filled up to all the fullness of God (Ephesians 3:14-19).

The ultimate male bonding occurs when the spirit of a man joins with the Spirit of God. The Lord then begins to shape the man's values and actions. Out of this mysterious dynamic, He brings forth that which is pure and true and right.

We can sum up the passages of manhood this way: The movement from mother to father is a critical *emotional* passage; the movement from father to male mentors is a major *personal* passage; and the movement from male mentors to the Lord Jesus Christ is an intensely *spiritual* passage—one that is marked by submission to the living God. All three steps are important. These steps may not occur in the order in which we have discussed them. They may overlap. Nevertheless, each one is crucial in the ascent to manhood.

Portrait of a "Real Man"

From the beginning of this chapter, we have been cracking the manhole cover. We began by examining the state of manhood today; next, we discerned the natural passages that propel a boy into manhood. At this point, a visual image will help immensely. In the book of Matthew, Jesus paints a portrait of a "real man." John the Baptist is a flesh and blood example of virile masculinity—one who lived out the ideals that are dear to the heart of God: "And as these were going away, Jesus began to speak to the multitudes about John, [asking] 'What did you go out into the wilderness to look at? A reed shaken by the wind?' " (Matthew 11:7).

Jesus recognized that the multitudes were drawn to John the Baptist. His life and character couldn't be ignored. Compelled by John's lifestyle and message, great crowds came to hear him preach. Jesus uses the imagery of a reed to underscore John's resolute conviction. Unlike a reed shaken by the wind, which connotes weakness and compromise, John was a man of courage. He wasn't afraid to stand against the winds of popular opinion and social pressure. He wasn't a wimp. Instead,

John the Baptist was a man of fierce determination and unshakable conviction: "But what did you go out to see? A man dressed in soft clothing? Behold, those who wear soft clothing are in kings' palaces" (Matthew 11:8).

John was not a reed shaken by the wind; neither was he a man dressed in soft clothes. John was anything but soft! On the contrary, he was rock-hard physically, emotionally, and spiritually. As we learn from Matthew 3:4, John adorned himself with "a garment of camel's hair, and a leather belt about his waist." This man would never have made the cover of *G.Q.*! What is the significance of John's clothing? Simply this: John the Baptist was motivated by a higher principle than personal comfort. He possessed what so many soft American males lack: life-giving energy. He was a man on a mission, and how he dressed and what he ate and what people thought of him was irrelevant.

Having posed a series of questions, Jesus now identifies the source of John's charisma. "But why did you go out? To see a prophet? Yes, I say to you, and one who is more than a prophet" (Matthew 11:9).

Why were the multitudes drawn to this camel-haired, honey-eating, repentance-preaching man? Because he was a prophet? Yes. But Jesus tells us John was "more than a prophet." What does this mean? We're not told. But I'd like to venture a suggestion. The multitudes were drawn to John because he was more than a prophet—he was a *real man*. And there is something attractive and compelling about real men. Real men lead with confidence; they speak with conviction. They have been captured by a vision and are indifferent to public opinion and cultural pressure. This is what the crowds ventured into the wilderness to see.

Israel had become a land filled with hypocritical leaders, unscrupulous merchants, and unrepentant pilgrims. *A real man proved to be a refreshing contrast to the status quo.*

The American family is desperate today for real men. Wives yearn for the leadership of real men. Not *males,* but *men*—real men like John the Baptist, whose lives are marked by two radical characteristics. First, the church needs men who are wildly submissive to the Spirit of God. Scripture tells us that John the Baptist was "filled with the Holy Spirit, while yet in his mother's womb" (Luke 1:15). This fullness continued throughout the remainder of his days. The Spirit of God compelled John to denounce hypocrisy and injustice; the Spirit empowered him to preach a message of repentance, and even to confront the adultery of one as high and mighty as Herod—a confrontation that ultimately resulted in John's death. The family is imperiled when men ignore the Spirit's voice and remain indifferent to hypocrisy and injustice.

John the Baptist was the quintessential "wild man"—but he was also wildly submissive to the call of God upon his life.

Second, today's family needs men who are irresistibly approachable. For all of his flamboyance and refusal to compromise spiritually, John the Baptist was irresistibly approachable. We know this because Matthew 3:5-6 states, "Jerusalem was going out to him, and all Judea and all the district around the Jordan; and they were being baptized by him in the Jordan River, as they confessed their sins." John was approachable. People don't confess their sins to an indifferent, hardhearted religious fanatic. The multitudes saw John as trustworthy and accepting. There was a transparency and vulnerability about his life that drew others like a planet's gravitational field. Sucked into this vortex of warmth and compassion, people responded spontaneously.

Wildly submissive (to God). Irresistibly approachable (to others). The American family hungers for a new generation of men who are willing to embrace these two characteristics of biblical manhood. Our culture is dying without them. What woman, what child, doesn't yearn for this kind of real man to love them and lead them?

It's Time to Grow Up

If I can speak directly to the Christian men reading these words, I'd like to draw a line in the sand and challenge you to step across to the other side. It's time to grow up. In his outstanding book, *The Masculine Journey,* Robert Hicks makes this statement about stunted growth on the path to manhood:

> Some men are very phallic-aware but have sort of fixated at the phallic stage of development. On the masculine journey they stopped at Phallicville, found a sex-object, and built their whole life there. I have met men in their fifties and sixties who still think below their belts most of the time. They have never grown up and moved on in their maleness.[7]

Whether the "permanent rest area" is a preoccupation with sex, material pursuits, an obsession with one's career or one's pleasures, *Men, it's time to grow up.* "When I was a child," writes the apostle Paul, "I used to speak as a child, think as a child, reason as a child; *when I became A MAN, I did away with childish things"* (1 Corinthians 13:11, emphasis mine). Did you hear the last line? There comes a time in a man's life when he must answer the call of God—the same call which John the Baptist heeded and obeyed. The call of God demands much of a man. It requires that he accept responsibility for his life, as well as the lives of his family and others within his community. It demands sacrifice and courage; there will be times of loneliness and isolation. Along the way, a man will experience deep pain and heartache as he sorts out the hurts of the past and the priorities of the present. Like "Christian" on his journey in *Pilgrim's Progress,* the ascent to manhood will be strewn with pitfalls and boulders.

But the call of God is not all duty. For along with these burdens there is also immeasurable joy. The godly man experiences a dignity that is conferred upon him by God Himself, a coronation that is recognized, and admired, by other men. This most precious gift is reserved for the brave, the proud, the few. These are the Green Berets in God's army, the leaders of His church and His families. This select group bears a singular title: MEN.

The line in the sand is crossed when a man completes the three stages of manhood. You may need to grapple with the following questions.

Stage #1: Have I broken the emotional bonds with my mother? Is she still exerting unwarranted and unhealthy influence in my life? Have I defined the parameters of my relationship with my mother? If not, why not?

Stage #2: Who are the mentors in my life? Am I afraid to open my life to the scrutiny of other men? What do I fear most about interpersonal relationships? How could I benefit from the influence of godly men?

Stage #3: What are the personal barriers to a deep, abiding relationship with Jesus Christ? What are my divinely appointed responsibilities at this season of my life? How can I contribute to the spiritual life of my family, my church, and my community?

To the average man, such questions are interesting but unimportant. To a *real man,* however, these questions are the beginning of the journey of a lifetime—the path to authentic manhood.

E. Anthony Rotundo, in his historical survey, *American Manhood,* cites an interesting observation by fellow historian Arthur Cole:

When historian Arthur Cole explored the lives of eighteenth-century merchants, he made a surprising discovery. These leading businessmen spent much of the day away from their businesses, investing large amounts of time in the public and religious affairs of their communities.... This was an era when a man's identity came as much from his family and its place in the community as from his own achievements. A merchant enjoyed a position of prominence in his community, so it was his duty to lead in matters of governance and religion.[8]

There are times when progress requires that we go backward, not forward. This is one of those times. My friend, you have been called TO LEAD. Your family, your church, and your community are starved for male leadership. For your leadership. Are you a reed shaken by the wind or are you a real man?

No one can answer that question...but you.

Notes

[1]Bill Haltom, "Demise of 'Real Men' Has Guys Wandering in the Woods," *Memphis Commercial Appeal,* 7 March 1992, A-15.

[2]Robert Bly, *Iron John* (Reading, Mass.: Addison-Wesley Publishing Co., 1990), 2-3.

[3]Stephen B. Clark, *Man and Woman in Christ* (Ann Arbor, Mich.: Servant Books, 1980), 636.

[4]Gordon Dalbey, *Healing the Masculine Soul* (Dallas: Word, 1980), 43.

[5]Dotson Rader, "What Love Means," *Parade,* 8 March 1992, 4.

[6]William D. Gairdner, *The War Against the Family* (Toronto, Canada: Stoddart, 1992), 85.

[7]Robert Hicks, *The Masculine Journey* (Colorado Springs, Colo.: NavPress, 1993), 24.

[8]E. Anthony Rotundo, *American Manhood* (New York: Basic Books, 1993), 167.

CHAPTER SEVEN

HOME-KEEPING HEARTS

*"The most remarkable achievement of feminism is the breakdown of the family....
The nuclear family is a goner."*
FEMINIST MARY O'BRIEN

It's Christmas morning. At the Zelin home in San Diego, California, seven-year-old Zachariah Zelin opens his present from Santa Claus. Bright-eyed with excitement, the youngster discovers that his wish has been granted—Santa has delivered the talking G. I. Joe doll he requested. On the surface, Zack's G. I. Joe looks just like any other G. I. Joe manufactured by the Hasbro Company. The miniature soldier is dressed in army fatigues. Grenades hang from his belt. He's gripping a machine gun and is ready for action. There is one flaw, however, with Zachariah Zelin's doll.

Joe talks like Barbie.

Chalk up another victory for the B.L.O.—the Barbie Liberation Organization.

The B.L.O. is a small group of feminists who claim to have switched the voice boxes in hundreds of G. I. Joe and Barbie dolls across the United States. The emasculated Joe now asks, innocently, "Want to go shopping?" The testosterone-laden Barbie on the other hand, says in a baritone voice, "Dead men tell no lies." These "babes in toyland" represent the relentless effort by the politically correct to redefine male and female roles in our society. Said one B.L.O. member who spoke anonymously, "Our goal is to reveal and correct the problem of gender-based stereotyping in children's toys."[1]

This cross-pollination of Joe and Barbie is a humorous snapshot of a much greater, and more disturbing, problem now gripping American society and the family in particular: Society and the family are being crafted, sculpted, shaped, and transformed by influential forces designed to "correct the problem of gender-based stereotyping." And the influence extends far beyond children's toys. At issue is the true nature of manhood and womanhood. Lest you think this is an inconsequential issue with few implications for daily life, consider this statement by John Piper.

> The tendency today is to stress the equality of men and women by minimizing the unique significance of our maleness and femaleness. But this depreciation of male and female personhood is a great loss. It is taking a tremendous toll on generations of young men and women who do not know what it means to be a man or a woman. Confusion over the meaning of sexual personhood today is epidemic.... The consequence is more divorce, more homosexuality, more sexual abuse, more promiscuity, more social awkwardness, and more emotional distress and suicide that come with the loss of God-given identity.[2]

In this chapter and the next, we will examine what it means to be a biblical woman in today's Bold New World. We will seek to answer two questions that are crucial to our understanding of this issue: First, *Has God placed a unique feminine calling upon the lives of women?* In other words, is there a divine blueprint that shapes a woman's life choices, a calling that defines the essential nature of womanhood? Second, *What can women do in the church?* Can women serve as pastors? Can women lead a congregation? Are women free to serve in the same capacities as men or are there restrictions? Both of these questions and their answers have tremendous implications on how men and women view each other. And those *viewpoints* have tremendous implications on how a family functions or fails to function.

The Feminine "Mistake"

The present confusion about womanhood had its genesis in the early 19th century. The matriarchs of the contemporary feminist movement were troubled by the persistent legal oppression of women. From the vantage point of the late twentieth century, many of their concerns were justified. Women at the time were denied the right to vote; they had little, if any, protection under the law; they were not recognized as legal property owners. Opportunities for education were also denied on the basis of gender.

In addition to these factors, a number of women began to speak out against what they perceived to be sexual oppression. They demanded the right to more liberal sexual expression and greater access to birth control. They also rebelled against the notion of the traditional family and the role of the wife as homemaker. The first Women's Rights Convention was held in Seneca Falls, New York, in 1848. The participants posted a list of grievances against men, summarized by the closing statement: "He [man] has endeavored in every way that he could to destroy her confidence in her own powers, to lessen her self-respect, and to make her willing to lead a dependent and abject life."[3] Throughout the nineteenth century, the battle for equality was fought primarily by isolated individuals such as Fanny

Wright, Lucy Stone, and Julia Ward Howe, women who sought to alter the structure of a male-dominated society.

Feminists in the following century stood tall on the shoulders of these matriarchs. Mary Ware Dennett founded the National Birth Control League in the 1920s.[4] Margaret Sanger, the driving force behind the development of new methods of birth control and the founder of Planned Parenthood, lobbied for legalized abortion. Like a rising tide, feminist ideology began to exert greater influence within American society. In 1963 the dam burst. After years as a fringe movement, feminism moved into the mainstream with the publication of a book by Betty Friedan called *The Feminine Mystique*. As David Halberstam notes, "It [*The Feminine Mystique*] started slowly, but word of it grew and grew, and eventually, with three million copies in print, it became a handbook for the new feminist movement that was gradually beginning to come together."[5]

Friedan's book fanned the flame that had been smoldering for one hundred and fifty years. The author interviewed hundreds of American women and discovered "a problem that has no name."[6] Friedan quickly identified the problem as the "feminine mystique." According to Friedan, the feminine mystique is nothing more than the systematic, cultural oppression of women. Women are trapped in a prison called "home," chained to the prejudices and expectations of a male-dominated culture in which there is no hope whatsoever of finding true happiness. The only alternative is rebellion.

> Once she begins to see through the delusions of the feminine mystique—and realizes that neither her husband nor her children, nor the things in her house, nor sex, nor being like all the other women can give her a self—she often finds the solution much easier than she anticipated.[7]

For the last thirty years our culture has been convulsing under the enormous weight of such feminist ideology. The influence is pervasive and all-encompassing. Feminism has given rise to numerous social experiments in childrearing and marital relations; it has been the driving force behind legalized abortion and wanton sexual expression. On college campuses, feminism has led to the specious reinterpretation of history and anthropology. Our government, our schools, even our churches have all been transformed by this cultural phenomenon. It is telling that Betty Friedan dedicated her book to "all the new women, and the new men," for there are now millions of them inhabiting the Bold New World.

Before we look more intently at the basic tenets of feminism, it will be helpful to make a distinction between two words: *concern* and *philosophy*. If feminism were a concern, interested solely in equal rights and justice for women, then I believe the evangelical church would embrace it passionately. For though the Christian church has erred at points toward women, it remains committed to justice and equality for all peoples. But feminism is much more than a concern. Ironically, many people embrace feminism with the notion that it is simply a concern. After all, it markets itself under the banner of "equal rights," and what reasonable person could possibly be against equal rights? But feminism is more than a concern; it is a *philosophy*.

Feminism is a comprehensive, humanistic view of life. Like a huge subterranean river, this ideology bubbles violently below the surface of our culture, defining and redefining what it means to be male and female, and reshaping our society at the very core. Feminism is hostile to Christianity—which it perceives to be a social competitor—and yet it works within the church, seeking to remake Christianity after its own doctrines. Promoted under the banner of "concern," many men and women have been fooled into embracing what amounts to nothing less than a philosophy.

The Tenets of Feminism

So what are the tenets of this philosophy called feminism? There are six.

1. Feminism teaches that *sameness* must replace *stereotypes* in the home, the church, and society in general. Feminists believe society has propagated a host of stereotypes that must be discarded and replaced by more enlightened concepts. In their minds, apart from the obvious physical differences, men and women are actually very much alike. Roles in marriage, career pursuits, responsibilities in the home and in church—all of these concepts must be altered radically to fit the feminist agenda. As Janet Radcliffe Richards put it, "It is not by nature that women are different so much as it's by contrivance."[8]

Our traditional understanding of male-female roles, say the feminists, is the result of two factors: cultural conditioning and male oppression of women. If these two factors are removed from the cultural equation, feminists believe they would achieve their ideal—a unisex world of sameness, a world devoid of stereotypes and outdated ideas.

But science has shown us that the differences between the sexes are primarily biological, not cultural. Attempts to raise children in androgynous environments have raised serious questions about the veracity of unisex education. Psychologists have discovered that girls and boys resist what I call "gender-neutral childrearing." Harvard researcher Dorothy Ullian has warned that sex role interventions could do serious psychological harm to children. Other case studies have revealed the inherent dangers of raising children in a unisex environment. Sociologists Lionel Tiger and Robin Fox sum up an impressive body of research by saying that the ways in which we see men and women relating to one another in society are not the result of culture, but "are rooted directly in the innate biological endowment of the human species."[9]

The point of all this is obvious: The stereotypes we see among men and women in every culture are to a large degree the result of our biological natures, not sexist conditioning. To countermand the forces of biology in a child's formative years through unisex education can do enormous psychological damage. Imagine for a moment what would happen if an entire culture was hell-bent upon making men and women from the same mold. The psychological fallout is predictable: identity confusion, low self-esteem, sexual disorientation, personal depression, interpersonal paralysis. This is the logical outcome of a "sameness" philosophy. Sadly, we are witnessing the first fruits of this philosophy in our world right now.

2. Feminism asserts that *independence* must replace *interdependence* as a lifestyle. The concept of independence is crucial to feminist ideology. Proponents such as Germaine Greer decry socially sanctioned relationships like marriage because they lead to "entanglements." Such arrangements limit individual autonomy and personal fulfillment. And while many feminists refrain from Greer's extreme position, they nevertheless hold tightly to the concept of independence. Power, control, and freedom are celebrated ideals.

For example, even though she is married, Patricia Ireland, former president of the National Organization for Women (NOW), continues to carry on a long-distance lesbian relationship because she has embraced wholeheartedly the feminist value of independence. Such infidelity is a natural outgrowth of feminist philosophy.

3. *Equal* division of labor must replace a *sexual* division of labor at home and at work. Everything must be 50/50. The key word here is *egalitarian*. Never mind that in every society, past and present, the tasks of men and women consistently break down along traditional lines. According to Stephen Clark of Yale University, "cultures assign men a primary responsibility for the government of larger groupings within a society, and to women [they assign] a primary responsibility for home and the care of young children."[10] This evidence begs a question—is putting women "in the home" and men "at the head" some nefarious plot hatched by a bunch of male chauvinists in a prehistoric cave? Or is it simply the outworking of natural law? I believe it is the latter.

4. Sexual *liberation* must replace sexual *restraint* as a personal value. Make no mistake about it, one of the most powerful forces (if not the most powerful force) driving radical feminism today is a commitment to sex without consequences. Margaret Sanger spoke directly to this point in 1920 when she published her first book, *Woman and the New Race.* Sanger, who abandoned her husband and children for the cause of sexual liberation, wrote these words:

> A free race cannot be born of slave mothers. A woman enchained cannot choose but give a measure of that bondage to her sons and daughters. No woman can call herself free who does not own and control her body. No woman can call herself free until she can choose consciously whether she will or will not be a mother.[11]

Margaret Sanger controlled her own body. Her biography, written by Ellen Chesler and dubiously titled *Woman of Valor,* is filled with one promiscuous encounter after another.

If you doubt the impact of feminism upon sexual attitudes, ask a son or a daughter if virginity is considered by peers to be a compliment or a curse. Recently I came across an article in the U.S.A. *Today* magazine written by Karen DeCrow, another past president of NOW. DeCrow chides younger women, especially college-age women, for their return to what she calls "a new puritanicalism." She writes: "The cult of female virginity and purity is part of the second class citizenship of women."[12]

This quotation leaves you wondering if Ms. DeCrow has ever heard of AIDS? Is a woman required to put her life on the line to be a *first* class citizen? This is a clear-cut example of values being shaped and defined by philosophy—the philosophy of feminism.

5. Careerism must replace a spouse and children as a woman's premier pursuit in life. Women who choose the home as a career are viewed as deceived, oppressed, and backward. A career is the vehicle feminists trumpet as the key to liberty and personal freedom. A career gives power and power translates into freedom—freedom from an awful, dreadful dependency which is the antithesis of a liberating independence. So repugnant is the choice "homemaker" that Simone DeBeauvoir said, "No woman should be authorized to stay at home and raise her children. In fact, women should not even have that choice, precisely because if they have such a choice too many women will make it."[13] To facilitate this objective, feminists seek to elect officials and pass legislation making the "career choice" more attractive. Tax laws begin to favor working women over stay-at-home moms.

Gloria Steinem developed a national program for the express purpose of taking daughters to work to give them self-esteem. Yet as innocent as this appears on the surface, it is a gentle reminder that leaving a daughter at home results in low self-esteem. The message is subtle, but powerful nonetheless: "Enlightened women must escape the drudgery and oppression of home and husband."

6. Religion, history, and scientific data are being reinterpreted to complement feminist ideology. In numerous fields of study, feminists are actively reinterpreting the facts to buttress their ideological positions. As Raymond Ortlund observes, "evangelical feminists cannot create a new feminist canon without losing their evangelical credentials. So they reinterpret the sacred canon that exists to suit their purposes."[14] "Sexist" terminology is being removed from the Bible—because it smacks of antiquated patriarchal oppression. Your sons and daughters will be taught in the universities about the existence of matriarchal societies, societies ruled and dominated by women. This is the supposed "proof" that male-female roles are culturally determined, not biologically predisposed. Never mind the fact that true matriarchies have never existed.[15] Lacking any tangible evidence to support this assertion, feminists continue to propagate the myth of historical matriarchy. By way of rebuttal, listen to the Queen of Anthropology, Margaret Mead.

It is true that all claims made about societies ruled by women are nonsense. We have no reason to believe that they ever existed. Men have always been the leaders in public affairs in general.[16]

As conclusive as this statement may be, your sons and daughters will probably never hear anything like it in the classroom. Instead, they will hear the matriarchal myth presented as fact.

Religion, history, and scientific data are being reinterpreted to complement feminist ideology. I discovered an example of this recently in the *San Francisco Chronicle*. The article cited a study conducted by Catherine Ross at the University of Illinois. It was entitled "Stay-at-home Moms Among the Most Depressed People in America." The title caught my attention because it contradicted a study we did with the members of our body. We hired an outside researcher to poll our membership—church members were asked one hundred questions. The research team received over one thousand responses. After the evidence was collated, the pollster called me with the results. He said, "Here's an interesting fact you need to know about your church. In doing our research we discovered that the happiest, most fulfilled people in your body are homemakers." This conclusion was contrary to the one reached by Ross, who was quoted in the article as saying, "Any plea to return to the traditional family is a plea to return women to a psychologically disadvantaged place."[17]

Of course, the happiest women in Catherine Ross's study were single women who worked full time. But as I read further, I discovered one statement that jumped off the page. It said, "Most depressed of all were mothers who work and have a hard time finding child care." The question I ask myself is: *Why wasn't this fact the focus of the article? Why didn't the editor title it "Working Mothers the Most Depressed"?* Sadly, I know the answer. Facts are being reinterpreted to cast feminism in a favorable light. It's politically correct to denigrate stay-at-home moms; it is anathema to do the same with working mothers.

A Divine Calling for Women

Such is the opposition lined up against the evangelical church today. Needless to say, it will take courage to embrace an alternate view, especially one that derives its message from a book written in the first century. The opposition is formidable, aggressive, and unrelenting. To throw your hat in this corner is to court ridicule and disdain.

I'm reminded of a famous advertisement the federal government ran in newspapers across America in 1942 when they were recruiting workers to build the Alaskan highway.

NO PICNIC. Men hired for this job will be required to work and live under the most extreme conditions imaginable. Temperatures will range from 90 degrees above zero to 70 degrees below zero. Men will have to fight swamps, rivers, ice and cold. Mosquitoes, flies and gnats will not only be annoying but will cause bodily harm. If you are not prepared to work under these and similar conditions, DO NOT APPLY![18]

I know what you're thinking: *Where do I sign up?* Right? Wrong. The evangelical Christian experiences this same hesitation when confronted with a rabid, irrational, highly politicized feminist culture.

But contrary to the tenets of contemporary feminism, in spite of the ideologues who have infiltrated the church, in defiance of those who would remake male-female roles along androgynous lines, I believe the Scriptures teach that God has a unique feminine calling for women, a calling that transcends time and culture and is crucial to the stability of both the family and American society.

The apostle Paul articulates this "archaic," "antiquated" position in the book of Titus.

> But as for you, speak the things which are fitting for sound doctrine. Older men are to be temperate, dignified, sensible, sound in faith, in love, in perseverance. Older women likewise are to be reverent in their behavior, not malicious gossips, nor enslaved to much wine, teaching what is good, that they may encourage the young women to love their husbands, to love their children, to be sensible, pure, workers at home, kind, being subject to their own husbands, that the word of God may not be dishonored (Titus 2:1-5).

It's clear from the broader context that Paul is speaking to a church under siege. There is a great deal of controversy and much social upheaval taking place on the Isle of Crete. This is apparent from Paul's observation recorded in Titus 1:10-11: "For there are many rebellious men, empty talkers and deceivers, especially those of the circumcision, who must be silenced because they are upsetting whole families, teaching things they should not teach, for the sake of sordid gain." Just as in our own day, the faith was being challenged. Whole families were being upset by those who sought to reinvent Christianity; empty talkers were altering the faith to make it more palatable to Cretian culture. Judging by the subject matter in chapter 2, the focus of the opposition appears to be the family.

Into this storm of controversy Paul interjects a unique, feminine calling for women. It is a calling that transcends time and culture and is crucial to the stability of both the family and society. I want us to consider four facets to this exquisite spiritual jewel.

Instead of Self, Significant Others

Older women are to encourage the younger women to "love their husbands, to love their children" (Titus 2:4). In light of Paul's earlier diatribe against evil influences (Titus 1:10-16), I wonder if he is countering the onslaught of first-century feminist philosophy. As we'll see in the next chapter, there is plenty of historical evidence to support this assumption. Paul is intent upon defining the roles of women in the home. He begins with an admonition to love—and the object of this love is husband and children.

The first facet of this spiritual jewel is sacrifice. Jesus coupled love with sacrifice when He said, "Greater love has no one than this, that one lay down his life for his friends" (John 15:13). Married women are called to sacrifice for their husbands and their children. In practical terms, this means viewing your family as your primary occupation. Many Christian women have said "no" to career pursuits for the singular purpose of raising godly children. Many Christian couples have sacrificed a second income to insure the nurturance of their children. The mom who sacrifices for husband and children makes an invaluable contribution to their lives, a contribution that becomes more and more apparent as time goes by. Listen to Eda LeShan as she describes the down side of feminine neglect. Her statement answers the question: "What happens when a mother *chooses* to work outside the home?"

> Now, after observing many young children and working mothers, I see genuine hazards: weary mothers who can give only minimal attention to their infants after a long day's work and babies who too often become extremely dependent as they reach nursery-school age;

who become withdrawn after having been surrounded by too many people, too much stimulation all day, and—feeling under nurtured at the beginning, when it counts the most—regress to babyish behavior at five or six. Elementary schoolteachers have told me they can often tell which of the children in their classes have been in group care the longest because many seem depressed.[19]

Researchers Raymond and Dorothy Moore made this observation: "America's decline in literacy from the estimated 90 percentiles in the last century to the 50 percentiles today parallels the parental scramble to institutionalize children at ever younger ages."[20] In his remarkable book, *The War Against the Family,* William D. Gairdner dismantles the feminist argument that daycare is harmless for children. He cites writer John Bowlby, who says, "The young child's hunger for his mother's presence is as great as his hunger for food, and her [the mother's] absence inevitably generates a powerful sense of loss and anger."[21] Dr. Harrison Spencer, chief of parasitic diseases at the Centers for Disease Control (CDC) estimates that "[daycare children] are at risk anywhere from two to eighteen times as much [as non-daycare kids] for certain infectious diseases that run the gamut from diarrheal diseases to respiratory and flu-like illnesses."[22]

Maternal neglect can have egregious long-term consequences:

> [Professor] Jay Belsky calls extensive daycare (in the twenty-plus hours a week range) a risk condition for children—and therefore for society as a whole. Why? Because—there is near unanimity on this point—*poorly attached children are sociopaths in the making* [emphasis is author's].[23]

Few things carry as much long-term impact for good or for evil as the involvement (or absence) of a mom.

Susannah Wesley, the mother of John and Charles, knew the importance of loving her family. There is no question why her sons eventually shook the world for Christ—they had a mom who sacrificed for their spiritual and emotional well-being. Mrs. Wesley described her commitment to childrearing this way:

> No one can, without renouncing the world, devote twenty years of the prime of their life in hopes of saving the souls of their children, which some women think you can do without much ado. But that was my intention, to give twenty years of my life to it.[24]

How different this is from today, when women are scrambling to "suck the marrow out of life" as Thoreau put it, but neglecting their husbands and children in the process. Ezekiel described the contemporary scene, though he himself was removed from it by twenty-seven hundred years:

> Behold, everyone who quotes proverbs will quote this proverb concerning you, saying, "Like mother, like daughter." You are the daughter of your mother, who loathed her husband and children. You are also the sister of your sisters, who loathed their husbands and children (Ezekiel 16:44-45).

When Napoleon was asked to identify the one thing that would restore the prestige and greatness of France, he offered only one solution: "Give us better mothers." Loving mothers. Sacrificial mothers.

Instead of "Supermyth," Common Sense

The second facet of this jewel is common sense. In Titus 2:5, Paul encourages women "to be sensible." The challenge here is to be realistic, to embrace a lifestyle that is reasonable and manageable.

Do you remember the Helen Reddy song from the 1970s, "I Am Woman, Hear Me Roar"? In the wake of a new definition of womanhood, millions of women in the '60s and '70s discarded traditional concepts and attempted to become "Superwomen." They took on countless responsibilities, juggled a career and a family, and competed with men for influence and power. But by the '80s and '90s, the roar had become a whine. Many women discovered they couldn't do what was being asked of them. One woman spoke for millions when she said, "I am spread so thin right now I don't think there is anything left of me. I am an overworked professional, an overtired mother, a part-time wife, a fair-weather friend."[25]

A biblical vision for women begins with the liberating idea that you don't have to be "Superwoman." Common sense tells a woman that she can't do everything, and that she must choose the *best* things, the things that really matter—like mentoring younger women, raising godly children, and establishing a home that honors Christ. Common sense tells a woman that her husband needs her, desperately, and that her contribution to the family is priceless. Common sense tells a woman that children need full-time moms and that the formative years cannot be neglected without severe, and in some cases irreversible, consequences. Common sense gives a woman the ability to say "no" with confidence to the thousand and one distractions pleading for her time.

The cartoon character Superman is susceptible to Kryptonite. "Superwoman" is susceptible to unguarded activity and multiple distractions outside the home.

Be sensible.

Instead of Careerism, Home-Keeping Hearts

If we've escaped the ire of feminists up to this point (which I doubt), our third facet is guaranteed to kindle an inferno. Paul uses the phrase "workers at home" in Titus 2:5 to describe a woman's chief occupation. Like claps of thunder rumbling in the distance, you can almost hear the cries of "liberated" women rising in strident opposition: "Oppressive!" "Archaic!" "Demeaning!"

But there it is. One little phrase that speaks volumes about a woman's premier pursuit in life: *They are to be workers at home.*

My grandmother, Katherine, left our family the legacy of "diligence at home." Mama Kate was a remarkable woman. She was well-educated and well-known throughout northern Louisiana for her many exploits. Kate was the head of a number of cultural and literary clubs, and she was an extremely influential person.

But the real passion of Mama Kate's heart was family.

Kate created a mantelpiece that symbolized her commitment to home. On her honeymoon in Colorado, this unique woman collected an assortment of rocks and spelled out the phrase "Home-Keeping Hearts," a phrase that was then set in a four-foot-long piece of concrete and placed over the fireplace in Kate's large plantation-style home. This priceless symbol now rests over the fireplace in our home.

If you had asked Mama Kate to place an accent mark over the most important part of her life, she would have simply pointed to the mantle above the fireplace. Home was the heartbeat of her life. It was here that she labored diligently. Outside interests were secondary to the creation and maintenance of this priceless treasure. "The wise woman builds her house, but the foolish tears it down with her own hands" (Proverbs 14:1).

Be diligent in the home.

Instead of Sameness, Support

Support is the fourth facet of the spiritual jewel called womanhood. This is the essential idea behind the much maligned phrase, "being subject to their own husbands" (Titus 2:5). The words "subjection" and "submission" connote inferiority today. But this is far from Paul's intention. Thomas R. Scheiner corrects our misunderstanding of these controversial terms.

> They [evangelical feminists] conclude that a difference in function necessarily involves a difference in essence; i.e. if men are in authority over women, then women must be inferior. The relationship between Christ and the Father shows us that this reasoning is flawed. One can possess a different function and still be equal in essence and worth. Women are equal to men in essence and in being; there is no ontological distinction, and yet they have a different function or role in church and home. Such differences do not logically imply inequality or inferiority, just as Christ's subjection to the Father does not imply His inferiority.[26]

While in no way compromising their essential nature, women are free to support their husbands. Instead of pursuing *sameness,* a biblical woman seeks to complement her husband. Her role is to empower her husband to responsible leadership. She is called to relinquish herself, not to a position of inferiority, but to a position of support—one that provides a priceless, irreplaceable, nurturing love unique to women. In yielding herself to this call, a woman discovers true freedom.

Where Are the Women?

I've set before you two systems, two philosophies of life. If you are a woman reading this text, I'd like you to consider some hard questions. Which set of values do you believe you should pursue within your home? Which set of values will result in true fulfillment? Which view of womanhood are you instilling in your daughters? Are your daughters being raised to respond to a divine call or are they being taught to yearn for a secular career as the *summum bonum* of life? Where are the older women of Titus 2:3 who are instructing the younger women? Where are the Christian women who are carrying the banner of biblical truth, women who are saying "no" to the pitfalls and lies of radical feminism?

Sadly, I don't have the answers to these questions. As one who is deeply concerned for the family, I can only ask the questions. What I *do* know is that future generations will be shaped by the answers we give in this generation.

Like mother, like daughter.

A Lesson for Allison

William Mattox took his daughter to work in April 1994. To celebrate "Take Your Daughter to Work Day," he arranged for his eight-year-old daughter, Allison, to accompany him to his place of employment in Washington, D.C. The morning of their adventure, Mattox detailed his plans in an article in the *Wall Street Journal.*

Allison was scheduled to meet with two women who call regularly on members of Congress. At lunch, the eight-year-old was going to talk with a female accountant who also does some public speaking. The afternoon was going to be spent in the company of a woman who once practiced law and now manages a team of writers. But the best part of Allison's education was going to occur in the car on the way home from work. Mattox writes:

> I am sure all of this will be interesting to Allison. But the time I am most looking forward to is the ride home. For it is then that I plan to point out to my daughter that some of the exciting tasks carried out by my female colleagues in the workplace are tasks my wife performed in jobs she held prior to motherhood. She used to meet regularly with congressmen and senators. She used to do some writing and public speaking. And she has a Phi Beta Kappa key from her college days.

After I remind my daughter of these things, I plan to turn to her and look her in the eye and say, "Allison, you must be a very special young girl. Your mother could be using her talents and skills in all sorts of jobs in the workplace, but she has chosen instead to use them at home teaching you. She must love you very, very, very much and think you are very, very important."

Somehow, I think that at that moment my daughter's self-esteem will rise to a level heretofore unimagined by the organizers of "Take Your Daughter to Work Day." And for that I owe a debt of gratitude to my wife, whose esteem-building job as a mother at home rarely receives the public esteem it deserves.[27]

Like mother, like daughter.

Notes

[1]Brigitte Greenberg, "G. I. Joe, Barbie Got Yule Switches," *Arkansas Democrat-Gazette,* 30 December 1993, A1.

[2]John Piper, "A Vision of Biblical Complementarity," *Recovering Biblical Manhood and Womanhood,* John Piper and Wayne Grudem, eds. (Wheaton, Ill.: Crossway, 1991), 33.

[3]Betty Friedan, *The Feminine Mystique* (New York: Dell, 1963), 84.

[4]Ellen Chesler, *Margaret Sanger: Woman of Valor* (New York: Simon and Schuster, 1992), 130.

[5]David Halberstam, *The Fifties* (New York: Villard Books, 1993), 598.

[6]Betty Friedan, *Feminine Mystique,* 15.

[7]Ibid., 338-339.

[8]John Stott, *Decisive Issues Facing Christians Today* (Old Tappan, New Jersey: Fleming H. Revell Company, 1984), 264.

[9]Stephen Clark, *Man and Woman in Christ* (Ann Arbor, Mich.: Servant Books, 1988), 435.

[10]Ibid., 413.

[11]Margaret Sanger, *Woman and the New Race* (New York: Macmillan, 1920), 94.

[12]Karen DeCrow, "Women Are Victims Again," U.S.A. *Today,* 5 October 1993, 11A.

[13]Nicholas Davidson, *The Failure of Feminism* (Buffalo, New York: Prometheus, 1988), 17.

[14]Raymond Ortlund, Jr., "Male-Female Equality and Male Headship," *Recovering Biblical Manhood and Womanhood,* 111.

[15]Stephen Clark, *Man and Woman in Christ* (Ann Arbor, Mich.: Servant Books, 1980), 414-415.

[16]Steven Goldberg, "Feminism Against Science," *National Review,* 18 November 1991, 30.

[17]Charles Petit, "Stay-at-Home Moms Ranked Among the Most Depressed," *San Francisco Chronicle,* 2 October 1992, A3.

[18]John Krakauer, "Ice, Mosquitoes & Muskeg—Building the Road to Alaska," *Smithsonian,* July 1992, 105.

[19]Eda LeShan, "Talking It Over," *Woman's Day,* 17 January 1989, 10.

[20]Raymond and Dorothy Moore, "When Education Becomes Abuse: A Different Look at the Mental Health of Children," *Journal of School Health,* Vol. 56, No. 2, February 1986, 73.

[21]William D. Gairdner, *The War Against the Family* (Toronto, Canada: Stoddart, 1992), 339.

[22]Ibid., 341.

[23]Ibid., 340.

[24]Dorothy Patterson, "The High Calling of Wife and Mother in Biblical Perspective," *Recovering Biblical Manhood and Womanhood,* 371.

[25]Robert Lewis and William Hendricks, *Rocking the Roles* (Colorado Springs: NavPress, 1991), 94.

[26]Thomas R. Schreiner, "Head Coverings, Prophecies and the Trinity," *Recovering Biblical Manhood and Womanhood,* 128.

[27]William R. Mattox, Jr., "A Lesson for Allison," *The Wall Street Journal,* 28 April 1994, A12.

CHAPTER EIGHT

AVOIDING EVE'S MISTAKE

"The goal of the women's movement is not about advancing women in positions in the church. It's about a complete change in theology."
DONNA STEICHEN

Has God placed a unique feminine calling upon the lives of *women?* The answer to this question is a resounding YES! Women are the priceless jewel in one of God's most treasured commodities—the family. They provide a nurturing love that is both invaluable and irreplaceable. This lofty vision of womanhood is unthinkable to most feminists, yet it remains a central component in the redemptive work of God.

Our second question is just as challenging and equally controversial: *What is a woman permitted to do within the church?* Can women serve as pastors? Can women lead a church? Are women free to serve in the same capacities as men or are there restrictions? And, if there are restrictions, what is the basis for those restrictions? And how does this affect the way we view families and family life, if at all?

A tumultuous debate is now raging within the world's religious community and even within the smaller sphere of evangelicalism. The debate centers around the role of women in the church. A number of recent developments highlight the urgency of this issue. For example, in 1989 the Episcopal Church broke with a two-thousand-year-old tradition and appointed a woman, Barbara Harris, to the heretofore exclusively male position of bishop.

At a church synod in November 1992, the Church of England paved the way for what previously would have been unthinkable—the ordination of 1,300 women for the priesthood. This decision by Anglican leaders was greeted with scorn by conservative church members. Said Ann Widdecombe, who quit the church following the vote: "Its [the Church of England's] doctrine is doubt, its creed is compromise, and its purpose appears to be party politics. This was just the last straw."[1] These developments and others are being hailed by feminists as a "second reformation."

We must ask this, however: Is "reformation" really what is taking place today? Are these events comparable in scope to the movement that thrust the Church back to the Bible and transformed the western world in the sixteenth century? Or conversely, is this merely a further alteration of Christian theology designed to keep pace with a secular culture?

Scratching Below the Surface

When you scratch below the surface of the debate over women in the church, you discover an ominous fact: This issue is much broader and more problematic than it appears at first glance. Most lay people, goaded by a secular media, have reduced the debate to a single issue: a woman's right to be priest, pastor, bishop, even Pope. But the truth is, the debate extends far beyond these borders into a land of New Age theology, brazen reinterpretations of Scripture, and overt challenges to orthodox Christianity. Richard Ostling writes, "The debate over the status of women, with all its theological and personal dramas, represents a *larger clash* between venerable religious beliefs and social movements that have affected much of the world over the past generation" [*emphasis mine*].[2]

With respect to the religious community, what are the broader issues at stake, the issues that are dear to the hearts of radical feminists? There are three.

1. The debate involves new ways of conceiving of God. God the Father has become God the Parent in some denominations. Some Methodist clergy conceive and speak of God as "Sophia, Goddess of Wisdom." The United Church of Christ has rewritten the Great Commission (Matthew 28:19). It now reads: "Go therefore and make disciples of all nations, baptizing them in the name of God the Father and Mother and of Jesus Christ the beloved Child of the Holy Spirit."[3] *Time* quotes Donna Steichen, author of *Ungodly Rage,* who has observed that "women have formed separatist 'Women-Church' worship, a New Age blend of feminist, ecological, neopagan and Christian elements. One book offers liturgies to celebrate the coming out of lesbians, teenagers' first menstrual periods and cycles of the moon."[4] Feminist Mary Daily summed it up: "If God is male, then the male is God." Hence the passionate rush to redefine the nature, and names, of God.

2. The debate involves the supremacy of biblical authority. The Bible, with its clear-cut statements on women's roles and masculine names for God, represents a formidable challenge to feminists. Radicals in the church have answered this challenge in one of two ways: they have either reinterpreted the Bible or discarded the sacred text altogether. Rosemary Reuther, an advocate for feminist ideology, is quite blunt about the changing role of Scripture. She argues that a chief priority of feminism is the displacement of the Bible as the normative source of Christian belief. In her words, "It [the Bible] becomes simply one source among many sources for women. What women should achieve within the church cannot be done from the existing base of the Christian Bible."[5]

How right she is. Clark Pinnock counters, "If it's the Bible you want, feminism is in trouble. If it's feminism you want, the Bible stands in its way."[6] To circumvent this impasse, feminists are undercutting biblical authority, striking a death blow to Christian orthodoxy.

3. The debate involves remaking Christianity itself. This point is a logical outworking of the first two. The editor of the *Catholic World Report,* Jesuit Joseph Fessio, summarizes the consequences of tinkering with tradition. "If you change the language of the liturgy and prayers and feminize it, you're ultimately changing the religion."[7] The religion espoused by a growing number of evangelical feminists is far afield from the faith of our fathers (and mothers, too, for that matter!).

On a personal level, many lay people from mainline churches ask me, "What in the world is happening to our denomination? Our hymns, our beliefs, our creeds—everything is changing!" My immediate response is that a complete social, moral, and theological overhaul is under way. We'd better wake up!

Denominations that once would not tolerate divorced ministers now find themselves debating whether to accept avowed lesbian ministers. "The movement's goal," warns Donna Steichen, "is nothing less than the overthrow of Christianity. It's not about advancing women's positions in the church. It's about a complete change in theology."[8]

All of these issues, and many others, now stand at the gate of evangelical Christianity. At the center of the firestorm are these questions which beg to be answered from an authoritative, biblical source: What can a woman do in the church? What roles do women play in the evangelical community? In the family?

One of the clearest biblical statements on women's roles is found in a letter written by Paul to a young preacher named Timothy. This young man was pastoring a church in Ephesus, a community which, surprisingly, mirrors our own in its material prosperity and open embrace of feminist ideology. If you've thought that radical feminism was strictly a twentieth-century phenomenon, then you'll be shocked by the social environment of this first-century community.

Feminism in the First Century

As every student of biblical interpretation knows well, context is everything. The specific context in which a book or letter was written is crucial to understanding its meaning. This basic hermeneutical principle is extremely important when we seek to interpret 1 Timothy 2:9-15. For too long, Paul's teaching on women's roles in this passage of Scripture has been denied the bias-eliminating voice of context.

Most exegetes begin with the mistaken assumption Paul is speaking in the midst of a patriarchal society. He isn't. Statements such as "I do not allow a woman to teach or exercise authority over a man" (v. 12) are understood as reinforcing a traditional chauvinistic social structure. Just the opposite is true. Far from reinforcing the status quo, Paul is enunciating a radical doctrine into a highly feminized culture. A brief survey of the historical context bears this out. Four snapshots of ancient Ephesus corroborate this important principle.

1. Ephesus was an extremely wealthy and prosperous city. The first snapshot concerns the standard of living in Ephesus. Located at the mouth of the Cayster River in the Roman province of Asia Minor, Ephesus was both a major export center and a natural landing point for ships from Rome. At this time in its history, Ephesus was one of the major financial centers within the Roman Empire. A twin city, Laodicea, located within walking distance of Ephesus, was equally prosperous (Revelation 3:17). The women of Ephesus shared in its wealth and prosperity. Many women lived lives of luxury and many fell prey to the "high life," becoming preoccupied with having "the right things." As we will see momentarily, this is the basis for Paul's admonition against such things as braided hair, gold and pearls, and costly garments (1 Timothy 2:9).

2. Women in Ephesus enjoyed social equality with men. There was a strong feminist spirit in Ephesus and throughout the rest of the Roman Empire as well. Historian Will Durant writes:

> Emancipation for women was as complete in those days as it is in ours. Women worked outside the home, in shops and factories. Some became doctors or lawyers, athletes, even gladiators. [And you thought women on "American Gladiators" was revolutionary!] Some became politically powerful.[9]

Social historian Jerome Carcopino adds this note in his book, *Daily Life in Ancient Rome:* "It is certain that the women of this epoch we are studying enjoyed a dignity and an independence at least equal if not superior to those claimed by contemporary feminists."[10]

I've sat through classes on university campuses and been fed the brazen lie that women in the first century were nothing more than beaten-down slaves. Such statements betray either faulty research or an audacious denial of historical fact. Certainly some women were oppressed. But many women in the first century, especially those in major urban centers of the Roman Empire, were experiencing freedoms on a massive scale. They were moving forcefully into society on multiple fronts. In fact, Carcopino says, "Women put their enthusiasm into an attempt to rival men, if not outclass them in every sphere of life."[11]

3. Religion in Ephesus was highly feminized. Lest we forget, the pagan deity that cast the greatest shadow in Ephesus was a *she*, not a *he*. The goddess Diana was a multi-breasted woman affectionately referred to by the populace as "the Mother of all life." The primary industry in the city was the manufacturing of silver shrines dedicated to this female goddess (Acts 19:23-25). Diana's temple was immense—so large, in fact, that it is considered one of the great wonders of the ancient world, comparable to Egypt's pyramids and the great hanging gardens of Babylon. Priestesses outnumbered priests in the temple. Thousands of women served alongside their male counterparts in religious worship. They held ecclesiastical offices for generations.

4. Women in Ephesus were leaving home and children for other pursuits. This was happening throughout the rest of the Roman Empire as well. Will Durant summarizes the opinion that many women held of the home: "Children were more of a liability than anything else for women in this day. Women wished to be sexually beautiful rather than maternally beautiful."[12] Carcopino says: "Before this time a woman took pride in her fertility. But now she fears it."[13] If a first-century woman did get pregnant, there was something she could do about it. Yes, women had a "choice," even in the first century. "So great were the abortionists potions," women were liberated from the bedroom.[14]

I have to ask myself, would Gloria Steinem have loved this place or what? Are you surprised this was the social climate of first-century Ephesus? If it sounds a lot like late twentieth-century America, then you have grasped the broader historical context of Paul's instruction to Timothy. Paul is not writing to buttress a degenerate, patriarchal society (as is commonly asserted in many quarters today); instead, he is countering a liberated, feminized culture much like our own. To argue that 1 Timothy 2:9-15 is invalid for today because "times have changed" is to miss the point completely. Paul's message is not one of *continuity,* but of *revolution.* In the face of first-century feminism run amuck, Paul instructs women to embrace a divine call. Their roles at home and in the church are prescribed by an immutable, wise God. The mandates of His calling are not archaic; instead, they are timeless. Neither are they bound by culture, but are tied to God's original design in creation.

The Role of Women in the Church

What role does Scripture prescribe for women in the church? Listen to Paul's instruction in 1 Timothy 2:9-15 and keep in mind that he is addressing, not a male-dominated society, but a feminized one.

> Likewise, I want women to adorn themselves with proper clothing, modestly and discreetly, not with braided hair and gold or pearls or costly garments; but rather by means of good works, as befits women making a claim to godliness. Let a woman quietly receive instruction with entire submissiveness. But I do not allow a woman to teach or exercise authority over a man, but to remain quiet. For it was Adam who was first created, and then Eve. And it was not Adam who was deceived, but the woman being quite deceived, fell into transgression. But women shall be preserved through the bearing of children if they continue in faith and love and sanctity with self-restraint.

The apostle begins with an emphasis upon a woman's heart (vv. 9-10). Two statements underscore this priority. The first, in verse 9, contrasts a woman's appearance with her character. Women are to adorn themselves "discreetly and modestly, not with braided hair and gold or pearls or costly garments." This verse has often been misinterpreted by some as a blanket statement against fashionable dress. I suspect, however, that this is a distortion of the truth. The force of the verse is found in two words—*modestly* and *discreetly*. Paul is not prohibiting ornate dress as much as he is emphasizing modesty and discretion. He does this for good reason. The wealthy women of Ephesus had become enamored with fashion. They were buying pearls and expensive gold and flaunting themselves to compete with one another in public. The *external* had supplanted the *internal.* Paul reminds his readers that true femininity is first and foremost a matter of the heart, not of appearance.

Second, women are to adorn themselves with good works (v. 10). This verse is a continuation of the previous one. It can be read this way: "but rather [let women adorn themselves] by means of good works, as befits women making a claim to godliness." What "good works" does Paul have in mind—works that befit women in particular? The list is long. Some of these good deeds, as we discovered in Titus 2, include: giving priority to the nurturance and rearing of children; being loving and supportive of husbands (not competing with them); and building home environments that are secure, creative, and full of acceptance. Women are called by God to nurture their children, not abandon them to daycare.

But the possibilities extend beyond the home. There are also a number of good works that women contribute to the life and health of the church. In fact, when you read the New Testament, you discover that there are *no limitations* on what a woman can do in the church. Women can teach, disciple, lead, administrate, sing, evangelize, prophesy, exhort, and counsel. The only limitation is one of *sphere,* not of *activity.* Women can serve in every conceivable area but they are restricted in one specific area, involving teaching and authority. If this sounds like a contradiction, let me explain.

Two Limitations

Paul had in mind the public worship service when he wrote: "Let a woman quietly receive instruction with entire submissiveness. But I do not allow a woman to teach or exercise authority over a man, but to remain quiet" (1 Timothy 2:11-12).

You can't be any more politically *incorrect* than this! Not in America. Nor in Ephesus. Scripture clearly mandates two limitations upon women in the church. Paul mentions both in verse 12: *teaching* and *exercising authority* over men. Let's consider each in turn.

The first limitation is teaching. Paul has in mind a specific form of teaching, that of authoritative public instruction. The word Paul uses for "teach" (*didasko*), is common in the New Testament. It refers to the public, authoritative exposition of Scripture.[15]

The second limitation deals with authority; more specifically, women exercising authority over men. The Greek word translated "exercise authority over" is the word *authenteo;* it means "to govern or to lead."[16]

When these two ideas, teaching and exercising authority, are considered together, I believe we arrive at a singular concept. In a phrase, I would call this concept spiritual leadership. Paul is saying, in effect, "I do not allow a woman to exercise *spiritual leadership* over a man." Women can teach other women. They can lead other women. But they cannot usurp the spiritual authority of men by exercising authority over them. The limitation, therefore, is not in what women do, but the context in which they do it.

As you might guess, this principle of spiritual authority is most often applied to the office of pastor, elder, or priest. Pastors and/or elders teach the Scriptures publicly and authoritatively to the whole church; they govern, lead, and oversee the body, exercising broad authority in matters of faith and doctrine. That the office of elder is limited to men can be confirmed by one incontrovertible fact: There are no female elders or pastors in the New Testament. None! The Scripture confers this spiritual leadership only upon men.

Jesus could have settled any future controversy by choosing a woman to join His original leadership team. Jesus was not bound by social custom or manmade traditions in any area, including gender. In fact, there were times when He was downright insensitive to such things: Attacking moneychangers in the temple, calling religious leaders "white-washed tombs," and trampling on the tradition of the Sabbath made Jesus a true social revolutionary.

We know from Scripture that many godly and capable women were with Christ from the earliest days of His public ministry. Some of them, I'm convinced, could teach and lead. And yet, when Jesus prayed all night asking His Father to show Him who would lead this spiritual revolution, the word He received was "MEN." Twelve MEN.

Paul's statement in 1 Timothy 2:12 is consistent with Jesus' selection of all-male leadership. But this Scripture is a declaration—a declaration that women are *not* to lead men spiritually. And *this declaration extends far beyond the office of apostle, pastor, or priest.* Please note this! It's very important. Paul didn't say, "I do not allow a woman to pastor." His declaration is broader than that. The principle stated here applies to *any situation* wherein women by their actions might "undercut, compete with, or usurp the spiritual leadership of men."[17] It's at this juncture that a real family value begins to emerge.

Today, we are constrained as biblical Christians to apply this principle *to the home,* as well as to small groups, Sunday school classes, seminars—in effect, to any domain wherein women sometimes take charge and exercise spiritual leadership over men.

If you think Paul's prohibitions sound patriarchal and oppressive, imagine how they must have sounded to the women of Ephesus. For generations these women had worshiped a female deity; they had thrown off the restraints of male domination; they had pursued equality in every area of life. Nevertheless, Paul says, "I do not allow a woman to teach or exercise authority over a man." These were brave words two thousand years ago; they remain equally so today.

A Theological Explanation

If I were a first-century woman hearing these revolutionary words for the first time, I would have demanded an explanation. Paul anticipates this inquiry and anchors his theological explanation in creation: "For it was Adam who was first created, and then Eve. And it was not Adam who was deceived, but the woman being quite deceived, fell into transgression" (1 Timothy 2:13-14).

The apostle bases his principle, not on culture nor personal opinion but, instead, upon the fact of creation. "Adam was created first, then Eve." The fact that Adam was created before Eve is more than a biblical nuance; it is a strong theological statement about man's role in creation, and how man relates to woman. Listen to Thomas R. Schreiner:

> Evangelical feminists often claim that any role distinctions between males and females are due only to the fall. But their argument fails for two reasons. First, Paul argues from creation, not from the fall. The distinctions between male and female are part of the created order, and Paul apparently did not think redemption in Christ negated creation....[18]

Commenting upon 1 Timothy 2:9-15, Douglas Moo states: "These restrictions are permanent, authoritative for the church in all times and places and circumstances as long *as men and women are descended from Adam and Eve*" [emphasis mine].[19] Spiritual leadership belonged to Adam by virtue of creation. In the same manner, the propagation of human life belonged to woman by virtue of her creation. To Paul, these differences must be respected—in every culture and in every age.

The account of the Fall in Genesis 3 gives us great insight into Paul's companion statement in verse 14—"And it was not Adam who was deceived, but the woman being quite deceived, fell into transgression." According to Genesis 3, both Adam and Eve disregarded God's original design. Eve usurped Adam's prerogative of spiritual leadership, and Adam acquiesced in his responsibility to lead. One cast aside divinely ordained limitations, the other sinned by becoming tragically passive. Eve charged independently ahead to create what she thought was a level playing field. While this was going on, Adam just stood there! Completely out of the loop, he relinquished his responsibility of spiritual leadership.

We shouldn't be surprised to discover these twin realities at work in American society today. Female control and male passivity are now endemic to men and women. A man's greatest temptation in the home is spiritual passivity—to acquiesce in his role as spiritual leader. A woman's greatest temptation is to usurp her husband's leadership. Feminism aggressively seeks to find a better way for both men and women. It endeavors to cast off past limitations, the constraints imposed upon women by culture and the church. Feminism seeks to reduce all of life— career endeavors, roles in marriage, parental responsibilities—to the benign level of *sameness*. When you add to the mix a generation of men who have no sense of their responsibilities, men who are passive in the home and spiritually limp, you have a prescription for disaster. This mixture is killing us. Literally.

So why does Paul limit the sphere of leadership for women? Not because women can't lead. They can. Not because women can't teach. They can. Paul limits the sphere of leadership for women precisely because *men have been called by God to lead*. It's creational, not patriarchal! Leadership is at the core of manhood, and women should be encouraging men to lead—not challenging this mandate, not usurping it or despising it. Deviating from God's design encourages bad things to happen. The church that dares to be politically incorrect will restrain its women and press its men toward responsible spiritual leadership—without apology to a feminized, disintegrating culture.

John Piper is painfully correct when he says, "If I were to put my finger on one devastating sin today, it would not be the so-called women's movement, but the lack of spiritual leadership by men at home and in the church."[20] Men today are grossly underchallenged. Most have an intolerable lack of vision of what a real man is, and few mentors to point the way (a subject we will address in chapter 9). Men today can work, play, and procreate, but fewer and fewer of them can lead. And yet leadership, the kind that draws admiration from a wife's heart and builds character in a child's soul, is the very essence of real manhood.

The church can change this deficit in men today but not by reinterpreting the faith. True change will come only when the church provides for and challenges men to answer God's call to be REAL MEN—men who lead their families spiritually, responsibly, and sacrificially; men who love their wives in a way that exalts and honors them as co-equals in life. Until this happens, expect women to feel oppressed.

And what about the women? Paul concludes this section by reminding women of their essential calling in life. "But women shall be saved through the bearing of children if they continue in faith and love and sanctity with self-restraint" (1 Timothy 2:15). This verse has led to a number of wild interpretations. Is Paul saying a woman's salvation depends upon her having children? No. The word translated "saved" is not addressing what we normally think of as salvation. "Saved" speaks of being delivered from the sin of Eve's foolishness (1 Timothy 2:14) in seeking to find life by seizing the throttle of spiritual leadership for both her and her husband.

The word "saved" also refers to "fulfillment." Paul is telling us that a woman will find her ultimate fulfillment in life, not by yielding gullibly to the empty promises of our world, but by pursuing God's unique design for her life. And for most women, this calling will involve children. In Paul's day, women viewed children as holding them back, spoiling their careers, and ruining their sexuality. Children were deemed a liability. Does that sound familiar? The apostle says just the opposite. He tells us that children are a means of salvation from an empty life and from a world that offers women, in every age, "forbidden fruit."

Children are a way to fulfill God's original calling on a woman's life, especially when those children grow up spiritually mature and socially responsible. This is the significance of Paul's qualifying statement in verse 15: "if they continue in faith, love, holiness and self-control." When a mother raises sons and daughters who go on to become men and women of character, faith, love, virtue, and power, she becomes a woman who is truly fulfilled. I'm afraid many women today will discover this reality when it's too late.

Turn Back the Clock

When I read Paul's closing statement in 1 Timothy 2:15, my heart grieves for America. What wouldn't our country give to have sons and daughters like this? But to have them we must have women who are devoted to their husbands and their children, moms who nurture and love and sacrifice for the next generation of Americans. The alternatives aren't working! Ironically, it's through the rearing of healthy, wholesome children that women ultimately exercise their greatest power, authority, and leadership in the world. The old proverb, "The hand that rocks the cradle, rules the world," is not far off.

Over 150 years ago, a Frenchman named Alexis de Tocqueville traveled to America to study the robust health of American culture. As a social scientist, Tocqueville was particularly interested in the fabric of our society; he wanted to discover the secrets underlying America's moral and social strength. He found it in the home:

For my part I have no hesitation in saying that although the American woman never leaves her domestic sphere and is in some respects very dependent within it, nowhere does she enjoy a higher station.... If anyone asks me what I think the chief cause of the extraordinary prosperity and growing power of this nation, I should answer that it is due to the superiority of their women.[21]

Am I suggesting that we turn back the clock 150 years to the old America? No, not at all. What I am suggesting, though, is that we turn our faith all the way back to creation—to rediscover the wonder of God's original design: its power and its promise. I'm asking you to see in this simple apostolic instruction the application of God's marvelous design for men and women. I'm asking you to see the redemptive power this design unleashes in society, especially when the church stays faithful to her call, and holds it up instead of caving in. I'm asking you to see the profound answer Paul gives to a very simple question: What can a woman do in the church? The answer is: "She can do everything"—as long as she gives her children priority attention and encourages her husband to responsible spiritual leadership.

Notes

[1] Richard N. Ostling, "The Second Reformation," *Time*, 23 November 1992, 53.

[2] Ibid., 53.

[3] Ibid., 54.

[4] Ibid.

[5] William Oddie, "The Goddess Squad," *National Review*, 18 November 1991, 45.

[6] Clark H. Pinnock, "Biblical Authority and the Issues in Question," *Women, Authority and the Bible*, Alvera Mickelsen, ed. (Downer's Grove, Ill.: Intervarsity Press, 1986), 57-58.

[7]Richard N. Ostling, "The Second Reformation," 53.

[8]Ibid., 54.

[9]Will Durant, *The Story of Civilization: Caesar and Christ;* 3 (New York: Simon and Schuster, 1944), 370.

[10]Jerome Carcopino, *Daily Life in Ancient Rome* (New Haven, Conn.: Yale University Press, 1966), 85.

[11]Ibid.

[12]Will Durant, *The Story of Civilization,* 222.

[13]Jerome Carcopino, *Daily Life in Ancient Rome,* 93.

[14]Will Durant, *The Story of Civilization,* 364.

[15]Almost without exception, *didasko* refers to the teaching of groups; hence, the idea of public instruction. See Roy B. Zuck, "Greek Words for Teachers," *Bibliotheca Sacra,* 122, April-June 1965, 159.

[16]G. Abbott-Smith, *A Manual Greek Lexicon of the New Testament* (Edinburgh, Scotland: T. and T. Clark, 1937), 68. *Authenteo* is a general word expressing authority in an overall manner. A. T. Robertson defines it as a vernacular term for "playing the master." A. T. Robertson, *Word Pictures in the New Testament;* IV (Nashville: Broadman Press, 1931), 570.

[17]Thomas R. Schreiner, "Head Coverings, Prophecies and the Trinity," *Recovering Biblical Manhood and Womanhood,* John Piper and Wayne Grudem, eds. (Wheaton, Ill.: Crossway, 1991), 133.

[18]Ibid.

[19]Douglas Moo, "What Does It Mean Not to Teach or Have Authority Over Men?" *Recovering Biblical Manhood and Womanhood,* 180.

[20]John Piper, "A Vision of Biblical Complementarity," 53.

[21]Alexis de Tocqueville, *Democracy in America,* trans. George Lawrence, ed. J. P. Mayer (New York: Doubleday, Anchor Books, 1969), 603.

CHAPTER NINE

CHILDREN DON'T BOUNCE...

They Break

"Children are the living messages we send to a time that we will not see."
NEIL POSTMAN

If I were a dog, I'd give a month's-worth of Kibbles 'n Bits to live in Germany. I would probably need to learn a new doggy language and even develop a taste for European table scraps. But these minor inconveniences would be well worth the move. You see, the Germans know how to care for their dogs.

According to a recent article in the *Frankfurter Rundschau*, the federal Ministry of Agriculture is about to release a sweeping policy guaranteed to improve the quality of life for canines. The new law is designed to ensure that dogs receive adequate "exercise and social contact." (I suspect this will reduce the number of dysfunctional dogs that now populate the German countryside.) Pet owners will be required to be within view or vocal distance of their dogs for at least eight hours a day. And "Dogs must be given direct attention several times a day, totaling at least two hours in one-dog households and a half-hour in multi-dog households." (Separation anxiety must be a leading cause of psychological disorders in German pets.)

Dogs kept in enclosures must be granted two hours of freedom a day. The government also mandates the size of dog houses. Pets weighing up to thirty-three pounds are now legally entitled to four square meters of space; larger pets are guaranteed eight square meters. According to Ilya Weiss, the director for the Association Against the Abuse of Animals, "The regulations show how little attention is paid to the justified demands of animal protection activists."

Aside from the parenthetical commentary, I'm not making this up.

I wonder if Germany has similar regulations pertaining to the daily care of children. I doubt it.

Please don't misconstrue my editorial comments. I like dogs. But something is terribly amiss when the needs of pets are legislated and the needs of children are ignored. William Penn was correct when he observed that "men are generally more careful of the breed of their horses and dogs than of their children."

In the final chapter of his alarming book, *The Rise of Selfishness in America,* historian James Lincoln Collier articulates the rampant disregard American parents have for their kids:

> In other words, parents today are making *the choice* to have children without accepting any concomitant responsibility for taking care of them. It is particularly the fathers who are to blame. Millions of American males are today refusing to accept any responsibility for the children that they have sired; and even more millions are escaping from those responsibilities as soon as they discover that childrearing is not always fun. It is more important for perhaps the majority of American

men to fulfill themselves than it is to see that their children get off to the best start in life.[1]

We know by experience that a positive, healthy childhood can be the genesis of great strength in a person's life. Our childhood lives on in us—shaping who we are, what we do, and how we feel. These inaugural experiences, when pleasant and rewarding, lead to solid character formation, psychological well-being, and healthy relationships. But equally true is the dark side of childhood. A dysfunctional beginning can unleash a plethora of personal demons that haunt an individual for a lifetime.

James Toney lives every day with the demons of his childhood. In May 1991, Toney became the International Boxing Federation's middle-weight champion of the world. He is a vicious competitor, with lightning quick hands and an explosive left hook. But James Toney's most notable characteristic is his anger. It motivates everything he does. And the object of that anger is his father:

"I fight with anger," explains James Toney, Jr. "My dad, he did my mom wrong. He left us, he beat my mother up all the time. He shot my mom, left her with a mark on her leg. He made my mom work two jobs, and he just left his responsibilities behind. I can never forgive that.... I hope he [his father] reads this, because if he ever decides to come out of the woodwork, I'll be ready for him. Everything I do is about that. I look at my opponent and I see my dad, so I have to take him out. I have to kill him. I'll do anything I have to do to get him out of there."[2]

America is populated today by millions of adults like James Toney—men and women who nurture and coddle a resentment borne of abuse, neglect, and rejection. Child psychiatrist Dr. Hugh Misseldine has witnessed this same pattern in thousands of patients.

As a child psychiatrist, I'm in a unique position to see in the adult what has happened in the child he once was. I often observe in their very origin the beginning of trouble-making adult attitudes beginning in the child. They are a child's way of dealing with the often unreasonable and excessive demands of his parents. And then I see the end result of these childhood reactions in the adult—loneliness, anxiety, sexual difficulties, depressions, fears, marital discords and compulsive addictive behaviors.[3]

To underscore this reality, Misseldine adds, "No one outgrows his feelings of childhood. For better or for worse, the child lives on in the adult."[4]

The Seeds of Anger

Adults in our generation are angry and bitter for one simple reason: Somewhere along the way their parents (and their fathers in particular) neglected a basic principle of Scripture. This principle is a foundational truth; it is the cornerstone, the plumb line that ensures healthy, emotionally stable children. What is it? "And, fathers, do not provoke your children to anger; but bring them up in the discipline and instruction of the Lord" (Ephesians 6:4).

This verse contains a positive exhortation and a negative prohibition. The exhortation is "bring them up in the discipline and instruction of the Lord." Fathers are called to nurture their children, to discipline them and encourage them in the "how-to's" of living, and to instruct them in the basics of spiritual life. Such involvement demands careful attention and divinely appointed patience. It is a challenge fraught with much discouragement; nevertheless, the rewards are indescribable.

Without a father's care for the souls of his children, a demon is unleashed. Note the choices in Ephesians 6:4. There are only two: Nurture your children or anger them. Either bring them up well or provoke them. Those are your only choices, and the latter is lethal.

The Bible uses two words commonly translated "anger." One is *thumos*. *Thumos* refers to "a strong passion or emotion of the mind."[5] The word connotes anger that is expressed, visible, often convulsive. The second word for anger is *orge*. This is the word Paul uses here in Ephesians 6:4. *Orge* is not necessarily an expressive anger, though it may erupt from time to time when one is provoked. Instead, *orge* is suppressed anger. This word refers to a deep-seated, smoldering inner rage that is the result of past abuse or neglect. The apostle employs an intensified form of the verb to stress the hidden rage inherent in this type of anger. Paul warns fathers against treating children in such a way that their kids grow up with a "deep-seated inner rage" born of abuse and neglect.

Sadly, this condition is all too common in today's world.

Singer Billy Joel simmers with rage, even at thirty-six years of age, because "he's still angry that his mother was left by his father..."[6] Baseball player George Brett grew up under a demanding, perfectionistic father. When his dad died in 1992, Brett struggled to sort out his convoluted emotions. He recalls his father's comments at the close of the 1980 season, a year when the young Brett flirted with a .400 batting average, and finished hitting .390: "Most people's dads would put their arms around you and say you had a good year.... My dad said, 'If you would have got five more hits you would have hit .400.'"[7]

Fathers aren't the only ones who sow seeds of anger.

In her book, *The Sisterhood,* Marsha Cohen explores the lives of feminism's most cherished leaders. One leader who bears the scars of maternal abuse is none other than Betty Friedan, the founder of the National Organization for Women (NOW), and the author of *Feminine Mystique,* feminism's equivalent of Marx's *Communist Manifesto.* Cohen discovered that Friedan's mother, to use the author's words, was "maternally inept." Betty's sister, Amy, describes their mother as one having a "complete inability to nurture.... We really absolutely did not have a mother loving us. She was there, but she didn't know how to mother."[8]

Friedan's mother was a critical woman who made Betty feel unwanted and ugly. "...And my mother," says Friedan's brother, "still thinks Betty had worked as hard as she could to make herself as ugly as possible."[9] Is it any wonder that Betty Friedan seeks to repudiate and overthrow the home, marriage, and motherhood? These cherished ideals are a continuing source of heartache for her.

Why is Paul's admonition against "provoking to anger" so important? Because to a certain extent, childhood is irretrievable. What happens in the first few years of a child's life will ultimately shape his or her personality, character, expectations, emotions, and so on. Listen to Paul Meier, co-founder of the Minirth-Meier Institute:

> One of the things I have learned in my psychiatric training is that approximately eighty-five percent of a person's ultimate personality is formed by the time he is six years old. Those first six years, therefore, are obviously the most crucial. This is not to say that after six years, it is too late to correct...but it becomes increasingly more difficult.[10]

How a baby's parents rear him or her during these crucial first six years will determine much of how that individual will enjoy and succeed in life during the other seventy to eighty years."

Kids Don't Bounce

Why do I present these stories and statistics, facts and information? I do so to unseat and dethrone a terrible myth, an egregious lie that reigns over so many American families and influences so many moms and dads. This myth has allowed mothers and fathers to vent unrestrained emotions upon one another and to act irresponsibly in front of their children. It has allowed parents to continue to pursue the "do your own thing" philosophy they first learned from the sixties. It has given still others the freedom to immerse themselves in careerism, to triangle sons and daughters into harmful adult relationships, and to press unrealistic expectations on their children. This myth has sanctioned divorce, even abuse. What is the myth? It can be stated in two simple phrases:

"THEY CAN HANDLE IT!"
"THEY'LL BOUNCE BACK!"

For example, a child walks into a room and witnesses mom and dad screaming at one another, exchanging four-letter words and other sundry unpleasantries. The parents glance at the child and think to themselves, "He can handle it." Or one day mom comes to junior and says, "Dad and I aren't doing very well..." and she begins to weep and starts looking to her son for affirmation. Or maybe dad deserts the family for another woman, choosing to believe the notion, "They [the kids] will bounce back."

There is something wrong with each of these scenarios. To ease the pain and assuage the hurt, American parents have perpetuated the lie that "The kids can handle it! They'll bounce back!"

A number of books have been published to give credence to this myth. A classic in this vein is *Creative Divorce: A New Opportunity for Personal Growth,* by Mel Krantzler. In a section entitled "Children Are Resilient," Krantzler regurgitates the pablum of pop psychology:

It goes without saying that children are enormously influenced by the quality of their family life and the relationship with their parents. However, short of actual neglect and physical abuse, children can survive any family crisis *without permanent damage* [emphasis mine]—and grow as human beings in the process.[11]

Oh yeah? A more accurate portrait of divorce and its consequences is painted by psychologist Judith Wallerstein. Wallerstein tracked 131 children of divorce for fifteen years to determine the long-term consequences. What did she discover? At the five-year mark, more than a third of those studied experienced moderate to severe depression.[12] By the tenth year, a significant number of these young adults were "troubled, drifting, and underachieving."[13] And by the fifteenth year, many were finding it all but impossible to develop stable love relationships. For her ground-breaking work, Wallerstein received a number of angry letters. She was ridiculed by the psychological community for her pessimistic views. Wallerstein concludes:

> Divorce is deceptive. Legally it is a single event, but psychologically it is a chain—sometimes a never ending chain—of events, relocations, and radically shifting relationships strung through time, a process that forever changes the lives of the people involved.[14]

The evidence is in: *CHILDREN DON'T BOUNCE. THEY BREAK.* Like an egg cast to the ground, kids develop cracks that linger for a lifetime. These cracks remain hidden; they sear a child's soul and mark his or her life in a thousand different ways. And much of a child's life will be spent trying to fuse the cracks together again.

Kids don't bounce; they break. Children are not rubber; instead, they are fine crystal, easily damaged.

A child is a terrible thing to break.

Exposing the Fault Lines of Childhood

What are the cracks that can damage a child for life? There are four.

1. The "love" crack. When a child's hunger for love is denied, he or she is placed at risk, emotionally and psychologically.

I'll never forget the man I met one Sunday afternoon in San Francisco. I was speaking at a Family Life conference and had just finished giving the "dad" talk when I noticed a huge hulk of a man walking slowly down the aisle toward me. This guy was as wide as he was tall; he had enormous arms and a gigantic neck. But at that particular moment, this man's most distinguishing characteristic was his face—it was covered with tears. He had allowed the suppressed pain of a lost childhood and an absent father to surface.

In the eleven years that I've spoken for Family Life, I've witnessed the same response, over and over again, to the "dad" talk. Men are overwhelmed by a sense of loss as they reflect upon their relationships with dad. I've watched hundreds of men weep openly, grieving for a childhood that is gone forever, never to be recovered.

My huge friend stood before me, reached out his arms, and embraced me. I noticed he was wearing a Super Bowl ring on his finger; I later discovered he was a coach with the Oakland Raiders.

He was the biggest baby I've ever held in my arms.

This broken man sobbed openly, not because he had lost a job or was divorcing his wife; he sobbed because the "love" crack had been exposed and his troubled soul could contain the pain no longer. There was a child trapped inside the body of a man, and the child was crying out for help.

I meet hundreds of men like him across the country; in fact, I encounter one every morning in the mirror. As the child of an alcoholic, I feel the "love" crack. Deeply. There are times when I'd like for somebody to take hold of my inner child and embrace him, and let him know that everything is going to be okay.

The pathologies men feel today as a result of this love deficit may well grow even stronger as we move into the twenty-first century. A mom deficit—not just a dad deficit—looms large on the horizon. Because of the pervasive influence of feminism, the next generation may not just be yearning for fathers, but for mothers as well. Today, fewer and fewer moms are nurturing their children through the first six years of development. Large doses of love are crucial at this season of a child's life. According to one study, fifty percent of all children under the age of five are now in some kind of regular daycare arrangement; half of these are under two years old. A Rand Corporation survey found that 38 percent of all women in America who become pregnant are back in the work force by the time their children are three months old.[15]

Women may "find" themselves in their careers, but lose their children in the process.

More than anything else, children need love—lots of it. They need warm hugs and encouraging words. Children need heavy doses of affection—affection expressed physically, verbally, and emotionally. Chuck Swindoll writes:

> Many a young woman who opts for immoral sexual relationships does so because she can scarcely remember a time when her father so much as touched her. Unaffectionate dads, without wishing to do so, can trigger a daughter's promiscuity. All of this leads me to write, with a great deal of passion, "Dads, don't hold back your affection." Demonstrate your feelings of love and affection to both sons and daughters, and don't stop once they reach adolescence. They long for your affirmation and appreciation. They will love you for it. More importantly, they will emulate your example when God gives them their own family.[16]

You can fail in many places as a parent but you cannot afford to stumble at this point. "Love covers a multitude of sins," wrote the apostle Peter. How true this is of parenthood.

2. The "sexuality" crack. There are few things as vulnerable, or as tender, as a person's sexuality—especially in the formative years. Many factors shape a child's sexual identity: childhood experiences, cultural standards, education, and the media. But as powerful as each of these factors may be, nothing exerts as much influence on a child's sexual identity as mom and dad.

One of the forgotten facts about the passionate debate over homosexuality today is that most homosexuals suffer from an emotional deficit with a same-sex parent. After years of research, Elizabeth Moberly reached this compelling conclusion:

> In the homosexual condition, psychological needs that are essentially pre-adult remain in the person who is in other respects adult. Homosexual activity implies the eroticization of deficits in growth that remain outstanding [from childhood].... This is fundamentally a confusion of the emotional needs of the non-adult with the physiological desires of the adult.[17]

During childhood, the homosexual, whether a man or a woman, has often suffered some form of deficit in the relationship with the parent of the same sex. Damaged, rejected, and traumatized, many homosexuals then seek to repair their lost childhood through homosexual activity.

The greatest safeguard against the "sexuality" crack is parental consistency—consistency in *behavior,* consistency in *discipline,* consistency in *fulfilling the parental roles mandated by Scripture.* Dr. Irving Bieber writes: "We have come to the conclusion that a constructive, supportive, warmly related father precludes the possibility of a homosexual man."[18]

3. The "trust" crack. Parent-child relationships, especially during the first six to ten years, provide the working model for all subsequent relationships in a child's life. And a critical component of the parent-child relationship is trust. Trust in a parent breeds security and confidence; it fosters emotional stability and defines ethical boundaries. But when trust is broken or violated, a child is injured at the core of his or her being. Charles Dickens recognized the significance of trust in a child's life when he wrote in *Great Expectations,* "In the little world in which children have their existence…there is nothing so finely perceived and so finely felt, as injustice." Trust can be broken in a variety of ways: through favoritism, cruelty, broken promises, and manipulation. Children are quick to detect the subtle, and overt, violations of this most precious commodity—trust.

The fact is, women who don't trust their dads growing up find it very difficult to trust their husbands in marriage. Our parental histories sail us from the safe or unsafe harbor of childhood into the rough and stormy (or smooth) seas of adulthood.[19]

4. The "affirmation" crack. The importance of affirmation is illustrated most forcefully in the life of our Lord. In Matthew 3, Jesus Christ is poised to begin His earthly ministry. Jesus is baptized by John, an act of obedience which inaugurates the final three years of His earthly life. As Christ emerges from the water, the Spirit of God descends upon Him, "and behold, a voice [spoke] out of the heavens, saying, 'This is My beloved Son, in whom I am well-pleased' " (Matthew 3:17).

What is the significance of this verse? Even though Jesus Christ was God in the flesh, He was nevertheless a man. Like you and me, Jesus was a human being who needed to be affirmed in His manhood, His character, and His mission. Every child—son or daughter—needs the blessing of parents. *The Blessing,* by John Trent and Gary Smalley, was written to stress the importance of parental affirmation.

One of the most common demons stalking adults today is the gnawing sense that they have never fulfilled their parents' expectations. Personal disappointment often disguises itself in a collection of destructive lies, such as "I'm not good enough!" "I'm not pretty enough!" or "I'm not successful enough!" And no matter how much a person achieves throughout his life, no matter how many rungs he scales on the ladder, he can never seem to fill the empty void created by the "affirmation" crack.

A scene from the movie *Field of Dreams* illustrates the human need for, and the awesome power of, affirmation. Do you remember when Shoeless Joe Jackson walks in the outfield near the corn patch with Doc Graham? Doc begins to reminisce about the time in his past when he chose the medical profession over a baseball career. You get the impression that Doc Graham had never been affirmed in his decision, that he longed for someone—anyone—to tell him he had made the right choice. Standing in the outfield while struggling with his identity, Doc Graham finally hears the words that every adult—and every child—longs to hear. Shoeless Joe Jackson tosses Doc the ball and says, "Hey, you're good! You're good." The viewer senses Doc Graham's rejuvenation and healing in this one powerful statement.

One wonders how many successful people, just like a Doc Graham and just like our Lord, are yearning desperately for their parents' affirmation of "You're good" and "I am well pleased."

Repairing the Cracks

The four cracks I've been discussing, developed in childhood, can last a lifetime. What can a parent do to prevent, or repair, these fault lines of destruction and despair? Let me speak first to those parents whose children are still in the home, under their parents' care. There are four action points you can implement right now to prevent the tragic consequences outlined above.

1. Love your children. Biblical love is not an ethereal concept; rather, it is practical and tangible. Give your children the gift of your time; set aside hours in the week to play with them and read to them and nurture them. On top of this, speak words of affirmation. Hug them and hold them; celebrate birthdays and achievements. Make your kids feel special.

2. Discipline your children. Kids need and want clearly defined boundaries. They must be given responsibilities and be held accountable for their tasks and chores.

3. Be consistent. As standard-bearers, parents must reinforce the values, goals, and expectations of the family, without compromise. A husband and wife must work in tandem, consistently reinforcing these ideals and modeling them for the younger members of the family.

4. Fathers must lead. Dads need to initiate spiritual conversation and help with homework. And they must initiate conflict resolution and family activities. A passive father is a harbinger of death to a young child. Listen to these words by David Stoops and Stephen Arterburn in their book, *The Angry Man:*

> Experience has shown us that the men who are happiest and most content in the masculine role today are those whose fathers invested [read "initiated"] a great deal of time and energy in their lives. These dads may have worked outside the home, as the vast majority of fathers today do. But they were committed to maintaining a positive, nurturing relationship with their sons.... As a result of their investment, their sons are among the most well-adjusted and peaceful husbands and fathers in our society.[20]

The parents who implement these four action steps—faithfully, consistently, authentically—can preserve the "fine crystal" of a child's psyche.

But what about those parents who failed miserably with their children, parents whose actions and behavior have engendered deep scars and emotional trauma? Is there any hope for them? Yes, there is.

I received a letter some time ago from a man who is wrestling with the demons of past parental failures. He writes:

Dear Robert,

I need some practical spiritual help from you. Our family was highly troubled for a long period of time leading up to my son's treatment for a severe compulsive disorder. Our difficult home environment was probably caused by a deterioration in my relationship with God and my lack of spiritual leadership in the home....

I have now renewed my relationship with God. I have assumed my family leadership role. And each of my children, including my son, have come to know and profess faith in Christ during this period. This is really as much as I could ask as a father and husband. But I am diligently searching now for a way to improve my son's situation. *Robert, I want my son back.*

How many thousands of parents eventually come to this place of heartache and pain, seeking desperately to undo the wrong choices and missed opportunities of the past? What can a parent do to begin the healing process?

Let me offer one recommendation. If you are a parent who has hurt your children, a parent who failed to love and to discipline, a parent who was inconsistent, even indifferent, don't deny your guilt. Begin right now by confessing all of your sins and failures to a gracious God. Claim the promise of 1 John 1:9, which reads, "If we confess our sins, He is faithful and righteous to forgive us our sin, and to cleanse us from all unrighteousness." Bring your sins one by one to the cross; allow the blood of Christ to wash each one away.

Once you've done this, meet with your adult child (even if you have to travel across the country to do so) and ask him or her to forgive you. Pursue reconciliation with uncompromising passion; don't rest until you've done everything in your power to make it right. And from this point on, commit yourself to being the parent God desires for you to be.

Others of you reading this chapter have been on the receiving end of parental abuse. You know the pain of love never given, discipline withheld, and needs ignored. One or all of the "cracks" we've examined have penetrated your life.

The challenge before you is to *forgive*.

Many adult children exact revenge on parents by holding their sins and failures over the offending parent's head. The abuses of the past are replayed over and over again in the child's mind; they are hinted at in conversations with mom or dad. These injustices then define the parameters of the parent-child relationship.

But until forgiveness is granted (whether it's asked for or not), the adult child remains a prisoner of the past, trapped in a victim mentality that prohibits real growth and maturity. Forgiveness is the inaugural declaration that I am a "change agent," not a "helpless victim," and that I am going to make choices to heal the wounds of my past.

The emotional and traumatic hurt experienced at the hands of another is painful. So many children today bear the emotional scars of words and actions perpetrated upon them when they were helpless and vulnerable. The effects are carried with them for years.

But eventually we come to the time in life when we must decide whether to remain with the ghosts of the past roaming throughout our personality, or to do some housecleaning.... You see, the responsibility for who we are and what we are does shift to us at some point in life.[21]

You are poised to take responsibility for your own life when you are ready to forgive.

Only the King Can Do It!

Each of us learned a classic nursery rhyme when we were children. It goes like this:

Humpty-dumpty sat on a wall;
Humpty-dumpty had a great fall.
All the king's horses and all the king's men
Couldn't put Humpty together again.

The image here is of a rotund, brittle, egg-shaped fellow who falls to the ground and suffers a mortal wound. His cracks are irreparable—much like the wounds of many adult children. According to the rhyme, a valiant effort is made to save Humpty. The king's horses are called upon first. As a metaphor of power, horses symbolize strength. Too many wounded souls in our day have turned to power in the hope of being healed: the power of achievement, the power of success, the power of material gain. But as was true in Humpty's case, power is an impotent healer. It only deadens the pain; it does not heal it.

The king's men are called upon next. What do they symbolize? How about therapists and counselors, the wise men of our day? These "gurus of the soul" have been deified in our generation. Their apotheosis has occurred in the absence of spiritual values. But once again, even the king's men are powerless to heal.

If I could finish this rhyme and give it a spiritual twist, I'd end it this way: "All the king's horses and all the king's men couldn't put Humpty together again—but...

THE KING CAN!

Only the KING of heaven can put Humpty-dumpty back together again. Jesus Christ said, "I came that they might have life, and might have it abundantly" (John 10:10). The new car and the new girlfriend and the new therapist are not the answers to the cracks in your soul. There is only one answer—His name is Jesus Christ. When you give *this* King your life, He begins to reconstitute the shattered pieces of your soul:

Then I will make up to you for the years that the swarming locust has eaten, the creeping locust, the stripping locust, and the gnawing locust, My great army which I sent among you (Joel 2:25).

Behold, I am going to deal at that time with all your oppressors, I will save the lame and gather the outcast, and I will turn their shame into praise and renown in all the earth (Zephaniah 3:19).

But for you who fear My name the sun of righteousness will rise with healing in its wings; and you will go forth and skip about like calves from the stall (Malachi 4:2).

The bad news is, *kids don't bounce, they break.* But the good news is, *the King delights in putting His kids back together again.*

My Hero

During the winter of 1993, workers at the Baseball Hall of Fame in Cooperstown, Ohio, made a remarkable, heartwarming discovery. While renovating a section of the museum, they found a photograph that had been hidden in a crevice underneath a display case. The man in the picture has a bat resting on his shoulder; he's wearing a uniform with the words "Sinclair Oil" printed across his chest; his demeanor is gentle and friendly.

Stapled to the picture is a note, scribbled in pen by an adoring fan. The note reads:

You were never too tired to play ball. On your days off, you helped build the Little League Field. You always came to watch me play. You were a Hall of Fame Dad. I wish I could share this moment with you.

Your Son, Pete

A son named Pete found a creative way to put his dad in the Hall of Fame.

Social critic Neil Postman has written that "children are the living messages we send to a time that we will not see." Encoded with our values, personalities, gifts, and attitudes, these living messages, if they are raised well, will one day speak out against sin, produce godly families, promote racial justice, champion the rights of the unborn, and regenerate the moral climate of America. But if they are raised poorly, these living messages will commit acts of violence, abuse drugs, burden the public dole, and contribute to the denigration of American society. Children don't bounce...they break!

America's future depends upon the messages we are crafting in our homes today.

It's up to us to send positive ones!

Notes

[1] James Lincoln Collier, *The Rise of Selfishness in America* (Oxford University Press, 1991), 253.

[2] Charles Pierce, "The Sins of the Father," *Sports Illustrated*, 20 March 1992, 40.

[3] Dr. Hugh Misseldine, *Your Inner Child of the Past* (New York: Simon and Schuster, 1963), 14.

[4] Ibid.

[5] Harold K. Moulton, *The Analytical Greek Lexicon Revised* (Grand Rapids, Mich.: Zondervan, 1978), 197.

[6] *Parade*, 24 October 1993, 1.

[7]Craig Horst, "Brett Dealing with Off-, On-field Problems," *Arkansas Democrat,* 28 June 1992, C4.

[8]Marsha Cohen, *The Sisterhood* (New York: Random House, Inc., 1988), 61.

[9]Ibid., 58.

[10]Paul Meier, *Christian Child-Rearing and Personality Development* (Grand Rapids, Mich.: Baker Book House, 1977), ix.

[11]Mel Krantzler, *Creative Divorce: A New Opportunity for Personal Growth* (New York: Signet, 1974), 173.

[12]Barbara Dafoe Whitehead, "Dan Quayle Was Right," *The Atlantic,* April 1993, 65.

[13]Ibid.

[14]Ibid.

[15]"Pregnant Women in the Workforce" (Table based on Rand Corporation Study); "Work Around Childbirth," *Wall Street Journal,* 6 February 1991, B1.

[16]Chuck Swindoll, *Father: Masculine Model of Leadership* (Portland, Ore.: Multnomah Press, 1990), 11.

[17]Elizabeth Moberley, *Homosexuality: A New Christian Ethic* (Cambridge, England: James Clarke and Co., 1983), 20.

[18]Dr. Irving Bieber, *Homosexuality: A Psychoanalytical Study* (New York: Busie Books, 1962), 303.

[19]John Bowlby, quoted in Elizabeth Moberley, *Homosexuality,* 15.

[20]David Stoops and Stephen Arterburn, *The Angry Man* (Dallas: Word, 1991), 28.

[21]H. Norman Wright, *The Healing of Fears* (Eugene, Ore.: Harvest House, 1982), 28.

CHAPTER TEN

DEFINING MORAL BOUNDARIES
for Your Family

"But in the modern world we are primarily confronted with the extraordinary spectacle of people turning to new ideals because they have not tried the old."
G.K. CHESTERTON

Forty years. That's how long it took Will Durant to complete his eleven-volume colossus, *The Story of Civilization*. Durant began his life's work in 1935 when he published *Our Oriental Heritage*. He finished the project in 1975 with the release of *The Age of Napoleon*. With a storyteller's wit and a historian's mind, Durant reconstructs the epic account of man's history. From the reign of the pharaohs to the fall of Rome, from the birth of Christ to the rise of Napoleon, the text reads like a Shakespearean drama. The glorious achievements and the savage brutalities of mankind are presented with clarity and conviction.

Will Durant wrote with principle. Immersed as he was in the details of human history, the author understood, better than most, the reasons for man's success and the roots of his failure. Though an agnostic, Durant recognized the undeniable importance of religion as a moral compass. He eschewed those who would deny the necessity, and the universality, of moral truth.

A year after the completion of *The Story of Civilization*, Durant and his wife, Ariel (who worked with him on the last three volumes of *Civilization*), synthesized their study in a fascinating book entitled *The Lessons of History*. *Lessons* is a bite-size smorgasbord of principles derived from years of historical research. In the chapter "Character and History," the Durants attack the contemporary folly of forfeiting the timeless traditions of the past. Their words are a sobering challenge to the amoral libertarians and iconoclastic prophets of our day.

> No one man, however brilliant or well-informed, can come in one lifetime to such fullness of understanding as to safely judge and dismiss the customs or institutions of his society, for these are the wisdom of generations after centuries of experiment in the laboratory of history. A youth boiling with hormones will wonder why he should not give full freedom to his sexual desires; and if he is unchecked by custom, morals, or laws, he may ruin his life before he matures sufficiently to understand that sex is a river of fire that must be banked and cooled by a hundred restraints if it is not to consume in chaos both the individual and the group.[1]

The present generation of Americans appears to have dismissed the customs, morals, and laws that have been our mainstay for hundreds of years. With bold and audacious arrogance, the tried and true values of Christian orthodoxy are being drawn and quartered, and cast aside on the refuse heap of traditional morality. Our moral malaise is most apparent on college campuses. Many teachers seem to delight in destroying the traditional faith and values of their students. Student housing reflects the sexually permissive values of the '60s, even though this is the age of AIDS. Male and female students are housed in co-ed living arrangements that send all the wrong signals. What's worse, parents pay for this "higher education."

The "college" section of *Rolling Stone* magazine recently carried a story about nudity on campus. The article highlighted the "best" events nationwide, such as the Watermyn Co-op Nude Party at Brown University. An annual affair, the Watermyn party has only one requirement: Students are required to shed their clothes within fifteen minutes. The University of Michigan has its Naked Mile; over four-hundred men and women participated this year. Once a month at Rice University, "students strip, lather themselves with shaving cream (in order to make body prints on windows and building walls) and run to the campus bar, where the raw racers drink a beer on the house."[2]

Our malaise is not confined to sexuality; the problem reaches far beyond the bedroom, pervading the institutions of education, business, politics, athletics, and every other domain of human existence. It's safe to say that America now finds itself in the midst of a moral abyss. Within this darkened cavern nothing is certain, nothing is secure, nothing is absolute. Right becomes wrong and wrong is often perverted to appear right. Every decision becomes a matter of personal preference, personal opinion, and personal choice. The end justifies the means. We no longer live in a society that recognizes or respects moral boundaries. For large numbers of Americans, the Judeo-Christian ethic has gone the way of the horse-drawn carriage—it was nice for a season, but is now nothing more than a museum piece.

Our moral ambiguity has created confusion and chaos; it has also generated a whole new entrepreneurial venture: ethical education. What was once known intuitively and accepted socially must now be taught institutionally. One of the greatest growth industries of the 1990s is ethics. Medical schools are sprouting ethics departments; business schools have added mandatory classes on moral decision-making. Harvard University was one of the first to require ethics classes for business students—this in response to the growing need for moral clarity in the business community.

For example, researcher John Pierce found that a majority of college and university business majors judge the climate of American business to be decidedly unethical. Professor Archie Carroll, of the University of Georgia, surveyed hundreds of corporate managers throughout the United States and found that 64 percent of respondents felt pressured to compromise their values to meet their companies' goals. For a generation we've been taught that integrity does not pay and that compromise is the golden road to success.

The chickens have come home to roost.

Americans sense the need for values and standards but are unable, or unwilling, to step into the light of absolute truth. The impotent ideas of the past continue to define our morality in the present. The prevailing idea seems to be that a universal ethic which would be definitive for all peoples for all time in all places is a myth. The acceptance of what is right and good is determined only by the culture in which that question arises. A professor at the Harvard Business School once opined: "We should make no attempt to impose any one system of values on our students."

These are statements from the abyss. They leave you mired in a quagmire (if I can change the metaphor). Such false wisdom breeds situational ethics. Moral decisions are made on a day-to-day basis. They become a series of choices that mirror one's personal preferences, and they lack any substantive character. For if there is no definitive standard guiding a peoples' behavior, if there is no universal ethic, then, by default, the *bottom line* becomes the ultimate value.

Don't be fooled. There is always an absolute value. The absolute value may be money or happiness or freedom. The individual decides. A cartoon I once read in *New Yorker* magazine captured this new ethic, what I call "Morality by Default." A group of glassy-eyed business executives are seated around a conference table; the company's C.E.O. is speaking about the merits of a new proposal. He says, "This proposal of course might not be ethical. Does anyone have a problem with it?" There is no response from his rubber-stamp employees. After all, who has the courage to transgress that greatest of contemporary values—the Almighty Dollar?

Even the religious community is increasingly unable to draw boundaries. In *Christianity Today*, William Willimon, a Methodist professor at Duke University, shares this example:

> In a course of mine, I asked seminarians to share case studies of their pastoral experience. One student pastor presented a case wherein a woman asked her pastor what the United Methodist Church believes about premarital sex. The pastor, a beneficiary of seminary training, asked, "What do you think about premarital sex?" The parishioner persisted. "I know that pastors don't approve," she replied. "Some pastors don't," he said, "primarily older pastors." "But isn't the Bible against people just living together?" she asked. To which he replied, "The Bible is a culturally conditioned book that must be read with interpretive sophistication. The main thing is that you are open, trusting, loving, and caring."[3]

Americans are like bungee-cord jumpers. They leap from the towering heights of self-arrogance and plunge into the rocky terrain of marriage, family, business, and education. Thinking they are restrained by a thick strand of personal morality, they discover to their horror that the bungee cord is wispy and inadequate. The adventure of life becomes a free-fall into chaos and confusion. Lacking clearly defined moral boundaries that are strong enough to hold them, these individuals plummet violently onto the jagged rocks of personal crisis: immorality, divorce, despair, and heartache.

As a pastor, I've counseled hundreds of men and women whose cords were severed by the harsh realities of life. Unable to define their values, unwilling to submit to biblical standards (or any standard, for that matter), they imperil themselves and the lives of their family members, often with tragic results.

Once again, Will Durant calls us back to the necessity of moral boundaries.

A little knowledge of history stresses the variability of moral codes, and concludes that they are negligible because they differ in time and place, and sometimes contradict each other. A larger knowledge stresses the universality of moral codes, and concludes to their necessity.[4]

A healthy family is one that isn't afraid to define itself or its values. A healthy family is one that thinks deeply about moral standards; it draws clearly demarcated boundaries and submits passionately to timeless truths. A healthy family expects its children to carry these precious gems of truth into the next generation.

Living within the Boundaries

After the nation of Israel entered the land of Canaan, the leaders of the twelve tribes subdivided the territory by drawing lots. Joshua records this process in chapters 15 through 21 of the book which bears his name. To be honest, these are some of the most boring chapters in the Bible. It matters little to me that the territory of Ephraim extended to the brook of Kanah in the west (Joshua 16:8), or that the territory of Asher reached as far as Cabul in the north (Joshua 16:27).

Archaeologists may find this compelling—but I don't. However, there is a symbolic truth here that underlies the mundane process of ancient surveying, and that is the importance of boundaries. In fact, the early books of the Bible deal primarily with boundaries. Adam and Eve were granted great freedoms but were also commanded to live by clearly pre-scribed standards. The Old Testament law is a combination of civil, moral, and religious boundaries given, as Moses says, not for our misery but "for our good" (Deuteronomy 6:24). The geographical boundaries of Joshua 15 through 21 were neces-sary to ensure the peaceful coexistence of the tribes of Israel. Autonomous, independent people recoil from boundaries but wise men and women embrace them as a source of life. Psalm 119 is a testimony by one who had discovered the life-giving power of moral and spiritual boundaries.

In a moral universe, happiness and morality are related concepts. The individual who seeks happiness by abandoning truth and responsibility violates this timeless principle. This is why Isaiah can write: "There is no peace," says my God, "for the wicked" (Isaiah 57:21). You can't violate the moral law and be at peace with yourself. For this reason, Jonathan Edwards stated: "True happiness consists in the possession and enjoy-ment of moral good, in a way sweetly agreeing with God's moral perfections."[5]

Real life is found in obedience to the ordinances of God. Like the Israelites, you and I must delineate our boundaries; we must define our moral standards—in accordance with the Word of God—and submit to them, regardless of the cost.

In Titus 2:11-12, the apostle Paul gives a succinct starting point for those who desire to fix boundaries. These verses appear at the end of a passage filled with practical admonitions to old men (2:2), old women (2:3), young women (2:4-5), young men (2:7-8), and servants (2:9-10). Throughout this section Paul has been delineating moral boundaries. In verses 11 and 12, he summarizes his teaching and identifies the moti-vation behind the admonitions: "For the grace of God has appeared, bringing salvation to all men, instructing us to deny ungodliness and worldly desires and to live sensibly, righteously and godly in the present age."

The Motivating Power of Grace

Grace. This is what inspired God to establish moral boundaries. It is what men and women experience when they submit to moral boundaries. And this is precisely where each of us must begin if we are to obey God's Word. When some people think of moral boundaries, they envision confinement and restriction. Even many Christians view moral obligation as burdensome. They see God as a heavenly killjoy, bent upon making their lives miserable.

If this is your attitude, then you have forgotten the grace of God.

Paul tells us that "the grace of God has appeared." He has in mind the glorious incarnation of Jesus Christ and His subsequent death and resurrection for our sins. He is the One who "takes away the sin of the world" (John 1:29). Jesus Christ came to give abundant life (John 10:10) and to call us out of darkness into His marvelous light (1 Peter 2:9). The apostle Paul experienced this grace on the road to Damascus (Acts 9). It captured his heart and his imagination and became the wellspring of his ministry (2 Corinthians 5:11-21).

No man or woman who has experienced, or continues to experience, the grace of God is able to conclude that moral boundaries are a burden. Instead, these constraints become a source of life, defining one's behavior in a fallen world. And grace becomes an ever-present source of joy, motivating the redeemed sinner to glorify his Savior in every facet of life.

The grace of God is the key to obeying the moral law. For apart from grace and the glorious reality of redemption, moral boundaries grate; they sear at our flesh and suffocate our souls. But grace liberates. It reminds us that all of salvation—justification, sanctification, glorification—is bestowed freely. What God accomplished on our behalf wasn't necessary. It wasn't meted out to deserving individuals, for none is deserving. From this vantage point, moral boundaries take on a whole new perspective. They become opportunities for worship, not reasons for despair.

This principle is illustrated in the parable of the two debtors. Jesus is dining in the home of a Pharisee when the unthinkable occurs: A woman enters the premises and brazenly worships the Lord. She wets His feet with her tears and anoints His feet with perfume. The host and the guests are aghast; they find this open display of affection offensive, for, as Luke notes, this woman was a "sinner" (Luke 7:37)—a prostitute. The disgust is heightened when the woman kisses the Lord's feet and then wipes them with her hair (Luke 7:38).

The dinner guests are offended by the woman; Jesus is offended by their attitude. In response to such open ingratitude, Jesus tells the parable of the two debtors.

And Jesus answered and said to him, "Simon, I have something to say to you." And he replied, "Say it, Teacher." "A certain moneylender had two debtors: one owed five hundred denarii, and the other fifty. When they were unable to repay, he graciously forgave them both. Which of them therefore will love him more?" Simon answered and said, "I suppose the one whom he forgave more." And He said to him, "You have judged correctly." And turning toward the woman, He said to Simon, "Do you see this woman? I entered your house; you gave Me no water for My feet, but she has wet My feet with her tears, and wiped them with her hair. You gave Me no kiss; but she, since the time I came in, has not ceased to kiss My feet. You did not anoint My head with oil, but she anointed My feet with perfume. For this reason I say to you, her sins, which are many, have been forgiven, for she loved much; but he who is forgiven little, loves little."

The truth of this parable is profound: *Grace always results in gratitude.* How could it be otherwise? Great forgiveness engenders great love. There is an absence of worship and devotion and obedience in the church today because there is a concomitant absence of God's grace. When the Christian grows callous to the grace of God (an oxymoron of the worst magnitude), devotion becomes duty; obedience becomes labor.

Paul speaks of grace in Titus 2 because he knows that grace motivates the discerning believer to submit to moral boundaries. This is a perspective that has been lost in our day.

The Disciplining Power of Grace

But grace doesn't just motivate, it also disciplines. It delineates boundaries. Paul informs us of two consequences of God's grace. He says, first, that God's grace has brought "salvation to all men" (Titus 2:11). Second, grace is continually "instructing us to deny ungodliness and worldly desires" (Titus 2:12). The word translated "instructing" in verse 12 is the participial form of the Greek verb, *paideuo. Paideuo* connotes the idea of instruction, but also implies a more rigid training regimen. In other passages of Scripture this word is translated as "training" (2 Timothy 3:16) and even "discipline" (Hebrews 12:5,7,9). Grace motivates. We know this by experience. But grace also disciplines. It constricts—not for the purpose of smothering, but for the purpose of giving life.

This one verse silences forever those within the church who support the unbiblical and heretical idea of *antinomianism*— the notion that the redeemed sinner is liberated from the moral law and is now free to live as he will "by grace." Poppycock! God's grace doesn't free a man to live as he will; instead, it empowers a man to live as he ought!

Motivated by grace, disciplined by grace, *the Christian is called to define a practical morality for himself in the present world.* The first two parameters of this boundary are negative: we are to "deny ungodliness and worldly desires." "Ungodliness" is a broad term encompassing all that is opposed to Christian life and spiritual vitality; "worldly desires" refers to those passions which promote secular thinking and a secular lifestyle. Taken together, these two negatives condemn any attitude or behavior that is antagonistic or disruptive to spiritual life.

But what qualifies as "ungodliness" today? Or how about "worldly desires"? The minute we ask these questions, many are thrown back into the closet of personal preference. Clearly, some issues are black and white; but many are not. A generation ago, it was easier to define boundaries. Today, many families toil in moral ambiguity. Words like "purity" are nebulous and amorphous. For example, when it comes to sex, some Christians interpret purity to mean anything less than sexual intercourse. I distinctly remember three members of our congregation marching out of the sanctuary one morning when I defined sexual purity in something more than culturally acceptable terms.

Let me draw a line in the sand to illustrate the point. Take the subject of movies. Can you remember the first time you saw someone naked on the screen? I can. The year was 1965. I was seventeen. I was a junior in high school, on a date with the woman who would eventually become my wife, Sherard. We were seated in the Dixie Theater in Ruston and, without warning, a woman on the big screen took off all of her clothes.

I had never seen anything like this before in my life. I remember walking out of the theater in shock. I felt ashamed. But there was a part of me that wanted more. After all, the sexual revolution was just beginning. In a very short time, the images became more and more graphic. I went off to college and soon became exposed to a sordid number of images on the movie screen. Since I wasn't a Christian at the time, I didn't feel the need to establish boundaries. Like many others, I was free-falling into a moral abyss.

What was just beginning to appear in the movies in 1965 is now common fare on television and cable channels. You don't have to go to a theater to indulge the desires of the flesh—you can now satiate your passions in the privacy of your own home. Like never before, there is a need to delineate boundaries. But where do you draw the line? What is permissible for the Christian? The minute someone says, "R-rated movies are wrong," a chorus of voices within the evangelical community will cry, "No, that's legalism!" So we keep our options open, all in the name of "grace." This makes me nervous. For the sake of "liberty," we countenance foul language and immorality. If naked bodies and four-letter words don't qualify as "ungodliness," then it's time to redefine the meaning of the word.

How are you going to morally define your lifestyle? The question is of vital importance. Paul provides three guidelines in Titus 2:12 to help dispel our confusion.

First, he urges us to "live sensibly." In simple terms, our lives should make practical sense to any observer. Realism is an appropriate synonym. The well-defined Christian is realistic about his family, his morality, his career, and his hobbies. The Christian husband apportions his time to adequately care for his wife and children; the Christian wife avoids the entanglements of outside attractions to nurture her husband and shepherd her children. In the area of morality, the Christian seeks to establish realistic standards that reflect the teaching of Scripture. When ambiguities arise, he chooses the high road. Matthew 7:13-14 is his guide:

> Enter by the narrow gate; for the gate is wide and the way is broad that leads to destruction, and many are those who enter by it. For the gate is small, and the way is narrow that leads to life.

Christian husbands and wives also forego career options that could have a detrimental effect upon their spiritual lives and their family. In short, they draw lines that make sense.

Second, we are to "live righteously." In other words, *we are to do right*. If I'm a businessman, I disperse profits in a way that is not just fair to me but fair to my employees, as well. As a parent, I do right by acting responsibly. I establish moral boundaries for my children—and I keep them myself. I practice what I preach.

Time magazine recently carried an article entitled "Safe Parents." (The title is a word-play on the concept of "safe sex.") Parents in California are networking with others parents to safeguard what their children watch on television. They want to be sure their youngsters aren't exposed to sex and violence when they spend the night at a friend's house. A "safe parent" is one who will chaperone your child when he or she is in that friend's home. They don't allow viewing of R-rated movies, or allow indecent videos to be viewed on the VCR. This is what it means to live righteously.

Third, we are to live "godly." To be *God-like* is the idea. The person who lives a godly life is proud to show his deeds, his behaviors, and his attitudes toward God. Just as your child runs into your arms after Sunday school and begins to relate the truths he or she has just learned, so the Christian is proud to display his life to God. This is what it means to be godly—to exhibit your public life, your recreational life, and your private life to the Lord—and know that He approves of the boundaries you have staked out.

Sensibly. Righteously. Godly. These are three boundaries that should surround the Christian family in the Bold New World. In my own life, I've used this plumb line to lay a spiritual foundation. These principles guide my attitudes and my behaviors in a variety of areas. In my job as a pastor, I strive to be at home four nights out of the week in order to keep my involvement with my family strong. In my relationship with my wife, I am committed to being a "one woman man," and I work hard to communicate with Sherard. In my spiritual life, I've made myself accountable to other men. In the area of giving, ten percent or more is my commitment to the Lord.

I set aside the Lord's Day and limit my weekend commitments to ensure my presence at church. I practice the spiritual disciplines of Bible study, prayer, solitude, and confession. In the area of entertainment, I've drawn the line at PG-13 movies, though I've discovered that even this boundary is slowly being overrun by a corrupt, socially irresponsible movie industry. My wife and I take creative vacations with our children. We monitor the information and images that are communicated through the television set. My lifestyle orbits around, and is defined by, these restrictive—yet liberating—proclamations: sensibly, righteously, godly.

The Benefit of Boundaries

In the process of marking off clearly defined moral and spiritual boundaries, I've discovered four important benefits.

1. When we establish standards, we come to know who we are. A lot of people in our world spend their lives trying to "find themselves." I can say, by the grace of God, that I know who I am. My life has been defined by the Word of God.

2. When we establish standards, we have more time for ourselves, not less. Fixed boundaries allow us to say "no" with confidence. The spontaneous attractions of life can be confronted with an assurance born of conviction and determination.

3. When we establish standards, our children develop a sense of security. Because a child's self-image and emotional well-being are shaped primarily by parents, it is paramount that mom and dad model moral security and confidence themselves. Hypocrisy kills. Morally confused parents breed morally confused children. If I'm perplexed about my standards, my children will be too. But the reverse is also true. Well-defined boundaries, buttressed by parental consistency, are the most potent weapon in your parenting arsenal. Children thrive in this atmosphere.

4. **When we establish standards, we become a lifeline to those who are lost.** It is axiomatic that moral ambiguity creates chaos and confusion. The world is populated by people starved for definitive answers to life's unanswered questions. As Christians, we have the answers. And these answers take on flesh and blood when they are exhibited in the arena of daily life. Morally defined Christian families are a bright light and a lifeline to other families who are lost.

There is a memorable line in a Harrison Ford movie that summarizes and illustrates the pressing need to choose wisely. In *Indiana Jones and the Last Crusade*, Harrison Ford seeks to find the chalice that Christ used at the Last Supper. In the closing scene, Indy and his friends are standing before a huge table; hundreds of drinking vessels are arrayed before them. An aged knight is guarding the treasure. Before Indiana is able to seize the chalice, his antagonist steps forward and chooses what he thinks is the prized vessel. This man puts the cup to his lips and drinks, hoping in the process to gain eternal life. Slowly, horribly, his body corrodes and disintegrates, and he dies. The knight then turns to Indy and states the obvious, "He did not choose wisely."

When it comes to defining a practical morality, your family had better choose wisely. Life and death, qualitatively speaking, hang in the balance. In the chapter that follows, I have provided an opportunity for you to set forth in writing the family values you consider sacred. *This would be a wonderful project for you and your mate to do together.* In the process, you may find a few family blanks that need to be filled in, or a few inconsistencies that need to be worked through. But don't let that stop you! Nothing of real value happens effortlessly, especially Real Family Values. So take your time! When you are finished, this moral Constitution may prove to be one of the most important achievements of your marriage, and one of the most important gifts you will ever give to your children.

Notes

[1]Will and Ariel Durant, *The Lessons of History* (New York: Simon and Schuster, 1968), 35-36.

[2]"Cheeky Monkeys," Michael Rubiner, *Rolling Stone*, 693, 20 October 1994, 87,89.

[3]William Willimon, "Risky Business," *Christianity Today*, 19 February 1988, 24-25.

[4]Will Durant in James L. Christian, *Philosophy: An Introduction to the Art of Wondering*, 4th edition (New York: Holt, Rinehart and Winston, 1977), 333.

[5]Jonathan Edwards, *The Works of Jonathan Edwards*, Edward Hickman, ed., 1 (Avon, England: Banner of Truth Trust, 1992), 284.

CHAPTER ELEVEN

YOUR FAMILY VALUES

"Choose life in order that you may live, you and your descendants."
DEUTERONOMY 29:19

"Do two men walk together unless they have made an appointment?"
AMOS 3:3

"...instructing us to deny ungodliness and worldly desires and to live sensibly, righteously and godly in the present age."
TITUS 2:12

Before you begin this project, let's identify the defining characteristics of a Real Family Value. Let's also recognize the fact that most families assume they have family values. Unfortunately, for some, these values are often highly generalized. To say, "I'm committed to my children," or "I'm for a clear sense of right and wrong," or "I believe in marriage" is encouraging, but these examples fall woefully short of a real value.

In other families, many values are still in the "undecided" category. This indecision undermines accountability and creates a good deal of moral duplicity which confuses and corrupts children. Exit moral convictions. Enter moral ambiguity.

So what constitutes a Real Family Value? There are three discernible characteristics.

1. A Real Family Value is *definable.* The more specifically and succinctly it can be stated, the better. "I believe in marriage," as we've said, is far too general. On the other hand, to say, "I believe marriage is a commitment before God of a man and a woman to each other for a lifetime," is better.

2. A Real Family Value is *supportable*. A real value must go beyond "because I said so." Real values need transcendent authority. They need to be supported with "God said." Therefore, standing next to each of your family values there needs to be at least one Scripture reference which *clearly* offers God-centered affirmation and support for the value. In our previous example of marriage being valued as "a commitment before God of a man and a woman to each other for a lifetime," one might attach to it Matthew 19:4-6, which reads:

> And He [Jesus] answered and said, "Have you not read, that He who created them from the beginning made them male and female, and said, 'For this cause a man shall leave his father and mother, and shall cleave to his wife; and the two shall become one flesh'? Consequently, they are no longer two, but one flesh. What, therefore, God has joined together, let no man separate."

Since children often ask "why?" wise parents will employ history, everyday events, statistics, and modern research, when applicable, to help reinforce for their children *why* God's Word is trustworthy. Deuteronomy 6:6-7 says:

> "And these words, which I am commanding you today, shall be on your heart; and you shall teach them diligently to your sons and shall talk of them when you sit in your house and when you walk by the way and when you lie down and when you rise up."

"Why?" questions from children are healthy. When questions are properly addressed by parents—using the support of Scripture as well as other available data, plus direct observations from life—the child's desire to learn can help him or her build deep convictions.

3. A Real Family Value is *observable.* A family value is not a theory. Regardless of what you espouse, if the value is not lived out, it's not a *real* value. Further, values that are lived out inconsistently or sporadically are not real values either. *A Real Family Value is what you say and do with consistency and regularity.* Values are the threads that weave together a lifestyle. Children will not carry out or pass on your theories. Instead, you will leave in your children what you have lived out in your home.

Definable, supportable, observable: These are the chief characteristics of a Real Family Value. They create harmony and understanding between husband and wife. They establish moral boundaries that children need and want. They help build strong, secure homes (Luke 6:47-48).

Your Family Values

I have separated your family values into three categories: marriage, children, and home. This will add to the project a certain measure of focus and order. Under each category, I have also provided a number of sample items to help you get started. By each item, define your family value with a concise statement. Then, cite at least one clear biblical text that would support this value. Finally, list one or two ways this value can be observed on a consistent basis in your home.[1]

I. Marriage Values

1. On the permanency of marriage, we believe:

Biblical support:
How observed?

2. On the purpose(s) of marriage, we believe:

Biblical support:
How observed?

3. On a husband's role in marriage, we believe:

Biblical support:
How observed?

4. On a husband's responsibilities in marriage, we believe:

Biblical support:
How observed?

5. On a wife's role in marriage, we believe:

Biblical support:
How observed?

6. On a wife's responsibilities in marriage, we believe:

Biblical support:
How observed?

7. What other values would you place under Marriage?
(Please use a separate notebook for these additional values.)

II. Children Values

1. On the importance of children, we believe:

Biblical support:
How observed?

2. On a father's responsibility for raising children, we believe:

Biblical support:
How observed?

3. On a mother's responsibility for raising children, we believe:

Biblical support:
How observed?

4. On career pursuits (of parents) and children, we believe:

Biblical support:
How observed?

5. On the spiritual instruction of children, we believe:

Biblical support:
How observed?

6. On character goals for children, we believe:

Biblical support:
How observed?

7. On abortion, we believe:

Biblical support:
How observed?

8. What other values would you place under Children?

III. Home Values

1. On the use of alcohol and drugs, we believe:

Biblical support:
How observed?

2. On prayer in our home, we believe:

Biblical support:
How observed?

3. On our movie and television standards, we believe:

Biblical support:
How observed?

4. On financial giving, we believe:

Biblical support:
How observed?

5. On the accumulation of debt, we believe:

Biblical support:
How observed?

6. On church attendance and involvement, we believe:

Biblical support:
How observed?

7. On speech and profanity, we believe:

Biblical support:
How observed?

8. On payment of taxes, we believe:

Biblical support:
How observed?

9. What other values would you place under Home?

A Tradition for the Future

Several years ago, a business consultant friend of mine asked me to define our staff values here at the church. "Staff values?" I responded inquisitively. "What are 'staff values'?" He went on to tell me that many corporations had found it extremely helpful and healthy to formalize a set of corporate values for all company employees to live up to. Each value selected was intended to shape and influence company culture. Each would be thoroughly explained to company personnel and from that point onward would serve as driving forces behind company performance.

Not long after that my son, Garrett, was in the hospital having minor foot surgery. When using a phone in the waiting room, I was struck by the sight of the hospital's "corporate values" being listed on the telephone receiver. Later, I saw that those values statements were displayed everywhere in order to remind personnel of the specific expectations for the care of hospital patients.

Today, every staff member's desk at our church, bears a small plaque with…yes, our staff values listed on it. The five values listed there are: Teamwork, Integrity, Loyalty, Innovation, and Excellence. We have found that formalizing our values as a church staff has been a tremendous benefit to us in setting the kind of working environment we believe is best for us. It also gives us specific points to celebrate when staff members excel in one or more of these areas.

I share this story with you to encourage you to *formalize your family values.* This chapter is a starting place but it is only a working draft. After you finish it, why not polish the language and create a formal family document with the title "Our Family Values" or "We Believe…" It could then be typeset and matted, placed in a special frame, and hung in a prominent place in your home. (*Note:* In the Appendix of this book— "Our Family Values…"—I have included two sample documents of formalized family values, written by couples who attend the church I pastor. These samples will provide some additional help in crafting your own family values document.)

Not unlike the coat of arms of medieval Europe—a combination of emblems, figures, and other elements which held special significance to the family or organization it represented—your document would be a constant reminder of the values which are expected to set the tenor of your home, from dad on down. It will also clarify what is to be celebrated and rewarded.

Over the years, this guiding family document could be made into a *family tradition.* Copies could be presented to your children as a wedding gift, or when they move out on their own, or when they have their first child. However you decide to do it, handing down and passing on your values ceremonially could become a powerful tradition for your children to build upon.

Proverbs 22:28 seems to back my suggestion. There, Solomon writes, "Do not move the ancient boundary which your fathers have set."

A BOUNDARY.

In today's toxic culture, every family needs one.[2]

Notes

[1]A recommended resource which I believe can aid you in establishing Real Family Values is "The Family Manifesto," published by FamilyLife. A copy of this helpful booklet outlining timeless family values can be obtained from FamilyLife by calling 1-800-FLTODAY.

[2]I would love to read your family values document when you complete it. Would you consider sending me a copy? Mail your document to Robert Lewis, 12601 Hinson Road, Little Rock, AR 72212.

YOUR FAMILY

and Ongoing Social Controversies

CHAPTER TWELVE

HOMOSEXUALITY

"A lot of these kids have absolutely nobody in the world.
They are hated and despised everywhere they go.
They are so isolated that it's not surprising
that a lot of them don't see a future."
LISA ROGERS

One of the most poignant moments in my life occurred in a church. A deserted church. On a bitterly cold night in December 1988, I sat in our sanctuary next to a person with whom I'd shared my whole life but had never really known. His name was Charles.

My big brother.

We had grown up side by side, along with our younger brother, John. Four years my senior, Charles and I muddled our way through childhood together. The Bible says that "a friend loves at all times, and a brother is born for adversity" (Proverbs 17:17). This was true for the two of us. Charles was the typical big brother: protective, yet condescending. I was the typical little brother: trusting, but annoying.

Like all brothers, we had our differences. But we were bound together by blood, and our relationship during the early years was a collage of shared experiences: Thanksgivings and Christmases, family holidays, trips to the beach, and innumerable football games.

These memories seemed distant and otherworldly that cold night in December. Charles and I were strangers now. Virtually the only thing we had in common was our last name. Little brother had grown up and become a pastor. Big brother was a lawyer and a member of the gay community in Houston. I pondered the differences as we sat, silently, in the darkened church sanctuary.

We had not been on the best of terms for a long time. The distance between us was aggravated by stereotypes—some true, others false. Over the years Charles had come to view me as a close-minded, heartless fundamentalist; I saw my brother as a *laissez faire* libertarian, a person who drank too much, partied too much, and whose values were directly opposite my own.

But the fact that we were together, in this place, meant only one thing: restoration was taking place.

The process of reconciliation had begun, as most do, with a crisis. A year and a half earlier, in the summer of 1987, Charles had taken me aside and informed me that he had contracted HIV. I was shocked. I shouldn't have been; I had suspected he was gay. But I *was* shocked. At first I didn't know what to say. But in that moment, as the words "I have AIDS" sank into my heart, the grace of God prompted me to do something that forever changed our relationship. I got up off the couch and walked over to my brother. I put my arms around him, and I hugged him. Then I said something I hadn't said in a long time. I said simply, "I love you, Charles. I love you."

In the months following this encounter, Charles and I began to converse regularly. At first it was awkward. We had so little in common. But slowly the relationship improved. And in December 1988, I invited my brother to join us for Christmas.

Charles accepted, but wanted to stay in a hotel. I insisted he stay with us. He did. We spent a wonderful week together. It was a week that altered our perspective of one another.

By this time the AIDS virus had decimated Charles' body. He was thin and frail, and there were times when he had to sit quietly and rest. Nevertheless, my brother spent hours playing with my children. One image is stamped indelibly on my mind. Charles was a gifted artist. He loved to draw and my kids were fascinated by the pictures he painted. One afternoon, Charles was seated in the kitchen, surrounded by the Lewis children. The artist was teaching four youngsters how to sketch faces. They were all laughing and hugging Uncle Charles. As I watched this scene from the living room, I realized, again, that Charles was my brother. Just my brother.

In that moment he ceased to be a sexual preference. He became a human being.

Later that evening I invited Charles to see our church, an offer he gladly accepted. While a cold north wind blew outside, two brothers sat in the darkened sanctuary, pondering the differences that had kept them apart. Something happened to my brother that night. Whereas I had experienced my moment of alteration a few hours earlier, I believe Charles experienced his change in the silence of our church. I could sense a number of emotions surging through his soul. Charles was wrestling with his feelings toward me, and reevaluating who I was. He was pondering the nature of God and struggling to understand the evangelical church.

When we left the church that night, things were different between us. Our relationship was marked by a new intimacy, a new rapport. There was a new respect for those areas in which we couldn't agree, and a determination to love one another—in spite of the differences.

I want you to know that my opposition to Charles' behavior didn't change. Neither did his commitment to that behavior. But a lot *did* change. And it all started with open arms and a hug a year and a half earlier.

I begin with this story because it illustrates the wide range of emotions and the complex issues which attend one of the most volatile social problems of our day—homosexuality. To help us make sense of this perplexing subject, it will help to understand that the homosexual community can be divided into three distinct but overlapping groups. For the evangelical church to transcend stereotypes and become strategic in the "gay" '90s, we must apprehend the differences and shape our responses accordingly. Those who are gay can be grouped into the following categories: 1) committed and coping; 2) radical and aggressive; 3) hidden and hurting. Each group masks a different set of needs and possesses a different agenda in the Bold New World.

Committed and Coping Homosexuals

Over the years, I have interacted with a number of homosexuals and lesbians, men and women who have struggled with the gay lifestyle. Many of these people are part of the same group to which my brother belonged; I would classify them as "committed and coping." They are committed to the lifestyle but coping with a host of issues that follow in the wake of such a commitment: "Who can I tell?" "Where and when can I be open about my sexuality?" "What do I do with my feelings of guilt and dishonesty?" "Who *am* I?"

Eric Markus, a former associate producer for *Good Morning America*, put it this way: "When I realized I was gay, I also realized I did have a choice.... I could choose to live in a closet, maybe even marry a woman and pretend to be who I'm not, or I could be honest about who I am and live my life openly—no easy thing to do."[1]

To live as a homosexual is no easy task. Those who are committed and coping spend most of their lives trying to understand who they are and seeking to discover how and where they fit in. They live with an array of conflicting values and emotions, all of which foster confusion and self-doubt.

My brother is a prime example. Charles spent years in therapy and support groups; he attended a very liberal church, seeking some kind of affirmation for himself as a person. And like many of his friends, Charles escaped into alcoholism. He embraced the gay lifestyle but felt overwhelmed by it at the same time. As far as I know, Charles wasn't a radical gay activist; he didn't march in gay parades, for example. He wasn't into *that* aspect of the movement. But Charles had resolved that he was homosexual. It was a conclusion that would define his life and, ultimately, determine his destiny.

Like my brother and Eric Markus and thousands of others, the "committed and coping" have made homosexuality the paradigm for their lives. Those in this group have trouble "coming out of the closet." In the months following Charles' death, as I traveled to Houston to settle his estate, I discovered he lived out of *two* closets—literally.

One closet was filled with the attire of the professional Charles—tailored suits, starched shirts, polished shoes. But then there was another closet. This one was full of evening gowns and slips and wigs and dresses. It contained a woman's cheerleading outfit, and hundreds of photographs that documented my brother's life within the gay community. In one picture, Charles is playing poker with a group of friends; everyone seated around the table is dressed in drag. There were pictures taken at elegant parties in Houston: They portrayed older men wearing tuxedoes and younger men in dresses.

It was a world to which Charles was committed, but also one which he was unable to reconcile with the rest of his life. The closets are a metaphor of his troubled existence. In one closet he declared himself gay, but only within a limited environment. The other closet was always nearby. This is the struggle of a large number of homosexuals. They're committed, but they're also coping—just trying to make sense of it all.

Radical and Aggressive Homosexuals

This second group comprises a much smaller percentage of the homosexual community than those who are "committed and coping." It's the group with which we as Christians are most familiar; we react to and talk about them most, and yes, we fear them most. They are the radical and aggressive homosexuals.

These are the gay activists we see on television and read about in the newspapers. They are hostile and angry and vocal about everything pertaining to the issue of homosexuality. The "radical and aggressive" group is represented by a number of *avant garde* organizations: the Gay and Lesbian Coalition, Queer Nation, Act-up. In 1993, Luke Sissyfag, a member of one these groups, stood up and dressed down President Clinton, charging that he wasn't doing enough about the AIDS crisis.

The "radical and aggressive" element is agenda-driven; they seek a special class status that goes beyond basic civil rights. They want educational programs to be taught in the public schools (beginning with kindergarten)—programs which affirm homosexuality as a valid lifestyle and homosexual behavior as legitimate and normal. This group wants the right to marry, and couples want the right to be defined as a legal family unit. They seek adoption rights and cultural acceptance by society as a whole. Gay writer Bruce Bawer summarizes the distinguishing characteristics of this small but vocal group: "For the subculture (i.e., radical gays), homosexuality is not simply a fact of sexual orientation but also an act of sexual emancipation, political rebellion, social experimentation and cultural self-assertion."[2]

The "radical and aggressive" group has a clear and concise agenda. They also have a distinct strategy: intimidation. In a growing number of cases, radical homosexuals have disrupted church services and employed violence to punish those who consider such behavior abnormal and unacceptable. These people bristle with hatred for one group in particular—evangelical Christians—whom they dismiss as homophobic and repressive. In short, they want full acceptance of homosexuality as an alternate lifestyle and are hell-bent upon realizing this objective. Their ultimate goal is captured in a slogan which you've probably heard now and again: "We're here, we're queer, get used to it!"[3]

How do radical homosexuals plan to gain acceptance? Their strategy takes four forms.

1. Radical Gays Press for Acceptance by the Use of Myths

Radical homosexuals press their agenda by employing a number of myths. These myths have altered the way in which the American public thinks about homosexuality. There are three which I will share with you.

1. "I was born gay." This is probably the most powerful myth being propagated by homosexuals today. We'll revisit this assertion later in the chapter, but for now, you need to know that there is no final evidence whatsoever to conclude that homosexuality is biologically determined. An array of scientific studies support the exact *opposite* conclusion. But incredibly, not a day goes by that we don't hear this myth being forced upon the American public as undeniable fact.

In response to a twenty-five-year-old lesbian's letter about her sexual orientation, Abigail Van Buren responded in her "Dear Abby" column this way:

Dear Lesbian: Thank you for your honesty. I have always believed that one's sexual orientation is genetically predetermined before birth. Homosexuals have, for too long, suffered because of fear, ignorance and prejudice. Homosexuals are born—not made.[4]

Ms. Van Buren offers no support of any kind for her conclusions. But anyone who disagrees with her conclusions is labeled fearful, ignorant, and prejudiced.

Some time ago, I was flipping through the channels on my television set and I landed on C-SPAN, just as a member of the National Press Club was introducing a spokesman for the Gay and Lesbian Task Force. This man approached the podium. His first statement to the National Press Club was strong and decisive. He said: "I was born gay." For this bold assertion, he received thunderous applause from the Washington media, rather than a vigorous line of questioning for scientific support of his claim.

Based on scanty, specious "evidence," the American public is constantly bombarded with the myth that homosexuals are "born this way." This "fact" is then enlarged until it becomes an inalienable right. (If adultery, alcoholism, anger, gluttony, and other undesirable behaviors have genetic links, should they become rights, too?)

2. "Ten to 13 percent of the population is gay." This is another myth that continues to be foisted upon the American public. It is simply untrue. The product of a flawed study by Alfred Kinsey, this figure has been cited for years by gay radicals to buttress their agenda. We still hear it thrown around as if it were fact.[5]

The real facts tell a different story altogether: "The Kinsey data, which suggested that 10 percent of males are homosexual, has now been convincingly discredited."[6] According to *Time* magazine, the actual percentage of those who would be considered homosexual is much smaller. In an article entitled "The

Shrinking Ten Percent," *Time* cites a number of studies that demonstrate conclusively that the percentage of men who had sex with other men over a ten-year period was only 2.3 percent.[7] Furthermore, those who had sex *exclusively* with other men—and their choice wasn't mandated by circumstances (e.g., life in prison)—was even lower: a mere 1.1 percent. One to 2 percent. Not 10.

3. "Homosexuals can't change." This third myth that gay radicals use to shape public opinion is a lie. I've seen homosexuals change. I've known men in the church who have changed their sexual orientation from homosexual to heterosexual. Do they still struggle? Yes. As sexual creatures we all struggle. But they have abandoned their homosexual behavior and are glad they did.

Still, the radical homosexual continues to propagate the myth that change isn't impossible, that people are born with this predetermined condition. Efforts to change are considered cruel and inhumane. With myth in hand, they elicit sympathy and acceptance at all levels of society. And in the process, they engender despair in the breasts of thousands of gay men and women who hate themselves, but are convinced that change is a pipe dream.

2. Radical Gays Press for Acceptance by Utilizing a "Pro-Gay Media"

Do you remember the book *Fahrenheit 451* by Ray Bradbury? You may have read it in high school or college. *Fahrenheit 451* depicts a fictitious time when truth was kept from the common man through the burning of books. Well, we don't live in a world called Fahrenheit 451; we live in a world called Fahren-*hype* 451. It's a place where truth is kept from the average American by dissemination of partial and outright false information and deception. The progenitor of this illusion is a pro-gay media which shields us from anti-gay scientific research and from specific gay behaviors that would shock our senses, focusing our attention, instead, on abstract gay rights.

The dark side of homosexuality lies entombed in the vaults of news organizations across the country.

Chances are you have never seen a gay-pride parade. Not the *whole* parade. Take the recent march on Washington in which 300,000 gays and lesbians protested for homosexual rights. The images which eventually made it to your television screen represent a sanitized version of the actual events. From the viewer's point of view, this march looked just like a civil rights protest of the '60s. It was anything but.

What you *didn't* see on the evening news were the hundreds of lesbians marching topless down Pennsylvania Avenue and the men engaged in simulated sex acts. You didn't hear the crowd shouting, "Ten percent is not enough—recruit, recruit, recruit!" You didn't see the guys dressed in drag, the leathers, the transvestites, the lesbians outside the White House shouting, "Chelsea! Chelsea! Chelsea!" You were shielded from the members of NAMBLA, the North American Man-Boy Love Association, who are seeking to repeal all laws prohibiting sexual relations with minors. All of these elements were surreptitiously deleted from every news broadcast other than C-SPAN.

You will not see the truth because a pro-gay, agenda-driven media will not show it to you. Their aim is to grant legitimacy to this offensive behavior.

3. Radical Gays Press for Acceptance by Reinterpreting Scripture

The Bible is being reinterpreted by homosexuals to lend credence to their chosen lifestyle. For example, Jonathan and David's relationship is said to be one of the purest expressions of homosexual love ever depicted anywhere. The judgment of Sodom and Gomorrah was not precipitated by the sin of sodomy; instead, God judged the people because they failed to show hospitality to the angelic visitors. This is gay theology at its best.

Direct statements condemning homosexuality in Scripture are to be understood as homosexual acts committed by heterosexuals *against their nature*. The sin is that of dishonesty, not perversion. Homosexuality is valid if it is *natural*. We are also told that Paul never condemned homosexual love between committed homosexuals; what he condemned was promiscuity by all people, regardless of their sexual preference. Gay theology. It rides the wave of tortured interpretation. Welcome to another edition of the politically correct Bible.

4. Radical Gays Press for Acceptance Through Education and Legislation

This is where the gay agenda gets scary for the Christian. Tolerance for a homosexual person is one thing; laws and educational materials that promote homosexuality as a valid lifestyle are quite another. Imagine how you would feel if you were a parent in the New York City public schools and your child brought home books with titles like, *Heather Has Two Mommies*, *Daddy's Roommate*, and *Gloria Goes to Gay-pride*. All three are a brazen endorsement of homosexuality as an alternate lifestyle. Is this what you want your first-, second-, and third-grade kids reading?

Such was the case in the boroughs of New York.

Parents in New York City cried "foul" and had the books removed. But this hasn't stopped the radical element from pressing its case at every turn. Militant gays are not just open about their sexuality; they are adamant that society embrace them—fully and completely.

221

Hidden and Hurting Homosexuals

Committed and coping; radical and aggressive. There is yet a third group—what I've called the "hidden and hurting." While it's difficult to quantify their numbers, I believe this group represents the majority of homosexuals. The "hidden and hurting" are disgusted with themselves and the feelings that dominate their lives. They don't like being gay and would change in a heartbeat—it they only knew how to do so. This group of people are caught in a quandary: They experience a powerful attraction toward members of the same sex, but they also live with feelings of self-contempt. Some have been involved in homosexual behavior; all endure lives that are marked by personal upheaval and loneliness.

On occasion I've had the opportunity to interact with members of this group. Their responses are representative of the heartache that characterizes the "hidden and hurting." One man told me: "Robert, whatever disgust you feel for me cannot even begin to compare with the disgust I feel for myself." Another said, "I hate dishonesty, but I always feel I'm living a lie." Then he added, "I am, but then, I am not."

In his book entitled, *How Will I Tell My Mother?*, Jerry Arterburn spoke for thousands when he penned these words:

> The whole scheme of two identities was quite tiring. It was hard to keep everyone satisfied and almost impossible to keep track of who knew what secret. I developed a paranoia caused from years of wondering whether I would be found out.... The energy that it took to maintain my double life left me feeling empty and wanting a way out.[8]

These are the hidden and hurting. I personally believe the evangelical church has abandoned this group of people in the Bold New World. The church has failed to provide a place for them to struggle, a place where they can admit who they are and be real. The hidden homosexual listens to conversations between evangelical Christians and hears caustic remarks about radical gays. Though he himself completely disavows the radical agenda and lifestyle, he is lumped into this group. The message propagated by the church is clear: "All gays are perverts," "All gays are pedophiles," "All gays are child molesters."

In the midst of these fallacious, derogatory statements, the hidden homosexual begins to wonder if there is any room in the inn for him. Exaggerations of this kind close the door completely to the possibility of confession and healing. The stigma is too great.

The hidden, struggling homosexual has a historical counterpart in the first century—the afflicted person we know as a "leper." Do you remember their plight? Lepers were forced to live outside the city. Wherever they went, they had to declare their presence by shouting, "Unclean. Unclean." Tragically, those who treated the leper with the greatest contempt were the religious leaders of the day. Rabbinic law mandated a strict separation between this embattled group and the rest of society.

Alfred Edersheim writes: "No less a distance than four cubits (six feet) must be kept from a leper; or, if the wind came from that direction, a hundred were scarcely sufficient. Rabbi Meir would not eat an egg purchased in a street where there was a leper."[9] Oftentimes, the contempt turned to violence. "Another Rabbi boasted that he always threw stones at them to keep them far off, while others hid themselves or ran away."[10]

In many ways this is the predicament of the hidden homosexual in the evangelical community today. He sees himself as too unclean to be accepted by "righteous" people. The church has alienated this segment of society by virtue of our ignorance and hypocrisy.

John Drakeford says it best in his book, *Forbidden Love.*

A man stands up in the church and tells his story of drinking escapades, his slide into alcoholism.... Another man admits to a life spent on drugs, and tells of his struggle with addiction across the years. In both cases, the man declares he is through with it all and he's immediately hailed as a trophy of grace.

But let a man stand in the church and tell of his struggle with homosexuality, and a strange hush will descend. The reality is that people will not want him to go on. In fact, they will not even want him to be a part of their community.[11]

Discerning the Differences

It is imperative that we understand the differences between these three groups: the "committed and coping," the "radical and aggressive," and the "hidden and hurting." The church and our families can no longer speak in stereotypes and generalities. Instead, we must address specific audiences and tailor our approach accordingly. Wisdom mandates that we clarify the distinctions.

First, let's consider the objectives and needs of each group. The "radical" homosexual seeks cultural and philosophical approval; he wants society to acknowledge the validity of his lifestyle and the propriety of his behavior. The "committed" homosexual seeks personal acceptance; he longs for others who will acknowledge and approve of him as an individual. The "hidden" homosexual longs for love—period.

There are differences as well in their attitudes. The "radical" is close-minded, hostile, contemptuous of the church, and spiteful of the suggestion that change is possible. The "committed" is largely indifferent but can become open to change in the face of personal crisis. The "hidden" is willing to change but is often perplexed by the issues and afraid to reach out for help.

While we are unable to fix percentages, I suspect that the "radicals" represent the smallest group of gay people in America.

Yet despite their numbers, the "radicals" are the loudest and most vocal. The "committed" represent a somewhat larger group and, generally, they are moderates—both philosophically and politically.[12] I believe the largest group of homosexuals is the "hidden." We discount their presence largely because they are quiet and unobtrusive.

Upon which of the three groups does the evangelical church focus most of its attention? The "radicals." They scare us to death. We recoil from them and are intimidated by them. The "committed" is the group that confuses us the most. We struggle with them because they are our sons and daughters, our friends, and the people with whom we work.

Then there are the "hidden" homosexuals. What does the church do with them? One word comes to mind—*ignore!* We know very little about this struggling group of people and, if the truth were told, many Christians don't really care.

Understanding Homosexuality

Before delineating a biblical response to homosexuality, we must return to a critical question; it is a question that impacts every facet of this sensitive subject. The question is, *What causes homosexuality?*

Is homosexuality biologically determined or is it the result of environmental conditioning? As you may know, two recent studies have lent support to the notion that homosexuality is biological. In one study, neurobiologist Simon LeVay discovered that homosexual men possess a smaller anterior hypothalamus (the region of the brain known to be the source of sexual urges) than do heterosexuals. The hypothalamus in this small sampling of gay men was found to be comparable in size to the hypothalamus of women. The results suggested a genetic predisposition.

In a study by Dr. Michael Bailey and Richard Diller, genetic differences were discovered between homosexual and heterosexual men. Both of these studies received widespread coverage in the press, and many people interpreted this as "proof" that homosexuality is biologically determined.

It is important to understand, however, that both studies suffer from severe limitations. LeVay himself stated that his findings contain no direct evidence that the smaller hypothalamus causes homosexuality.[13] One scientist who is acquainted with LeVay's work adds this caveat: "Simon is very good; he's extremely well-equipped to make those observations. But we ought to put off big speculation until it is confirmed."[14]

As far as the research is concerned, these studies raise a number of questions but they don't prove anything. In fact, a more compelling case can be made to support the notion that homosexuality is not biological but is environmentally caused. William Byrne and Bruce Parsons, members of the Department of Psychiatry at the Columbia University College of Physicians and Surgeons, have stated just the opposite. They write:

> Recent studies postulate biological factors as the primary basis for sexual orientation. However, there is no evidence at present to substantiate a biologic theory.... Critical review shows the evidence favoring a biologic theory to be lacking.[15]

A parade of evidence, both old and new, indicates that homosexuality is caused by hurtful experiences endured in childhood, not by a gene or a brain abnormality.

Listen to the conclusion reached by Masters and Johnson:

> When dealing with problems of sexual preference, it is vital that all health care professionals bear in mind that the homosexual man or woman is basically a man or woman by genetic determination, and is homosexually oriented by learned preference.[16]

Charles Socarides writes: "Homosexuality is not innate. There is no connection between sexual instinct and the choice of sexual object. Such object choice is learned, acquired behavior."[17]

The most compelling piece of evidence is that presented by Dr. Elizabeth Moberly of Oxford University. Based on a comprehensive study, Dr. Moberly reached the following conclusion.

A homosexual orientation does not depend on a genetic predisposition, hormonal imbalance, or abnormal learning process, but on difficulties in the parent-child relationship, especially in the earlier years of life. The underlying principle is that the homosexual has suffered from some deficit in the relationship with the parent of the same sex.[18]

While there will be exceptions to the rule, studies indicate that 80 to 90 percent of gay men have suffered some type of severe emotional deficit in their relationships with their fathers. This reality has prompted Dr. Irving Bieber to conclude: "We have come to the conclusion that a constructive, supportive, warmly related father precludes the possibility of a homosexual man."[19] Victimized in childhood, these individuals feel alienated and alone. Such a deficiency creates a raw psychic wound, a wound that is salved later in life by homosexual relationships.

The scientific evidence is compelling and persuasive: The majority of homosexuals have suffered some kind of psychic or emotional break with a same-sex parent early in childhood. I know this was true with my brother. It is also true for every other homosexual I've known. These individuals each suffered an emotional deficiency with a same-sex parent.

Here's what occurs in the wake of this emotional void. As an injured child moves toward adulthood, this psychological deficit is internalized. It simmers for years within a troubled soul. During adolescence, it becomes eroticized, blossoming into sexual feelings toward persons of the same sex. We should note that the individual doesn't choose his orientation; it simply develops within him. As a result, this strong compulsion toward others of like gender leads one to believe, "I'm a homosexual and I've always been this way."

But the truth is, he wasn't *born* that way, he was *wounded;* and the wound caused him to deviate from normal sexual development. Unfortunately, to choose homosexuality and its attendant behavior as a solution only masks the pain and deepens the wounds.

Before we leave the scientific evidence, let me say again that *if* (and it's a big *if*) it can be proven that homosexuality is in part genetically proscribed, that in no way legitimizes the behavior. What other culturally censored behaviors would we then need to reclassify as legitimate for the same reason? Since when does genetics dictate culture? Isn't civilization in part the result of the suppression of certain specific, natural human inclinations through law?

The Biblical Position

We've considered the scientific evidence. Now let's turn our attention to the Scriptures. Does the Bible teach that a person is born gay? The answer is *no*. The Bible teaches that we are born *sinners*, which means we are separated from God and endowed by our forebears with an innate, natural propensity for self-protection and self-promotion, without regard to morality. Thrust into a corrupt world and confronted with a multiplicity of choices, our corrupt natures select those options which we believe will promote us and protect us. Our specific family backdrops may incline us to a particular unholy behavior. But the real root of our behavior is not in genetics, but in Genesis. We are born sinners, not homosexuals.

The Bible enunciates five truths concerning homosexuality.

1. Scripture considers homosexuality a behavior. Consider 1 Corinthians 6. In the second half of this chapter, the apostle Paul exhorts the Corinthian Christians to moral purity. He prefaces his remarks with a statement in verses 9 and 10 which read:

> Do you not know that the unrighteous shall not inherit the kingdom of God? Do not be deceived; neither fornicators, nor idolaters, nor adulterers, nor effeminate, nor homosexuals, nor thieves, nor the covetous, nor drunkards, nor revilers, nor swindlers shall inherit the kingdom of God.

Paul is enumerating *behaviors* here. A person becomes a thief when he steals; a man becomes an idolater when he worships idols. In the same vein, an individual becomes a homosexual when he engages in homosexual behavior.

Conversely, labels become meaningless when behavior *stops*. When does a thief cease to be a thief? When he no longer steals. A drunkard ceases to be a drunk when he no longer drinks. Likewise, a homosexual ceases being a homosexual when he no longer engages in homosexual behavior. It is not what one *feels*, but what one *does* that counts.

2. Homosexual *behavior* is sinful; homosexual *needs* are not. Let's deal with each of these in turn.

Homosexual behavior is sinful. Paul uses the word "unrighteous" in the Corinthian passage to characterize its essential nature. But a caveat is necessary. Did you notice the location of the word "homosexual" in the apostle's list? It doesn't come first; instead, it is fifth. Many in today's evangelical community would place it squarely at the beginning. Paul doesn't. Is this significant? I think so. Homosexuality is a sin but it is not *the* sin. It is one sin among many others. In other words, homosexuality doesn't stand out the way we make it stand out—as the ultimate sin. Parents, please note this. Many tend to diminish the sins of idolatry and adultery but elevate homosexuality to a level of abject perversity. Homosexual behavior is sinful. Much of it is indeed perverse. But in God's eyes, it is not *the* sin.[20]

Now to the second half of the equation: Homosexual behavior is sin; *homosexual needs are not.* We must distinguish between the behavior itself and the needs which give rise to the behavior. The former is offensive to God; the latter represents a legitimate hunger for love and acceptance.

The struggling homosexual can end his behavior. Many have done so. But true healing requires more than the cessation of gay behavior. There must be something more, something deeper. For true change to occur, the homosexual must experience the grace of God and the unconditional love of his or her family, as well as the love of a committed, supportive community of Christians. These two relationships—with God and others—provide the struggler with the love and acceptance he or she so desperately desires. Legitimate desires, which formerly were satisfied in abnormal ways, need to be met within the body of Christ. What an incredible challenge this is to our families and our churches!

3. Homosexuals can change. Paul says as much in 1 Corinthians 6:11. Referring to the list of behaviors given in verses 9 and 10, Paul writes: "And such were some of you; but you were washed, but you were sanctified, but you were justified in the name of the Lord Jesus Christ, and in the Spirit of our God."

There were ex-gays in the Corinthian church. And ex-transvestites. Along with ex-drunkards and ex-adulterers. The gospel had penetrated sin-hardened hearts and worked miracles of transformation. The Lord of heaven and earth accomplishes the same miracles today.

4. Cultural acceptance of homosexuality signals real danger. Once again, the prophet Hosea speaks to our day with bold and confrontive words. In Hosea 9, the prophet lashes out at a society that was wildly prosperous but brazenly wicked. Israel had become a quagmire of moral and spiritual corruption. An air of arrogance permeated the lives of Hosea's rebellious countrymen. In Hosea 9:7, this man of God enunciates the coming judgment of the Lord.

> The days of punishment have come, the days of retribution have come; let Israel know this! The prophet is a fool, the inspired man is demented, because of the grossness of your iniquity, and because your hostility is so great.

What had precipitated the divine judgment? Hosea tells us in verse 9: "They have gone deep in depravity as in the days of Gibeah; He will remember their iniquity, He will punish their sins."

Do you remember the events surrounding "the days of Gibeah"? It is an allusion to one of the most egregious events in Israel's history. The story is recorded for us in Judges 19. A Levitical priest travels to Gibeah with his concubine. After a wearying journey, the party lodges in the city. Later that same night, the men of the town pound on the door and demand that the owner of the house send out the male visitor, "that we may have relations with him" (Judges 19:22). The owner refuses these homosexuals' demands; the mob is given his concubine instead. They rape this woman repeatedly throughout the night, causing her death. To protest such an atrocious act, the priest hews his concubine into twelve pieces (one for each tribe in Israel), and sends her body throughout the territory of Israel.

"They have gone deep in depravity as in the days of Gibeah." This was Hosea's judgment upon the Israel of his day. The lesson is clear: When a society licenses homosexuality, when the mob reigns, when people call good evil and evil good, divine judgment is imminent. Let Israel know, "The days of punishment have come...because of the grossness of your iniquity."

The cultural acceptance of homosexuality signals danger.

5. Family and church acceptance of hurting homosexuals signals real maturity. First Thessalonians 5:14-15 says, "We urge you, brethren…encourage the fainthearted, help the weak, be patient with all men…always seek after that which is good for one another and for all men." It takes a mature family and a mature church to enter into the lives of men and women, sons and daughters, who are struggling with homosexuality. But without such beacons of hope and conduits for change, what alternative is there for the homosexual desiring change? It will take courageous Christians to meet this challenge.

Action Points

For too long, the Christian community has gone to one of two extremes in dealing with the issue of homosexuality: We have either ignored it completely or confronted it with a hostility that belies the message of the gospel. This must change. The situation mandates that we become "wise as serpents and innocent as doves." We must seek to implement the following action points.

1. As you engage the world, learn to practice *tolerance* **and** *intolerance.* Extend tolerance toward homosexuals of all kinds, whether radical or hidden, for they too have been created in the image of God. Homosexuals deserve to be treated with dignity and respect. Please, never forget this: These people are not just homosexuals; they are also human beings, like you and me. Provide them with the same measure of civility and civil rights that are accorded to all Americans. That's tolerance.

We must also learn to practice *intolerance.* Scripture exhorts us to stand up against any effort—social, political, or otherwise—that seeks to sanction homosexuality as a valid lifestyle. We must speak out. Parents must be heard in the public schools; voters must be heard in the public square. This will not be easy. The opposition is well-financed and passionate about its cause. They have the powerful support of the media. Intimidation will cause some to shrink back in fear. Stand your ground as a soldier of the cross. Have the courage to say "This is not right," and the wisdom to articulate the truth.

Balancing tolerance and intolerance is a delicate task. The insight of Msgr. Fulton Sheen will help us walk this tightrope. Over sixty years ago, the Catholic priest penned these timeless words: "Tolerance is an attitude of reasoned patience towards evil…a forbearance that restrains us from showing anger or inflicting punishment. Tolerance applies only to persons…never to truth. Tolerance applies to the erring, intolerance to the error."[21] We must be tolerant with people and intolerant when the truth is maligned.

2. As churches and families, we must be open and caring. We can't close ourselves off from the hidden homosexuals in our midst. They are dying, literally, for someone to embrace them as brothers and sisters in Christ. An open church will recognize the desperate plight of these fellow strugglers and seek to heal their broken hearts. Our church has taken some first steps toward addressing the needs of hidden homosexuals. We have extended love and acceptance to them from the pulpit. We have also become part of a national organization called "Homosexuals Anonymous." This support group, which meets weekly, gives homosexuals a place of refuge. It allows them to confront their struggles in an environment that is protective, while at the same time affirming them as individuals.

We must be open and caring. At this point, I feel compelled to issue a strong challenge. As the brother of a homosexual who died of AIDS, let me say, firmly but lovingly, *Watch your words!* It would be difficult to count the number of times I've winced at the insensitive jokes and comments spoken by fellow Christians. Humor that reinforces stereotypes has no place whatsoever in the vocabulary of God's people. Such callous language drives the hidden homosexual further from the throne of grace. Please be careful.

3. Within your own family (I'm speaking primarily to parents here), invest in your children. Dads must be emotionally involved in the lives of sons and daughters. To repeat an earlier statement by Dr. Irving Bieber, "We have come to the conclusion that a constructive, supportive, warmly related father precludes the possibility of a homosexual man." While there may be exceptions to the rule, the mandate is clear: No one influences the sexual identity of a child like dad.

Requiem

Charles Lewis died of AIDS in August 1990. His funeral wake was attended by hundreds of people, most of them members of the gay community. To the best of my knowledge, Charles never resolved the conflict between his behavior and his faith. My brother believed in Christ but he was also adamant that homosexuality was a legitimate lifestyle.

This conviction followed him to the grave.

In the years since he departed this life, I've often wondered how different things might have been if, early on, Charles had encountered Christians of a special stripe. Not the kind who tell gay jokes and mimic effeminate manners. Not the kind who hurl verbal firebrands of condemnation. Not the kind who turn an indifferent cheek. What if Charles had met a courageous band of Christians who love the struggler, regardless of his or her behavior; Christians who reach out and fearlessly embrace gay men and women; Christians who speak the truth wrapped in love?

These are good questions for churches and families in dealing with the ongoing social controversy of homosexuality.

Notes

[1] Eric Markus, "They're Not Telling the Truth," *Newsweek*, 14 September 1992, 41.

[2] Bruce Bawer, *A Place at the Table:* (New York: Poseidon, 1993), 38.

[3] It is interesting to note that many "committed" homosexuals are offended, even disgusted, by the radical elements within the gay community.

One individual summed it up this way: "The only time I ever feel ashamed of being gay is on Gay Pride Day" (Bruce Bawer, *A Place at the Table*, 153). The contempt they feel, however, is not for moral reasons but pragmatic ones. It is difficult to become mainstream when the fringe elements paint a picture of perversion and debauchery. Bawer adds: "The whole idea of gay politics, after all, should be to stop heterosexuals from thinking of gays as the most 'other' thing around" (39).

[4]Abigail Van Buren, "Dear Abby," *Arkansas Democrat-Gazette*, 30 December 1994, 4E.

[5]In an interview in *The Advocate*, a gay publication, Surgeon General Joycelyn Elders regurgitated the 10 percent figure. "The Condom Queen Reigns," *The Advocate*, 22 March 1994.

[6]"The Homosexual Movement," *First Things*, March 1994, 18.

[7]Priscilla Painton,"The Shrinking Ten Percent," *Time*, 26 April 1993, 27-29.

[8]Jerry Arterburn with Steve Arterburn, *How Will I Tell My Mother?* (Nashville: Thomas Nelson, 1988), 98.

[9]Alfred Edersheim, *The Life and Times of Jesus the Messiah* (Grand Rapids, Mich.: Eerdman's, 1971), 495.

[10]Ibid.

[11]John Drakeford, *Forbidden Love* (taken from a sermon by John MacArthur, titled, "What God Thinks of Homosexuals—Part 1 of 2"), published on audio cassette by Bible Believers Cassettes, Inc., Springdale, Arkansas.

[12]Almost one-fifth of American gays voted for the Bush-Quayle ticket in 1992. See Bruce Bawer, *A Place at the Table* (New York: Poseidon, 1993), 34.

[13]"Is Homosexuality Biological?" *Science*, Vol. 253, 956.

[14]Ibid.

[15]"Human Sexual Orientation: The Biologic Theories Reappraised," *Archives of General Psychiatry*, March 1993, 228.

[16]William Masters and Virginia Johnson, *Homosexuality in Perspective* (Boston: Little, Brown and Co., 1979), 271.

[17]Dr. Charles Socarides, *The Overt Homosexual* (New York: Grune and Stratton, 1968), 45.

[18]John Stott, *Decisive Issues Facing Christians Today* (New Jersey: Fleming H. Revell Co., 1990), 358. Dr. Elizabeth Moberley's *Homosexuality: A New*

Christian Ethic (Cambridge, England: James Clarke and Company, 1983) is a must for any Christian who is researching the subject of homosexuality.

[19]Dr. Irving Bieber, *Homosexuality: A Psychoanalytic Study* (New York: Busie Booles, 1962), 303.

[20]As we will discover momentarily, while homosexuality is not the sin among sins, it does signal the decline and demise of a culture. The society that openly embraces such behavior stumbles in the twilight of its own existence.

[21]Patrick Buchanan, "Why Are We Surprised by the State of Society?" *The Conservative Chronicle*, Vol. 9, No. 15, 13 April 1994, 24.

CHAPTER THIRTEEN

RACISM

"It is still true that eleven o'clock Sunday morning is the most segregated hour in America."

ANDRES TAPIA

I was fortunate. Even though I grew up in the deep South, I entered adulthood with a heart schooled to resist the venom of prejudice and bigotry. That I leaned away from this blight of the spirit is a testament to the powerful convictions of the two most influential people in my childhood—my mom and dad.

The South of the 1950s and '60s was a cultural anachronism, a land which time forgot. While the rest of the United States made measurable progress toward racial equality, the former Confederate States remained staunchly defiant. Southern leaders and cultural elites fought to preserve a social structure that had existed since the days of Reconstruction. It's not surprising, then, that the conflagration for civil rights was ignited, and burned brightest, in the South.

These were the days of Jim Crow—the forced segregation of blacks and whites. In my hometown in Louisiana, the invisible barbed wire of racism cast an evil pall over an otherwise peaceful community. A few images, like spectral figures, haunt the shadowy recesses of my mind. I can still see the public restrooms divided into three categories: "Men," "Women," and "Negroes." I can recall sitting in a movie theater and looking up into the balcony—the section reserved for blacks. I remember being shown the picture of a black man who was lynched outside town in the 1940s. And I can still hear my cousin, a man who prided himself on his collection of racial jokes, spinning one tasteless epithet after another. It was all around me—the overt discrimination, the subtle innuendo, the hidden rules that determined the social strata of one small Southern town.

Even at the tender age of nine, I was well on my way to becoming a racist—not a cross-burner or an ardent segregationist, mind you, but the more subtle kind. I was one who felt a sense of racial superiority, one who made distinctions between whites and blacks in everything. The seeds of racism, which lie dormant in the heart of every young child, were being nurtured in me by a bigoted society. Attitudes were crystallizing; convictions were taking shape. Only a dramatic experience could halt my descent into the stagnant waters of racial pride.

Thankfully, that experience occurred when I was nine years old.

Both of my parents worked full-time jobs. For this reason, mom and dad were forced to employ people from the community to watch the three Lewis boys when we came home from school. One of those who cared for us was a black teenager named James Jones. As I recall, James didn't have a father. His family lived in very impoverished conditions, and James took odd jobs to supplement his mother's meager income. Throughout my early years, this young man became a fixture in our home. After school and occasionally in the evening, James would do his best to keep the "little rascals" in their places. No man ever faced a more daunting challenge. The job required the courage of Indiana Jones, the wisdom of Yoda, and the strength of Arnold Schwarzenegger. But James was worthy of the task. He was a good baby-sitter and a great companion for three rambunctious kids. We developed a camaraderie with James and enjoyed his gentle, but firm, style.

But in my ninth year, the tranquillity was shattered by one ugly, hideous encounter. For the first time in our relationship, race became an issue. James was the victim. I was the culprit.

My folks had gone out for the evening. In their absence, I got into a fight with my older brother, Charles. Determined to resolve the dispute, James stepped into the fray and attempted to sort things out. He did his best to reconcile two hostile siblings. The terms of the agreement didn't sit well with me and I got sideways with James. When James brought his authority to bear in the situation, I reached my boiling point. Unable to contain myself any longer, I said something I've regretted ever since. With the arrogance of a fool, I looked James squarely in the eyes and shouted, "You're a nigger, James; that's all you are, a nigger! You don't have any right to say that to me!"

James Jones was a gentle man, but he wasn't about to ignore this egregious offense. Our baby-sitter threw me across his knee and paddled my posterior until my eyes streamed with tears. Angry and unrepentant, I leaped to my feet and made a halting pronouncement that must have made James' blood run cold. "When—my—dad—comes—home," I said, coughing out the words between sobs, "I'm—going—to—tell—him—what—you've—done!"

I can only imagine the fears that raced through James' mind over the next few hours. Like so many other blacks in the late 1950s, this man's fate would be decided by the capricious attitudes of a white man. For all James knew, there would be no appeal to a moral law. There were no guarantees of justice. You see, in the South of the 1950s, James Jones was what Ralph Ellison so astutely identified as an "invisible man."

I am an invisible man. No, I am not a spook like those who haunted Edgar Allan Poe; nor am I one of your Hollywood-movie ectoplasms. I am a man of substance, of flesh and bone, fiber and liquids—and I might even be said to possess a mind. I am invisible, understand, simply because people refuse to see me. Like the bodiless heads you see sometimes in circus sideshows, it is as though I have been surrounded by mirrors of hard, distorting glass. When they approach me they see only my surroundings, themselves, or figments of their imagination—indeed, everything and anything except me.[1]

My parents returned to the scene of the crime. The moment of reckoning was now at hand. The nine-year-old racist ran into his father's arms and argued his case, fully convinced that James would be punished and he would be vindicated. In the middle of my stammering defense, James stepped forward and, in a quiet but firm voice, spoke the words that justified his actions only hours before. "Mr. Lewis," he said, "your son called me a nigger." As soon as the words exited his mouth, I knew I was in trouble. My father grabbed my arm, lifted me off the ground, and paddled my posterior until my eyes again streamed with tears.

It was a rough day.

When he finished, Dad spoke the words I will never forget. "Robert, don't you ever say that again! EVER!"

In the years that followed this painful experience, a remarkable relationship developed between my mom and dad, and James. My father helped James secure a job at a respectable clothing store in town. With that help, James went on and got the first-ever college degree in his family.

At my father's funeral, as I stood mourning the loss of the man I called "Dad," I felt the compassionate touch of a strong hand on my shoulder. It was the hand of James Jones. He had come to pay his respects to the man who had respected him.

For the next few minutes, my mother and James shared a time-less moment together. Along with a warm hug, James expressed heartfelt appreciation for the contribution that my father had made in his life. In the conversation that followed, my mother bragged on James' many accomplishments. She took pride in pointing out to me that all three of James' children had graduated from college. As the discussion continued, I stood marveling at a beautiful relationship that could have been destroyed by something as benign as the color of one's skin.

It was the best lesson on race relations anyone could ever receive.

The Tragedy of Mistrust

I share my personal experience because I believe it captures the essence of Martin Luther King's dream for America. When Dr. King stood on the mall in Washington, D.C., that hot August day in 1963, I believe the impassioned preacher envisioned something greater than integration. King's vision was for *reconciliation*. He said, "I have a dream that one day, on the red hills of Georgia, the sons of former slaves and the sons of former slave owners will be able to sit down together at the table of brotherhood."

Brotherhood. That's not integration, that's reconciliation. Brotherhood is a concept that goes far beyond civil rights and integrated schools and minority representation. Important as these things are, brotherhood is something much higher, something much more noble. It is a quality that is deeply spiritual, intensely relational, and life-affirming. Brotherhood is a desire to confer upon another human being their God-given dignity—regardless of that person's color.

Today we have integration without brotherhood. We have race relations without racial reconciliation. It is dangerous ground we tread as a nation. The prophecy in the Kerner Report, a six-hundred-page document produced by the National Advisory

Commission during the Johnson administration, has now become a reality: "Our nation is moving toward two societies," the report concludes, "one white, one black. A house divided cannot stand."[2] Harry Ashmore confirms this sad truth in his book, *Civil Rights and Wrongs*. He writes: "If *e pluribus unum*—from the many, one—still represents the nation's goal, we have been moving away from it for two decades."[3]

America is *integrated* but increasingly *segregated*. This condition has fostered two seemingly insurmountable social realities. The first is a visceral black rage that whites simply don't understand. Can I state the obvious? Black Americans are angry. Not all of them are, but many. We saw their anger expressed in the streets of Los Angeles following the decision in the Rodney King beating case; we hear their anger in the violent lyrics of rap music. The memory of past injustices and the experience of present discrimination combine to ignite a smoldering bitterness that is palpable.

In an *Essence* magazine article entitled "Keeper of the Rage," writer Lula Strickland-Abuwi recounts an experience with her son, Khalid. "As we watched the documentary *Eyes on the Prize*, my 17-year-old son, Khalid, and I shared a new bond: rage. His was fresh and new, mine smoldering and rekindled."[4] For Ms. Strickland-Abuwi, this rage is a good thing—as long as it is pointed in a positive direction.

The first reality is a visceral black rage that whites don't understand; the second is an impatient white bewilderment that blacks don't understand. White Americans have grown impatient with the plaintive black refrain that interprets every rejection in the marketplace, every unfavorable response, as racially motivated. They are bewildered by an affirmative action policy at work and on the university campus that penalizes them for being white. They have grown impatient with a welfare system that eats away at their income and produces no tangible, lasting changes in the inner city.

The clash of these two realities has created what I call the "tragedy of mistrust." Both blacks and whites are guilty. In too many cases we do not see others as individuals—we see them as part of a group (white, black, Hispanic), and we immediately attach labels to them that are as superficial as one's skin color. We don't relate to individuals as *individuals*; instead we relate to a misconception, a mythical image born out of stereotypes and generalities.

A doctor friend of mine related a story to me that illustrates this point. During the summer of 1993, four nurses traveled from Little Rock to Las Vegas for a nursing convention. The first night in Vegas, these women decided to try their luck at gambling. One of the gals got on a roll and won several hundred dollars. Her three friends weren't so lucky and, since it was now past midnight, they retired to their hotel rooms for the night.

The lucky gambler decided to stay. She continued to win money. An hour or so later, it struck her: She had hundreds of dollars in her pocket, she was in a strange city, and worst of all, she was now alone. Gripped by fear and suspicious of everyone, this gal scurried across the lobby and waited nervously for an elevator. When one finally arrived, she rushed inside and pushed the button for the sixth floor. Just as the doors were about to close, four black men got on board. The steel doors shut behind them, and one of the men turned to her and said, "Hit the *FO*."

In a state of delirium by now, what this frightened women *thought* she heard was, "Hit the floor." That's precisely what she did. Convinced she was going to be robbed, this gal collapsed to the floor, sobbing. "Don't hurt me," she cried. "I've got hundreds of dollars in my pocket; you can have it all, just don't hurt me. My friends are in room 625. You can have their money, too; just don't hurt me."

She was still in a horizontal position when the elevator stopped at the fourth floor and the four black men, convulsing with laughter, headed to their rooms.

The next morning there was a knock at room 625. A bellhop handed her a dozen roses with a hundred dollar bill suspended from each one. A note was attached to the bouquet. It read: "Thank you for last night. I haven't laughed that hard in years." The note was signed, "Eddie Murphy."

Such deep mistrust, nurtured by stereotypes, is sometimes humorous. Often it is demeaning, degrading, and inexcusable. Worst of all, deep mistrust can sabotage honest, thoughtful attempts at reconciliation. On too many occasions this has been my experience as a pastor. For the last fifteen years in Little Rock, I've attempted to build a racial bridge to members of the black community. Quite frankly, I've had my feelings hurt a number of times. Honest, heartfelt efforts at reconciliation have been greeted with suspicion, cynicism, and anger. I've walked away frustrated and a little embarrassed for even trying.

I know now how John F. Kennedy must have felt when he traveled to the Berlin Wall in 1963 and tried to identify with the citizens of Berlin. After a rousing rhetorical flourish, Kennedy wanted to end his speech with the phrase, *"Ich bin Berliner!"* ("I am a Berliner!") However, the president inadvertently placed an article in front of the last word. What came out instead was *"Ich bin ein Berliner—*("I am *the* Berliner!") Unknown to the president, "The Berliner" was a giant jelly donut popular in Berlin at the time. As he stepped from the platform, Kennedy probably thought the Germans were cheering; the reality was, they were laughing at a president who had just called himself a jelly donut!

Now, was he trying to identify with the German people? Was he trying to communicate? Yes. But the president came across looking more like an incompetent buffoon than a head of state. Attempts at reconciliation between whites and blacks often end this same way. My small attempts at bridge-building have resulted in frustration and misunderstanding. When statements intended to reconcile are greeted with a suspicious air and reinterpreted through the wounds of the past, bridge-builders become discouraged. They ask themselves, "What's the use?" and often give up. This is the tragedy of mistrust.

Where Is the Church?

America is at a racial crossroads. Hate crimes are on the rise. In rural America, in the cities, and, surprisingly, on university campuses (the most "enlightened" environments in America), incidents of racism have increased dramatically. In his book *Inside American Education,* Thomas Sowell quotes a professor from the University of California at Berkeley who has witnessed the recent spread of racism: "I've been teaching at U.C. Berkeley now for 18 years and it's only within the last three or four years that I've seen racist graffiti for the first time."[5]

Says Daniel Levistas, the executive director for a national organization that tracks hate crimes, "The level of bigoted violence has reached epidemic levels in America."[6] After three decades of political legislation, affirmative action, and forced integration, we are no closer to attaining Dr. King's dream of brotherhood than we were in 1963.

Our predicament begs an ominous question, and that is, *Where is the evangelical church?* What steps has she taken to reconcile blacks and whites? If the pulpit is a good barometer, the answer is a discouraging one. I've been a Christian now for twenty-seven years. During this time I have listened to thousands of sermons. Incredibly, I've never heard a single message, ever, on the issue of racism. Have you?

The silence is deafening, isn't it?

This muted response by evangelical pulpits to the problem of racism suggests one awful possibility: Maybe we just don't care. Confronted with the enormity of the issue, and with so many other problems commanding our attention, the evangelical church seems to have abandoned all efforts toward reconciliation. Are you bothered by the fact that "eleven o'clock Sunday morning is the most segregated hour in America"?[7] I am. Our silence on this issue is a tragic indictment of the evangelical community.

All of which leads to an even more troubling question: *Is the evangelical church racist?* While no evangelical churches (that I know of) actively promote segregation, I know too many that fail to promote reconciliation. They are content to remain silent and uninvolved.

And what about Christian families? What have Christian moms and dads done to stir up a sense of racial reconciliation in the hearts of their children? If we are honest, very little. Somehow, this critical issue is never addressed as a family value. In the void, racism takes root.

Kay James is the executive vice president for the Family Research Council, a Christian group headquartered in Washington, D.C. She is a highly respected, influential leader within the organization. Kay also is black. Some time ago, Kay James was the victim of racism. The perpetrators of the crime, sadly, were her sisters in Christ and their families.

While living in Washington, Kay became involved in a women's Bible study that met weekly at a white church. As the year went by, Kay began to hear talk about an upcoming trip to Myrtle Beach. She discovered that the trip was an annual affair, a summer celebration that marked the completion of the Bible study. Throughout the year, Kay overheard so many references to previous trips that she began to revel in the excitement of the upcoming event. What a great time it would be.

Summer was fast approaching. Kay caught snatches of conversations about Myrtle Beach—her friends were making travel arrangements—but the discussions terminated whenever she came near. And then, to Kay's utter disappointment, the group left without her.

I never felt so betrayed and rejected. Eventually, embarrassment and hurt died down enough for me to ask one day why Charles and I weren't included in the beach trip. An uncomfortable silence followed. One said, "Well, Kay, we just felt that, well, you know, there aren't very many black people at Myrtle Beach, and we just thought you would be uncomfortable." Then I thought, "They were concerned about us? Didn't they see this irony?" It took all my courage to say something and I did. I said, "Well, I guess I thought that if we wouldn't be accepted at a certain vacation spot, you would choose another one rather than leave us out." Nothing more was ever said about it.[8]

Didn't they see the irony? But I wonder—was it really irony or a form of passive racism?

As I write this chapter, Americans are looking forward with enthusiasm to the 1996 Olympic Games in Atlanta, Georgia. The event has precipitated a discussion about the state flag of Georgia, a symbol that harkens back to the Confederacy and painfully reminds black Americans of their subjugation and oppression. My initial reaction to this brouhaha was a superficial, "What's the big deal—it's just a flag!" But the very fact that blacks have to raise the issue is what makes them so mad. The fact that whites can't, or won't, see the symbolism is what angers them so deeply.

Let me put the principle in another context. Assume for a moment that your best friend's son is killed by a red convertible. The child's death is a source of untold grief and sorrow to your friend. Every time he sees a red convertible, it reminds him of that fateful day when he lost his boy. Now, would you go out and purchase a red convertible, just because it's your right to do so? Would you do this to a friend?

Do you see the parallel?

At the heart of black rage today is a burning sense that whites really don't care about them. And don't care to care.

A Starting Point

In Acts 17, Paul gives us a starting point, a beginning perspective that helps us make sense of the racial quagmire we find ourselves in today. In this passage of Scripture, the apostle is in Athens, one of the most cosmopolitan and diverse cities in the ancient world. Ethnic, cultural, and religious pluralism abounded in the capital of Greece. Athens was a social and religious melting pot. People the world over would travel to Athens to consummate business deals, court political favors, and worship multiple deities. The city was filled with shrines, altars, and statues, many of which survive to this day.

Of this ancient capital, one Roman satirist remarked that, "It is easier in Athens to find a god than a man." At the Areopagus, a small hill northwest of the Acropolis, Paul the preacher stood and proclaimed, to his pluralistic audience, two great truths that enlighten our understanding on the subject of race relations.

> The God who made the world and all things in it, since He is Lord of heaven and earth, does not dwell in temples made with hands; neither is He served by human hands, as though He needed anything, since He Himself gives to all life and breath and all things; and He made from one, every nation of mankind to live on all the face of the earth, having determined their appointed times, and the boundaries of their habitation (Acts 17:24-26).

How does this passage inform our understanding of race relations?

1. It is clear that we all worship the same God. Black, white, red, or yellow, to be a Christian is to worship the one true God—the Lord of heaven and earth, He who gives life and breath to all. When my black brothers and sisters in Christ gather together on Sunday mornings, they are worshipping the same God I worship; they pray to the same God to whom I pray. This God doesn't boast a black face or a white face—His face is, as Scripture says, too glorious to behold, "for no man can see Me and live" (Exodus 33:20).

Our worship may take different forms—it may find expression in the traditional hymns of white churches or the energetic praise common to black churches. Nevertheless, the *object* of our worship is static, fixed, unchanging.

2. Paul tells us that we have a common ancestor. He says that God "made from one, every nation of mankind to live on the earth" (Acts 17:26). Made from *one*. Not *many*. The apostle is speaking here of the homogeneity of the human race. As different as we may seem today, we have a common ancestor. Commenting upon the Acts passage before us, William Baker writes:

> What that means, of course, is that all humanity had the same start. No alleged deficiencies among races or nationalities can be laid at the door of origins as described in the Bible.... The biblical teaching is that Adam is a common ancestor, and this lays to rest any claim of superiority due to some natural variation in evolution, at least as far as the Bible-believer is concerned.[9]

This truth is confirmed, not by Scripture alone, but by secular sources as well. According to *Time* magazine, a number of anthropologists now believe human beings have a singular parent, a literal Eve. Noted physical anthropologist Ashley Montague states:

> Concerning the origins of the living varieties of man, we can say little more than that there are many reasons for believing that a single stock gave rise to all of them.... All varieties of man belong to the same species

and have the same remote ancestry. This is a conclusion to which all the relevant evidence of comparative anatomy, palaeontology, serology, and genetics points.[10]

What, then, is the significance of the homogeneity of the human race? There is only one logical conclusion. If our beginning is the same, if the source of our being is the same, if our constitution is the same—regardless of color—then we *are* the same. Like the first human beings and every human being ever created, we have been imprinted with the *imago dei*, the image of God (Genesis 1:26-27). For this reason, we all possess dignity; we are all worthy of respect. No one has put it better than C. S. Lewis:

> There are no *ordinary* people. You have never talked to a mere mortal.... But it is immortals we joke with, work with, marry, snub, and exploit—immortal horrors or everlasting splendors.... Next to the Blessed Sacrament itself, your neighbor is the holiest object presented to your senses.[11]

Our Constitution summarizes this profound truth in one powerful five-word phrase. The statement "all men are created equal" is a biblical doctrine as well as a political reality. To deny this truth is to subvert both the Constitution and the clear teaching of Scripture. It is an even greater tragedy when this truth is not proclaimed powerfully by parents to their children, and by churches to their parishioners.

The Source of Reconciliation

We worship the same God; we have a common ancestor. These are great truths. Nevertheless, the final reconciliation of black and white (or any other racial conflict) can be realized only through the blood of Christ. Understanding our similarities and appreciating our differences in no way resolves the one overriding problem that keeps us apart—our pride.

However we choose to label racism, we cannot escape the word that Scripture uses. The Bible calls racism "sin." *Racism is sin*, and racial pride manifests itself in a thousand different ways. For whites, such hubris is communicated through racial slurs, subtle put-downs, and an air of superiority. For blacks, racism is communicated through allusions to past injustices, reminders intended to deepen white guilt and accentuate racial separation.[12] As Christians, we can put a good face on our actions; we can justify them in light of our own experience. But we can't escape the pulsating presence and the debilitating effects of our own pride.

If the final barrier to racial reconciliation is pride, the only solution is the cross. In Ephesians 2, the apostle Paul turns his attention to the problem of segregation. His challenge to us (black, white, brown, or yellow) is to come together around the one object that humbles our pride, denigrates our conceit, and shackles our arrogance—the cross of Jesus Christ.

In verse 11, Paul makes reference to the most difficult problem that confronted the first-century church. It was the one problem that appears again and again throughout the book of Acts, the one problem that required a church council to resolve (Acts 15). The problem to which Paul refers is the inclusion of Gentiles into the kingdom of God.

> Therefore remember, that formerly you, the Gentiles in the flesh, who are called "Uncircumcision" by the so-called "Circumcision," which is performed in the flesh by human hands—remember that you were at that time separate from Christ, excluded from the common-wealth of Israel, and strangers to the covenants of promise, having no hope and without God in the world (Ephesians 2:11-12).

Paul has in view two distinct groups of people. The first are the spiritually privileged, those whom he identifies as the "Circumcision." The "Circumcision" were those Jews who by birth inherited the rich spiritual heritage of their forefathers—the Law, the covenants, the temple ceremonies. This privileged group is contrasted with the "Uncircumcision," or the Gentiles. The apostle reminds the Gentiles that there was a time, not long past, when they were alienated from God, a time when their lives were characterized by despair and futility.

Enter Jesus Christ. Through the blood of the cross, Jesus Christ made it possible for the Gentiles to enjoy the same access to God formerly reserved for Jews alone: "But now in Christ Jesus, you who formerly were far off have been brought near by the blood of Christ" (Ephesians 2:13).

The inclusion of Gentiles into the kingdom of God sent shock waves throughout the Jewish community. We don't have to search long and hard to understand why. The Jewish Christians, or "Circumcision," brought many of their separatist attitudes into the church. Though objects of divine favor (with no special claim upon God's grace), this group had come to see themselves as superior to others. They forgot that spiritual privilege was a *gift*, not a *right*. This privileged class looked with condescension upon the "Uncircumcision." They viewed Gentiles as inferior, vile, wretched.

Even the Jewish use of the word "Uncircumcision" was pejorative; it smacked of racial and cultural superiority. Jewish rabbis even codified a legal system that fanned the flames of prejudice. Edersheim writes:

> Even the Mishnah goes so far as to forbid aid to a [heathen] mother in the hour of her need, or nourishment to her babe, in order not to bring up a child for idolatry. But this is not all. Heathens were, indeed, not to be precipitated into danger, but yet not to be delivered from it. Indeed, an isolated teacher ventures even upon this statement: "The best among the Gentiles, kill; the best among serpents, crush its head."[13]

These segregationist attitudes, over a thousand years old and taught from birth in every Jewish family, collided with the inclusionary teachings of Jesus Christ. Jewish Christians discovered they were to love those whom they had been taught to look down on:

> For He Himself is our peace, who made both groups [Jew and Gentile] into one, and broke down the barrier of the dividing wall, by abolishing in His flesh the enmity, which is the Law of commandments contained in ordinances, that in Himself He might make the two [Jew and Gentile] into one new man, thus establishing peace, and might reconcile them both in one body to God through the cross, by it having put to death the enmity (Ephesians 2:14-16).

How did reconciliation become a reality? As Paul says in verse 14, Jesus "broke down the barrier of the dividing wall." Archeologists have discovered that there was a literal wall that divided the inner court of the temple (where the Jews worshiped) from the outer court (where the Gentiles worshiped). An inscription on the wall, unearthed in 1871 at the site of the temple, carried these words: "No man of another race is to proceed within the partition and enclosing wall about the sanctuary; and anyone arrested there will have himself to blame for the penalty of death which will be imposed as a consequence."[14]

This wall extended far beyond the temple; it became a symbolic wall in the psyche of the Jews. It reflected the Jewish sense of religious and moral superiority. Jewish attitudes toward the heathen became fixed and unforgiving: "We're God's chosen; you're not! We're special; you're not! We're of Abraham; you're not! Stay away!"

This same wall divides whites and blacks today. One of the things that angers black Americans is an unspoken white superiority. It's an attitude that says "We're special; you're not! We're superior; you're not! Stay away!" It's the same self-righteous arrogance the Jews held toward the Gentiles.

The wall of bigotry, both ancient and modern, can be dismantled only through the life and death of Jesus Christ. When Christ appeared, He destroyed the arrogance that set a man against his neighbor, a Jew against a Gentile, a white against a black. Our Lord lived an impeccable life. His moral perfection exposed the hypocrisy of religious arrogance and pride. The Jew understood for the first time that he, like the Gentile, stood equally condemned before a holy God. All were equal— equally sinful!

> The person who lays heavy stress on the social, national, racial, physical, political, intellectual, moral, or religious differences among men has overlooked the one difference that dwarfs all others into comparative insignificance. They have not learned that there's only one crucial difference in life. And this is not the difference which separates the Assyrian from the Jew, nor that which separates the suave cosmopolitan from the swarthy farmer, nor even that which separates the saint from the sinner. The only really crucial difference is that which separates the Creator and creature.[15]

The cross obliterates all man-made distinctions. It alters our perspective and exposes the real issue at stake—our sin. The redemptive work of Christ spills over into our social relationships as well. One of the consequences of true redemption, according to the apostle, is reconciliation: God "makes the two [Jew and Gentile; black and white] into one new man" (Ephesians 2:14). He's talking about a synthesis of people—in effect, a *third race*. Gentiles didn't become Jews; Jews didn't become Gentiles. Instead, with ethnic distinctions intact, they both became something altogether new—Christians—a people who transcended racial distinctives and cultural differences and found common ground in the most desolate of places—the foot of the cross.

Common ground is a hill called Calvary. At Calvary, blacks don't have to become white; whites don't have to become black. Neither race is good enough for peace. But we must become *Christian*—in our attitudes, our language, and our behavior. For too long we have fixed our attention solely upon the *differences.* In our prejudice and pride we see only walls. It is time for the wall of racial pride to come down. Like the Berlin Wall, it must be dismantled, bit by bit. In our churches. In our families. In our hearts. The credibility of the gospel hangs in the balance. The legacy of race relations in America can and will be determined by the present generation of Christians:

> If segregation is wrong, we alone must bear the responsibility for the perpetuation of a segregated society. While we may trace its existence to the sinful choice of a previous generation, we cannot justify its perpetuation on this ground. If perpetuated beyond this generation, it will be due chiefly to the sinful choice of this generation. If we would, we could reduce the evils of segregation.[16]

A Place to Start

As Christians who live in the midst of a racially charged society, healing must begin with you and me. Therefore, let me suggest three steps of racial reconciliation you can take for the sake of your family, your community, and the gospel of Jesus Christ.

1. Confess and repent of any racial sins. Do you harbor feelings of superiority or attitudes of bitterness toward people of another color? Have you referred to others using derogatory words? Do you indulge the temptation to reinforce racial stereotypes or traffic in racial jokes? Regardless of your upbringing or past experiences, the Bible is the final arbiter of truth.

Every human being has been created in God's image, and for this reason is worthy of your respect. The golden rule is not color-blind. Confess your sins to the Lord and make a commitment to relate to others as Jesus Christ did—with integrity and grace and respect.

2. Pray. Pray for your church and the families represented there. Pray for your community. It's time for all of us to wake up and take an active role in reconciliation. Passivity won't work. Billy Graham has said that "racial and ethnic hostility is the chief social problem in our world today." He adds: "Of all people, Christians should be the most active in reaching out to those of other races instead of settling for the status quo." We must pray that individuals and families will begin to take seriously their calling as "ambassadors for Christ" (2 Corinthians 5:20).

3. Commit yourself to acts of reconciliation. We need to join with our brothers and sisters (of all races) and take an active part in destroying the walls that exist between us. For example, our church sponsors a helping hand program that is designed to build relationships with those within the inner city. Hundreds of people from our body donate their time and invest their lives year-round to help make reconciliation a reality. We have also joined with black churches and civic groups to work together on a number of special projects. Our goal is to bridge the chasm that separates white from black; to build authentic relationships.

But even more important than programs are the individual and family acts of reconciliation that all of us can practice: a kind word, a helping hand, an invitation to dinner, a genuine friendship. Ultimately, these are the only qualities that can dismantle the wall of separation and make the church what she was created to be: one body—the body of Christ.

In March 1981, three Ku Klux Klansmen drove the darkened streets of Mobile, Alabama, intent upon killing a black man. They were upset because a Mobile jury had recently failed to convict a black defendant charged with murdering a white policeman. These men were determined to exact vengeance upon the first black they could find. Their unfortunate victim that winter night was nineteen-year-old Michael Donald.

The three Klansmen spotted Donald on the street and enticed him to their car by asking for directions to a night club. They grabbed him and drove the young man out of town. Michael Donald was beaten senseless. His throat was slashed with a knife and his body was hung from a tree in Mobile. The killers then lit a cross on the front lawn of the county courthouse.

Two of the three men were brought to trial. Tiger Knowles was sentenced to life in prison; Henry Hayes was given the death penalty.

Six years passed.

In February 1987, Michael Donald's family decided to bring a civil suit against the Klan for their part in Michael's death. The Donalds filed a seven-million-dollar lawsuit against the organization, seeking compensatory damages for the brutal slaying. The stage was set for high drama. Yet no one could have anticipated the miraculous turn of events that would transpire at the outset of this second trial.

Following his conviction for murder, Tiger Knowles had become a Christian. Knowles now felt deep remorse for his part in the killing. As he entered the courtroom, Knowles approached the mother of the slain teenager. Michael's mother, Beulah May, had been so upset by her son's death that she had been unable to attend the first trial. Tiger Knowles stood before Mrs. Donald and, in a quivering voice, spoke the following words: "Mrs. Donald, I want you to know that if I could change places with your son right now, I would do so. Will you forgive me?"

This godly woman, who knew all too well the painful agony of grief, didn't hesitate in her response. She said, simply, "Son, I've already forgiven you."

Only the cross could stir a killer to ask for forgiveness; only the cross could bring a grieving mom to accept it.

This is the miracle of reconciliation.

In this chapter I have focused on the struggle between black people and white people because I'm from the South; this is the racial conflict I'm most familiar with. But *all* racial strife is abhorrent to our Lord. Christians must seek reconciliation with one another—we are all part of one Body.

At the culmination of human history, one group of people will stand in the presence of the King of kings. Their distinguishing marks will not be the color of their skin, nor the tone of their voice. That which sets this group apart will be their delight in Jesus Christ. When the Book of Life is opened, the twenty-four elders who worship before the Lamb will cry out:

> Worthy art Thou to take the book, and to break its seals; for Thou wast slain, and didst purchase for God with Thy blood men from every tribe and tongue and people and nation. And Thou hast made them to be a kingdom and priests to our God; and they will reign upon the earth (Revelation 5:9-10).

Beulah May Donald will be part of this group. So will Tiger Knowles. Red, yellow, black, and white. They are, and will be, precious in His sight. It's time to believe and embrace this biblical reality. It's time to teach our children this real family value, too.

Notes

[1] Ralph Ellison, *Invisible Man* (New York: Vintage Books, 1990), 3.

[2] Jared Taylor, *Paved with Good Intentions* (New York: Carroll & Graft Publishers, Inc., 1992), 11.

[3]Harry S. Ashmore, *Civil Rights and Wrongs:* (New York: Pantheon Books, 1994), xvi.

[4]"Keeper of the Rage," *Essence*, February 1991, 28.

[5]Thomas Sowell, *Inside American Education* (New York: The Free Press, 1993), 132.

[6]"America's Youthful Bigots," U.*S. News and World Report*, 7 May 1990, 59.

[7]"The Myth of Racial Progress," *Christianity Today*, 4 October 1993, 16.

[8]Ibid., 19.

[9]William H. Baker, *In the Image of God: A Biblical View of Humanity* (Chicago, Ill.: Moody, 1991), 124.

[10]M. F. Ashley Montague, *Man's Most Dangerous Myth: The Fallacy of Race* (Oxford, England: Oxford University Press, 1942; 5th edition revised and enlarged, 1974), 74.

[11]C. S. Lewis, *The Weight of Glory* (New York: Macmillan, 1962), 19.

[12]In his book *The Content of our Character*, black professor Shelby Steele argues that "the unconscious replaying of our oppression is now the greatest barrier to our full equality" (49). Egregious as past injustices may be, when any man, black or white, rehearses the pain of the past, it carries over into the present. It would be unfair to treat a man cruelly simply because his grandfather was a murderer. It is equally unfair to treat a man cruelly simply because his ancestors were racists.

[13]Alfred Edersheim, *The Life and Times of Jesus the Messiah* (Grand Rapids, Mich.: Eerdman's, 1971), 91.

[14]Everett Tilson, *Segregation and the Bible* (Nashville: Abingdon Press, 1958), 66.

[15]Ibid., 120-121.

[16]Ibid., 127-128.

CHAPTER FOURTEEN

THE UNBORN

"The sacred rights of mankind are not to be rummaged for among old parchments or musty records. They are written, as with a sunbeam, in the whole volume of human nature,...and can never be erased or obscured."

ALEXANDER HAMILTON

Carol Everett is a defector. For years this talented woman used her business skills to administrate four abortion clinics in Dallas, Texas. Under Carol's management the corporation's income skyrocketed. She was also an aggressive marketer. At the behest of junior high and high school administrations, Carol conducted sex education seminars—and received a $25 commission from the clinic for every referral that ended in abortion. It didn't matter whether the girls were pregnant or not, the clinics performed the procedures anyway.

The passion Carol brought to her career was motivated by the need to justify her own abortion years earlier. "If all these women are having abortions," she reasoned to herself, "then my own abortion was okay."[1]

When Carol's boss refused to give her a bigger share of the income, she opened two abortion clinics across town. The entrepreneurial venture proved to be a cash windfall. Miss Everett brought home nearly $13,000 a month.

The cumulative statistics of Carol's abortion venture boggle the mind. By her own estimation, Carol was responsible for the death of thirty-five thousand children. She also knows of nineteen mothers who were "maimed" while undergoing the procedure. One mother died.

Then the defection occurred. Just as God had intervened in the life of a slave trader named John Newton over two hundred years ago, God intervened in the life of Carol Everett. In 1983 Carol severed her involvement with the abortion industry. A local pastor shared Christ with Carol, and for the first time in her life, this sinner-turned-saint began to observe, and admit to, the horrors of legalized abortion.

> After I prayed with Jack [the pastor], I went back [to the clinic] a few hours later. When I walked in the door, I saw that everyone in the waiting room was crying—something I'd never noticed before. I began talking to these girls, and for the first time I listened instead of trying to sell them an abortion....

> Later that afternoon, I went back to the room where the doctors were performing second trimester abortions. Although I called fetuses "babies," I hadn't considered them to be human; I rationalized that God didn't intend for aborted fetuses to live. But I suddenly thought, "These babies have all the organs they need to sustain life." At that moment, I knew God had not intended for them to die—that these fetuses were human beings.[2]

Today Carol Everett heads a new venture—Life Network—a non-profit corporation that provides post-abortion counseling to women like herself who have been traumatized by this insidious evil many call "choice." Carol travels the country—speaking to churches and testifying before Senate subcommittees—for the express purpose of telling the truth about abortion.

The Truth about Abortion

What is the truth about abortion? Consider a few facts. Fifty-five million abortions will be performed worldwide this year, 1.6 million in America alone. That works out to more than 4,000 every day, 177 every hour. In fact, in the minute that it took you to read the first page of this chapter, three more innocent lives were terminated, violently. The numbers are mind-boggling. But they're just that—numbers. The most you'll ever hear from our liberally biased media are numbers. After all, numbers are benign; they lack personality and identity. Numbers don't cry when they're scalded by saline solution or bleed when they've been pierced by the "surgeon's" knife.

No, to get to the truth about abortion, you have to ask hard questions the kind of questions most of us would just as soon ignore. Questions such as: *When does human life begin? Is the unborn child a person? What really takes place in an abortion clinic? Why do many women still feel guilty years after undergoing an abortion? Why do many abortion providers (doctors, nurses, counselors) wrestle with shame and guilt themselves? What are the driving forces behind abortion?* These are just a few of the questions that rarely see the light of public discourse but which are key to our understanding the truth about abortion.

For most of us, the truth about abortion is simply too hard to bear. The response of many inside the church is denial; the response of many outside the church is *anger.* A few years ago I had the opportunity to speak to the senior class at the University of Arkansas Law School, here in Little Rock. We discussed a number of moral issues, but when the question of abortion was broached, one female student shouted at me: "We're not going to agree on this, so let's not talk about it." For a few moments, the entire class was silent. I said, "No, I disagree. I think there are many things that we could learn from one another; we need to talk." But no one wanted to talk. Not about this subject. So we moved on.

The issue of abortion has polarized a minority of Americans into one of two camps: those who refer to themselves euphemistically as "pro-choice," and those who are staunchly pro-life. Emotions tend to run so high that there is little or no constructive interaction between these two groups of people. And caught in the middle is a vast majority of Americans and American families who are either ignorant of, or indifferent to, the most convulsive social issue of our generation.

Our president mirrors the prevailing confusion and self-contradictory nature of many, if not most, Americans. I recall sitting in then Governor Bill Clinton's office years ago, hearing from his lips that he believed abortion was the taking of innocent human life. I've since read statements by President Clinton to the effect that "abortion is almost always wrong." But this is the same Bill Clinton who signed into law the most sweeping pro-abortion legislation in American political history.

The American public consistently tells pollsters that they are disturbed by abortion, that they don't like it and just wish this practice would go away. But this same public continues to elect legislators and pass laws ensuring legal access to abortion on demand.

Driven by Desire

When you get beyond the specious rhetoric deceptively labeled "choice," you discover that the abortion-rights movement is being driven by three powerful forces. "A Woman's Right to Choose" is simply a cheap storefront that hides a much more subtle, insidious agenda.

1. The first force driving the abortion rights movement is radical feminism. As we noted earlier, the goal of radical feminism is not simply justice and fairness; instead, the goal is *sameness*—abolishing any distinctions whatsoever between male and female. Sameness means being able to enjoy all of the male vices—wanton careerism, self-indulgence, sexual adventurism—

with equal passion and liberality. Radical autonomy—without restraint, without obligation—is the ultimate objective of radical feminism.

It is precisely at this point where abortion enters the equation. As many feminists see it, children are a social and economic liability (or more accurately, a "disability"). Women are disadvantaged from birth by the ability to conceive. In their view, women must be freed from their ability to conceive if they are to have the same adventures in life as men.

A Planned Parenthood advertisement I once saw in *Ms.* magazine clearly identified the link between feminism and abortion: "Abortion makes all other rights for women possible." How ironic it is that for feminists to obtain the "rights" of men, they must deny the rights of unborn children. In seeking liberation, they become oppressors. Noting this bald, audacious contradiction, Sidney Callahan writes:

> If women can either confer or withhold fetal right by private choices, then logically a woman's own rights are endangered when she is no longer wanted. In fact, women were all too recently legally defined, like the fetus today, as subordinate appendages to their husband-owners, considered part of a one-flesh dyad which the husband controlled at will.[3]

Radical feminists refuse the fetus the same basic human consideration they have fought to secure for themselves. This inversion of logic and morality has spawned a new generation of victims—the smallest members of the human family, our unborn children.

2. A second force behind the abortion-rights movement is sexual liberation without consequences. While this point could be subsumed under radical feminism, it deserves special consideration. There is much debate in the public arena today about the propriety of sex education: advocates argue, "kids are going to do it anyway," while opponents decry the exposure of young minds to "age-inappropriate" material. To appease their opposition, a growing number of sex educators reluctantly teach abstinence—often with a condescending attitude.[4] Others refuse to teach it at all. Why this aversion to abstinence? Does this attitude derive from the benign conclusion: "They're going to do it anyway"? I don't think so.

We are totally hoodwinked if we believe abstinence is pooh-poohed in the public schools because educators believe kids are going to have sex regardless of what they are told. There is a more sinister explanation. For many sexual educators, especially pioneers of the movement, abstinence is anathema for a different reason. At the core of their humanistic belief system, this potent group of people believes that consensual sex at almost any age is permissible, even desirable. Children should seek to express themselves sexually without reservation; they just need to be sure to use a condom.

Does this sound incredible? Let me give you an illustration. A few years ago I happened to be watching *Firing Line*. This particular night Gary Bauer of the Family Research Council was debating a sex educator employed by the U.S. government. Bauer and his female counterpart were arguing the pros and cons of sex education. As you can imagine, the dialogue grew rather heated at times. When the issue of abstinence was broached, this woman attacked the concept, dismissing it (as they often do) as a religious idea.

But in the midst of the woman's diatribe, Gary Bauer went on the offensive. He said, "I think it would be helpful if you told us what *you* believe." Then, going for the jugular, Bauer added, "Is it right or wrong for my twelve-year-old son to have sexual intercourse with your eleven-year-old daughter?" Clearly stuck for an answer, she fired back, "Gary, that's not the real issue here!" "No," replied Bauer, "this is the real issue, because how you answer this question ultimately determines what our children will be taught about sex." Still she hesitated. Like a bulldog, Bauer bore down, pressing for an answer. Finally, after a few minutes of verbal fisticuffs, the answer squeaked from her lips. To Bauer's question, "Is it okay for my twelve-year-old son to have sex with your eleven-year-old daughter," the woman replied, "Yes."

This is a very damning admission. Yet it is perfectly consistent with the basic tenets of sex-education philosophy. Sexual liberation without consequences, as an operative principle, drives and defines every facet of sex-education in the public arena—especially abortion. The founder of Planned Parenthood, Margaret Sanger, articulated this agenda in her book, *Woman Rebel*: "A woman's right is to live, to love, to be lazy, to be an unwed mother, to create, and to destroy."[5] In Sanger's mind, abortion was necessary to ensure sexual freedom for women. In 1916 she said, "Our business is unlimited sexual gratification without the burden of unwanted children."[6] Abortion is only a means to an end in the Bold New World. Sexual liberation without consequences is the real agenda.

3. The final force behind the abortion-rights' movement is money. Planned Parenthood is a corporate giant, worth in excess of $167 million.[7] Much of this corporation's money derives from federal grants and state subsidies. Planned Parenthood operates 879 clinics nationwide, and is staffed by more than 30,000 employees and volunteers.[8] What is often forgotten in the abortion debate is the fact that abortion is big business. And the "profit motive" adds a whole new dimension to this hideous subject. For example, abortion industry insider Carol Everett was privy to an all-too-common practice, that of reducing the dosage of birth control pills.

> The doctors at the clinic prescribed low-dose birth control pills with a high failure rate, knowing they needed to be taken accurately at the same time every day or pregnancy would occur. This ensured that teens would

be my best customers, since they usually aren't responsible enough to follow such rigid medication guidelines on their own.[9]

Driven by the profit motive, many clinics will perform abortions on women who are not even pregnant; or they will advertise free pregnancy tests and then charge a fee when one is administered. Crouching surreptitiously behind the banner of "choice" is an insatiable appetite for MONEY.

The Inescapable Question

No movement, regardless of its objective, can be considered legitimate if it condones and practices the indiscriminate slaughter of human life. Women's rights, sexual liberation, money—none of these goals justifies the unmitigated destruction of human beings, if this is in fact what is taking place. When you cut away the protests and the rhetoric, the politics and the passion, you are left with one inescapable question: *When does human life begin?*

Could there be a more significant family value than this? "I don't know" simply won't work. The issue is too important. The implications are too serious. Is the fetus (Latin for "young one") a human being, endowed by our Creator with the same inalienable rights set forth in our Constitution, or is it merely "a blob in the belly," as one ACLU member once told me?

To answer this question, let's consider three authorities with a vested interest in the abortion debate: science, the Bible, and the state. It will help us to begin by differentiating between each of these arenas. Science, the Bible, and the state each play a distinct role in answering the question: When does human life begin? Science deals primarily with *facts*—truths that can be known by empirical evidence. The Bible deals primarily with *faith*—truths that can be known intrinsically; these truths are intuitive and cannot be proven scientifically. The third authority, government, deals primarily with *rights*.

It's important to remember that the state, regardless of the testimony of science and the Bible, is the one agency which bears the responsibility of conferring *legal rights* within a given society.

This is an important distinction because when these three streams are intertwined, people become confused. For instance, when the Supreme Court handed down its decision in the *Roe v. Wade* case, the justices were not dealing with the scientific evidence of when human life begins. Instead, they were concerned with that point in human development when a fetus could be granted the legal rights of *personhood*. The justices chose what they considered the moment of "viability." But this was a *legal* declaration. They were not speaking scientifically. The *Roe v. Wade* decision determined (or more accurately, "denied") the legal status of personhood for the unborn child; it did not answer the question: When does human life begin?

The difference between the two is crucial. Personhood is a legal status, recognized by the courts. Life itself is something far more profound; it is conferred, not by judicial proclamation but by a wise, omniscient God. As Alexander Hamilton stated: "The sacred rights of mankind are not to be rummaged for among old parchments or musty records. They are written, as with a sunbeam, in the whole volume of human nature,...and can never be erased or obscure."[10] Not even by legal proclamation.

It is crucial that we recognize the distinctions between science, the Bible, and the state. Each speaks with a different voice, to a different objective. For example, when Molly Yard, former president of NOW (the National Organization for Women) declares "If you [have] ever seen an abortion...nothing comes out except a bunch of blood," you must realize that she is making a statement of *faith*, not of *fact*, for science tells us that an aborted fetus is much more than "a bunch of blood."

Or consider this statement in a pamphlet published by the National Abortion Rights Action League (NARAL): "Personhood at conception is a religious belief, not a provable biological fact." Personhood is a religious belief? No, it isn't! Personhood is a legal declaration; it's something conferred by the state. Any black person living in the 1850s, or any legally oppressed woman living in the early twentieth century would have seen through this faulty line of reasoning. Oppressed blacks and oppressed women laughed and loved and bled and cried. But the state, for whatever reasons, refused to confer upon them the legal standing of full *personhood*. Personhood is a legal declaration, not a religious belief.

The Testimony of Science

With these three distinctions in mind—science, the Bible, and the state—let's again turn to the question at hand: When does human life begin? Consider now the testimony of science. The objective observer makes a startling discovery when he examines the facts of science. In bold, unabashed logic, the scientific evidence shouts unequivocally that human life begins at conception! At no other time in the gestation period can we conclude that life suddenly, miraculously appears. It doesn't occur during the five- to nine-day period when the egg is implanted in the uterine wall; it doesn't occur when the fetus takes on a human-like appearance at eight weeks of age. Life doesn't begin at the point of quickening (four to five months into pregnancy), the moment when the mother begins to feel her baby move inside the womb, nor does it begin at the point of viability.

Science is absolutely clear on this point. The testimony of science is undeniable—*human life begins at conception*. At conception the unborn child is endowed with a genetic code related to, but distinct from, his or her mother. In other words, the developing unborn child is not an "appendage" of the mother, but a unique and separate living being who, for a time, is "attached" to the mother.

In his outstanding book, *The Moral Question of Abortion*, Stephen Schwarz presents the compelling, unique, and miraculous characteristics of this slowly developing human life. "The child and mother" writes Schwarz, "do not exchange blood, the child having from a very early point in its development its own and complete vascular system."[11] (This explains why only 30 percent of newborns born to AIDS-infected mothers acquire the virus themselves; in most cases, infection occurs when the child is exposed to the mother's blood in the birth canal.) Science has proven that the fetal heartbeat, detected at five and a half weeks, is "essentially similar to that of an adult in general configuration."[12]

Brain waves have been observed as early as forty-three days.[13] (Note: The unborn child possesses a heartbeat and brain waves much earlier than when the vast majority of abortions are performed.) From the moment of conception, the essential nature of the fetus is unchanged. He or she simply grows older, bigger, and more complex. There is no "other moment" of life.

Like Carol Everett, Dr. Bernard Nathanson is also a defector from the abortionist camp. The co-founder of NARAL, Dr. Nathanson established the most prodigious abortion clinic on the Eastern seaboard. His New York clinic had ten operating rooms and employed thirty-five doctors and eighty-five nurses. They performed 120 abortions a day, seven days a week. Directly or indirectly, Dr. Nathanson was involved in 75,000 abortions.

But his attitude toward abortion changed drastically in 1983. At that time, a number of new technologies were flooding the medical profession. With the advent of ultrasound, fetal heart monitoring and fetoscopy (an optical instrument inserted into the womb to observe the fetus), Dr. Nathanson became aware of a hidden world he had never seen before. What he saw changed his life.

As a result of all of this technology—looking at this baby, examining it, investigating it, watching its metabolic functions, watching it urinate, swallow, move and sleep, watching it dream, which you could see by its rapid eye movements via ultrasound, treating it, operating on it—I finally came to the conviction that this was my patient. This was a person! I was a physician, pledged to save my patients' lives, not to destroy them. So I changed my mind on the subject of abortion.[14]

Nathanson adds: "There was nothing religious about it. This was purely a change of mind as the result of this fantastic [scientific] technology, and the new insights and perceptions I had into the nature of the unborn child."[15]

There are many others within the scientific community who, much like Dr. Nathanson, have reached the same conclusion. Dr. Landrun Shettles, the pioneer of sperm biology, makes this statement: "I oppose abortion. I do so because I accept what is biologically manifest. My position is scientific, pragmatic, and humanitarian."[16] French doctor Jerome LeJeune, the discoverer of the chromosome pattern for Downs syndrome and one of the leading experts in the world in genetics, is even more blunt:

After fertilization has taken place, a new human being has come into being.... It is not my opinion. It is the teaching of all the genetics that I was given. There's no doubt it is a human being....

In testimony before a Senate subcommittee, Dr. LeJeune added:

Whether it has rights or not is not my field [do you hear the distinction between science and government?]. Whether it's a person, the law has to decide. But I'm going to tell you, if any of my students walked into my class and looked at a zygote [a fertilized egg cell before cleavage] or a five-day-old cell structure and said that it's not a human being, I'd throw them out of the class. It *is* a human being."[17]

The evidence is overwhelming. Amazingly enough, even the pro-abortionists have conceded the fact. The majority of pro-abortionists admit that life does indeed begin at conception. They hate to talk about it; they'll dodge this issue like the plague. But in a calculated sleight of hand, they shift the focus from *life* to *personhood.* And when the American public hears any discussion concerning personhood, it assumes we are talking about life. But the enemy is not talking about life. That topic is too dangerous. They want to discuss legalities—and whether or not this entity has the same rights as other persons.

The pro-abortionists dismiss the scientific arguments—they are too conclusive. Likewise, they dismiss the religious arguments—after all, who wants religion to dictate the affairs of daily life? Lacking any tangible evidence, this group uses the weapon of the state. And in a gnarled twist of logic, personhood has been separated from biological life. It happened to black Americans one hundred and fifty years ago; it is happening to unborn children today.

Abortion has now become a legal issue for the government to decide. Pro-abortionists argue that a woman's legal right to self-determination takes precedence over a human being in the womb. If this sounds a little sinister, it is. It's cold and calculating. It is also the culmination of a philosophy that ignores science in the name of self-fulfillment. As Sidney Callahan states, "Basic human rights in an egalitarian morality must be inalienable and not subject to the arbitrary decisions or desires of those who can dominate through strength, social resources, or other forms of privilege and power."[18]

When the intrinsic value of the individual is denied, when the facts of life are ignored, personhood (and our legal definition of personhood) becomes relative to a given culture. This is a very dangerous place to be. The implications extend far beyond the womb—to everyone. For now, this abortion of reason has created the twentieth century equivalent of child sacrifice. In Old Testament times, it was the father who took the child to the priest, to be offered up to Baal; in America, it is the mother (and her lover) who now brings the sacrifice.

The Testimony of the Bible

So much for the undeniable facts of science. What answer does the Bible give to the question: "When does human life begin?" The scriptural response is just as unequivocal. Old Testament scholar Meredith Kline states:

> The most significant thing about abortion legislation in biblical law, is that there is none [on the subject of abortion]. It was so unthinkable that an Israelite woman should desire an abortion that there was no need to mention this offense in the [Old Testament] criminal code.[19]

All that was necessary to prohibit abortion for centuries was just simply the command, "You shall not murder." Every Israelite woman and man knew that the pre-born child was a sacred human being.

From the very first chapter in the book of Genesis, we witness God embossing His image upon the highest of His creatures—man. The image of God in man is the divine signature of man's uniqueness (Genesis 1:26-27). This image is to be revered, even avenged when innocent human life is destroyed (Genesis 9:6). As theologian Millard Erickson writes:

> Because all are in the image of God, nothing should be done which would encroach upon another's legitimate exercise of dominion. Freedom must not be taken from a human who has not forfeited this right.... This means, most obviously, that slavery is improper. Beyond that,

however, it means that depriving someone of freedom through illegal means, manipulation, or intimidation is improper.[20]

Man's creation in God's image endows him with dignity. It raises man to the pinnacle of the created order. From beginning to end, the Bible reasserts the sacredness of human life. This sacredness is explicit in the sixth commandment: "Thou shalt not murder." It is equally explicit in Exodus 21, where God speaks directly concerning the value of unborn children:

> And if men struggle with each other and strike a woman with child so that she has a miscarriage [literally, "the child comes out"], yet there is no further injury, he shall surely be fined as the woman's husband may demand of him; and he shall pay as the judges decide. But if there is any further injury, then you shall appoint as a penalty life for life, eye for eye, tooth for tooth, hand for hand, foot for foot, burn for burn, wound for wound, bruise for bruise (Exodus 21:22-25).

The picture here is of two men fighting; a pregnant woman gets involved in the conflict and is struck by one of the combatants, causing her to deliver prematurely. On the surface, this passage seems to refer to stillbirth, thus implying that fetal human life is of lesser value than non-fetal human life. The confusion arises over the editors' translation (in this case, the NASB) of the Hebrew word *dalay*—"miscarriage." But as Robert N. Congdon points out in an article on this passage, this Hebrew word "always means 'living child' or one capable of living outside the womb."[21]

I talked personally with Old Testament scholar Walter Kaiser about this particular verse. His response was emphatic: "It does not mean 'miscarriage.' " In Exodus 23:26, Moses uses a different word commonly translated "miscarriage." This word was in his vocabulary, but he didn't use it here. The prophet is not referring to miscarriage; instead, he is addressing a live birth. So here's the logic: A man strikes a woman, causing her to deliver prematurely. If there is no further injury (to the child or mother), then the man shall pay a fine. But if further injury occurs (to the child or mother), then the guilty party shall pay according to the judicial principle of *lex talionis*—life for life.

This principle would have made perfect sense to an Israelite, for the simple reason that God affirms the value of fetal life throughout the Scriptures. Speaking of the prophet Jeremiah, God says: "Before I formed you in the womb, I knew you, and before you were born, I consecrated you" (Jeremiah 1:5). The psalmist David, in one of the most forceful statements in the Bible, recognizes and affirms God's intimate relationship with the unborn child:

> For Thou didst form my inward parts; Thou didst weave me in my mother's womb. I will give thanks to Thee, for I am fearfully and wonderfully made; wonderful are Thy works, and my soul knows it very well. My frame was not hidden from Thee, when I was made in secret, and skillfully wrought in the depths of the earth. Thine eyes have seen my unformed substance; and in Thy book they were all written, the days that were ordained for me, when as yet there was not one of them (Psalm 139:13-16).

When we come to the New Testament, we discover this same divine endearment for fetal life. Announcing the presentation of the Messiah, the angel of God says, "Behold, the virgin shall be with child" (Matthew 1:23). Not "potential human life." Not the impersonal "fetus." Matthew uses the word "child," denoting *full personhood.* When Elizabeth was six months pregnant with John the Baptist, and Mary, the mother of Jesus, had come to visit her, Luke tells us that "the baby leaped in her womb" (Luke 1:41). The *baby.*

Probably the greatest witness to the biblical position is seen in the transformation that occurred throughout the Roman

Empire as Christians mixed with a secular society. For most pagans, abortion was an easy (and common) alternative to childbirth and parenting. It was not uncommon for Roman women to have three, four, even *five* abortions during their lifetime. But as the early Christians fanned out across the Empire, disseminating their convictions about the sacredness of human life, profound changes took place. Historian Lawrence E. Stager summarizes the influence these first Christians exerted upon their promiscuous culture:

> Jews and Christians took a pro-natalist attitude toward conception and children. This attitude must have contributed significantly to prohibitions against homosexuality and bisexual behavior. They were adamantly against contraception, abortion, and infanticide, whereas the Romans were not....[22]

Confronted by a permissive society, early Christian apologists began to articulate the biblical teaching on abortion. Their statements served to buttress what was clearly manifest in the scriptural record. For example, in the early second-century Epistle of Barnabas, it says, "You shall love your neighbor as your own life. You shall not slay a child by abortion." *The Didache*, a second-century teaching manual, contains these words: "Do not murder a child by abortion or kill a newborn infant." Clement of Alexandria, a church leader in the second- century, wrote these words: "Those who use abortifacient medicines to hide their fornication cause not only the outright murder of the fetus but of the whole human race as well." And Tertullian said: "It does not matter whether you take away a life that is born, or destroy one coming to the birth. In both instances, destruction is murder."

Such historical documentation is so pervasive that Dr. Bruce Metzger, renowned New Testament scholar, was forced to conclude: "It is really remarkable how uniform and how pronounced was the early Christian opposition to abortion."[23]

Going one step further, Harold O. Brown summarizes the teaching of Christian leaders down to the present:

> The overwhelming consensus of the spiritual leaders of Protestantism, from the Reformation to the present, is clearly anti-abortion. There is very little doubt among biblically oriented Protestants that abortion is an attack on the image of God in the developing child and is a great evil.[24]

The Biblical position is CONCLUSIVE. Nevertheless, Christians in America's churches are confused. They watch church leaders and denominations step forward in support of abortion rights, they hear charismatic religious leaders say "a woman ought to have the legal right to abortion," and they wonder to themselves, *Is this a toss-up? Why is there so much dissension, even within the religious community, over this issue?*

The answer is crystal clear. It is vital that you realize that, when church leaders speak out in support of abortion rights, they have broken with both the authority of Scripture and the long-standing historical tradition of orthodox Christianity! Many of these leaders have even repudiated the very founders of their denominations—to crawl pathetically behind a degenerate culture. They affirm the guilty and betray the innocent. And most tragic of all is the fact that these heterodox Christians do it all in the name of justice!

The Final Witness—Experience

The testimonies of science and the Bible are overwhelming: Human life begins at conception. The state, as the divine instrument of justice, is obligated to protect the rights of all its members, a role which our highest court has abdicated in regard to unborn human life. Before summarizing our defense of the unborn child, let's consider the testimony of a final witness—experience. If abortion is right, then a woman should be able to undergo an abortion and feel good about her decision.

But just the opposite is what most often occurs. A vast number of women never seem to be able to forget the day when they aborted their baby. Many women now suffer from "post-abortion syndrome"—they experience flashbacks to that fateful day in the abortion clinic and are consumed with unrelenting guilt and shame, both of which haunt them for a lifetime.

I have counseled a number of women who agonize over this experience. They sob uncontrollably, grieving for a lost child whom they envision constantly—imagining him or her playing baseball, heading off to school, running down the hall-way. The most difficult day of the year for most of these women is the day their child was due to be born—a day which never arrived.

Skeptics will listen to the testimony of experience and dismiss it as religiously motivated. After all, they argue, these are women in the church. They've been made to feel guilt and shame by judgmental Christian leaders.

But this is a hollow defense.

The guilt and shame are real. The surest evidence for this is found in an unlikely source—the abortion providers them-selves. At the other end of the spectrum, among those who are ardently pro-abortion, we witness this same self-doubt, agony, and gut-wrenching pain. Consider the following article from the national *American Medical Association* newspaper, entitled "Abortion Providers Share Their Inner Conflicts." I quote it at length:

> The notion that the nurses, doctors, counselors and others who work in the abortion field have qualms about the work they do is a well kept secret. But among themselves, at work or at meetings with other providers, they talk about how they really feel. About women who come in for "repeat" abortions. About women whose reasons for having abortions aren't ones they consider valid. About their anger towards women

who wait until late in their pregnancies to have elective abortions. And about the feelings they have toward the fetus, especially as gestational age increases. They wonder if the fetus feels pain. They talk about the soul and where it goes. And about their dreams in which aborted fetuses stare at them with ancient eyes and perfectly shaped hands and feet asking, "Why? Why did you do this to me?"

Oddly, many of the issues that disturb abortion foes also seem to trouble the providers.... One counselor from Kansas said, "This may sound like repression; however, it does work for me. When I find myself identifying with a fetus and I think the larger it gets, that's normal...then I think, 'It's OK to consciously decide and remind ourselves to identify with the woman. The external criteria of viability really isn't what it's all about. It's an unwanted pregnancy and that's the bottom line....' "

A nurse who had worked in an abortion clinic for less than a year said her most troubling moments came not in the procedure room, but afterwards. Many times, she said, "Women who had abortions would lie in the recovery room and cry, 'I've just killed my baby; I've just killed my baby!' I don't know what to say to these women," the nurse told the group. "Part of me thinks, 'Maybe they're right.' "[25]

Even at the farthest end of the spectrum, the conscience screams: "Human life begins at conception!"

Speak Up!

In the face of such overwhelming evidence, the Christian is left with a singular response: "I've got to do something." Let me give you four action points you can implement to make a difference in our Bold New World.

1. Use correct terminology. This may seem like a small point, but it is extremely important. Make a determined effort to speak of "abortion," not "choice." You may have noticed that the phrase "pro-choice" has not appeared previously in this chapter. "Choice" is not a synonym for "abortion." Choice is a euphemism for death. Pro-abortionists have surreptitiously coined the phrase to move the issue away from the central tenet of the debate—life itself. When you engage your world in dialogue, remember that life is the crucial question. Use correct terminology.

2. Speak out for the unborn at every opportunity. These defenseless children have no voice—other than yours. Speak out in your school and at work; write editorials to the local newspaper in support of our unborn children. Psalm 82:3-4 admonishes us to "Vindicate the weak and fatherless; do justice to the afflicted and destitute. Rescue the weak and needy; deliver them out of the hand of the wicked." John Leo, writing in *Time*, has observed correctly that the pro-life argument will eventually win because truth ultimately rests in their camp. We *will* win. But how many more must die before God's people speak up?

3. Encourage women with unplanned and unwanted pregnancies to seek adoption. If you were to come into my office at church, you would discover the picture of a baby boy on my desk. This little guy is one of the great joys of my life. His mother, a single woman, became pregnant and turned to me for counseling. I encouraged this young woman to bear her child and place him up for adoption—advice she wisely heeded. And as a gift to me, this courageous woman named her son Robert—after me. Somewhere in the United States, a beautiful, blonde-haired baby boy is bringing untold joy to a couple who couldn't have children of their own—all because one brave woman refused to make two mistakes instead of one.

4. Support the crisis pregnancy centers and adoption agencies in your community. These agencies are in desperate need of your volunteer time and your money. You can make a tangible difference for life—if you are willing to pay a small, but invaluable, price.

LIFE...WHAT A BEAUTIFUL CHOICE!

Notes

[1]"Amazing Grace," *Today's Christian Woman*, March/April 1993, 29.

[2]Ibid., 31.

[3]Donald P. Judges, *Hard Choices, Lost Voices* (Chicago, Ill.: Ivan R. Dee, 1993), 156.

[4]When abstinence is taught in the public school, it is often presented as an alternative to "safe sex," just another choice among many others. But as William Kilpatrick points out (*Why Johnny Can't Tell Right from Wrong*, Simon and Schuster, 1992, 97-98), this is tantamount to giving someone the choice of running in a marathon when he has failed to train for it. "An individual can't choose to do something if he lacks the capacity for it. For example, running the Boston Marathon is not a choice for those who are out of shape. It only becomes a choice for those who are willing to put in many months of training." Kilpatrick correctly identifies the relationship between choices and habits. Abstinence only becomes a choice when it is purchased with self-discipline. To present it as one choice among many, apart from a training regimen, is ludicrous.

[5]Don Feder, *A Jewish Conservative Look at Pagan America* (Lafayette, La.: Huntington House Publishers, 1993), 182.

[6]William Gairdner, *The War Against the Family* (Toronto, Canada: Stoddart, 1992), 464.

[7]"Abortion, Inc.," David Kupelian and Jo Ann Gasper, *New Dimensions*, October 1991, 12.

[8]Ibid, 16.

[9]"Amazing Grace," 77.

[10]Donald P. Judges, *Hard Choice*, 118.

[11]Stephen Schwarz, *The Moral Question of Abortion* (Chicago, Ill.: Loyola University Press, 1990), 3.

[12]Ibid.

[13]Ibid.

[14]David Kupelian and Mark Masters, "Pro-choice 1991: Skeletons in the Closet," *New Dimensions*, October 1991, 40.

[15]Ibid.

[16]Landrun Shettles and David Rorvik, *Rites of Life: The Scientific Evidence of Life Before Birth* (Grand Rapids, Mich.: Zondervan Publishing House, 1983), 103.

[17]"Subcommittee on Separation of Power to Senate Judiciary Committee S-158," 97th Congress, First Session, 1981. Dr. LeJeune has been called upon to testify many times on behalf of the unborn child. His testimony is always powerful and compelling.

[18]Donald P. Judges, *Hard Choices*, 156.

[19]Meredith Kline, "Lex Talionis and the Human Fetus," *The Journal of the Evangelical Theological Society*, September 1977, 193.

[20]Millard Erickson, *Christian Theology*, 2 (Grand Rapids, Mich.: Baker, 1984), 517.

[21]Robert N. Congdon, "Exodus 21:22-25 and the Abortion Debate," *Bibliotheca Sacra*, Vol. 146, April-June 1989, 138.

[22]"Eroticism and Infanticide at Ashkelon," Lawrence E. Stager, *Biblical Archaeology Review*, July-August 1991, 9.

[23]Michael Gorman, *Abortion and the Early Church* (Downer's Grove, Ill.: InterVarsity Press, 1982), 9.

[24]"Abortion," Harold O. Brown, *The Evangelical Dictionary of Theology*, Walter A. Elwell, ed. (Grand Rapids, Mich.: Baker, 1984), 5.

[25]Diane M. Gianelli, "Abortion Providers Share Their Inner Conflicts," *American Medical Association* newspaper, 12 July 1993, 3.

Final Thoughts

IF it is true that our world is in the midst of a great transition and a new world is being birthed, fundamentally different from the one we have known, *THEN* we can either surrender to the currents of change and let them take us wherever they will, or we can discern our times and set out courageously to reestablish a biblical way of life that will first redeem our families and then our nation.

But it all starts with family…and Real Family Values.

> My orders are to fight;
> Then if I bleed, or fail,
> Or strongly win what matters it?
> God only doth prevail.
> The servant craveth naught
> Except to serve with might.
> I was not told to win or lose—
> My orders are to fight.

> —*Ethelyn Wetherald*

APPENDIX

"What We Believe..."

TWO FAMILIES SHARE
THE REAL FAMILY VALUES
PRACTICED IN THEIR HOMES.

Marriage Values

- We believe it is not good for man to be alone (Genesis 2:18).

- We believe God has provided a suitable woman (Genesis 2:18) for a man and brings them together in marriage to enjoy a life-long union (Matthew 19:6), to become one flesh (Genesis 2:24; Ephesians 5:31), to fulfill sexual desires (1 Corinthians 7:2-3), to build a strong family unit (Titus 2:4-5), to raise up godly offspring (Deuteronomy 6:4-9), and to provide a picture to the world of Christ's love for His body, the church (Ephesians 5:22-23).

Husband's Role and Responsibility

- We believe the husband is the servant-leader of the marriage and family (Luke 22:25-27; Matthew 20:28; Ephesians 5:23; 1 Timothy 3:2-4,12), lover (Ephesians 5:25,28,33; 1 Peter 3:7-8), protector and provider (Ephesians 5:29; 1 Peter 3:7), and encourager (1 Peter 3:8; Proverbs 31:28-30) of his wife and family.

Wife's Role and Responsibility

- We believe the wife is the helper/supporter (Genesis 2:18; 1 Corinthians 2:18), lover (Titus 2:45; 1 Peter 3:1-6), admirer (Ephesians 5:33; Song of Solomon 5:10-16), sexual responder (Song of Solomon 3:4; 1 Corinthians 7:2-3), willingly submitting to her husband (Ephesians 5:22-24; 1 Peter 3:1-6), and working to build up her home to know, love, and follow Christ (Proverbs 31:10-31; 1 Timothy 2:15; Titus 2:4-5).

Fidelity

- We value sexual purity and lifetime devotion in marriage—one man, one woman for life (Matthew 19:3-6; 1 Corinthians 7:1-5).

  (Observed: Keep wandering eyes and thoughts in check. Make mate a consistent focus of attention and affection. Regularly and freshly verbalize attraction and devotion to each other.)

Communication

- We value open, honest, transparent interaction intended to increase intimacy, strengthen oneness, and stimulate understanding and growth (Proverbs 18:13; James 1:19; Ephesians 4:29; Colossians 3:16-17; Ephesians 4:15).

  (Observed: Have regular planned [meal times, etc.] or spontaneous occasions where issues are raised, concerns are shared, laughter, sorrow, love, and disappointments are expressed with kindness. Cultivating understanding is the goal.)

Team-effort Parenting

- We value the complementary contribution that each parent's love, personality, background, spiritual maturity, modeling, devotion, and convictions makes to the raising of each child.

  (Observed: Praying, planning, practicing; using a different parenting approach for different children or special circumstances.)

Parenting Values

- We value our children as gifts from God (Psalm 127:3-5—rewards/blessings), worthy of honor and development.

- We believe Dad is to model and teach spiritual life (Deuteronomy 6:4-9), discipline (Hebrews 12:6-13; Ephesians 6:4), set goals, and lead children in the discovery of Christ, life, personal responsibility, and celebration (Psalm 78:72).

- We believe Mom is to love her family (Titus 2:4-5) and give health to her home by nurturing, supporting, and encouraging her husband and children (Proverbs 31).

- We believe spiritual instruction should be consistent, relevant, fresh, conviction-forming, and designed to stimulate our children to love and obey God (Psalm 1; Matthew 22:37-38; 2 Corinthians 5:9; Colossians 1:28), love others (Matthew 22:39-40), and live out their God-given life and mission (Ecclesiastes 12:13-14; 2 Timothy 1:6).

- We believe in developing the character qualities of integrity, forgiveness, service to others, love (1 Corinthians 13:4-8), communication, respect, and spiritual growth.

- We believe God has created each person with purpose, design, and intimate knowledge (Psalm 139:1-6, 13-18). We believe life begins at conception and that human life uniquely displays the image of God and is worthy of protection and nurture. We believe in the sanctity of life.

Career

- We value Mom being at home to provide stability, security, and oversight (training) for the children. We value making decisions affecting Dad's career based on the dynamics of our family (Psalm 8:72). While children are young, we feel it is best for Mom to stay home and be a "worker at home" (Titus 2:5; 1 Timothy 5:14).

Home Values

- While the Bible does not prohibit alcohol use, we do not use alcohol in our home, at family gatherings, on special occasions, or when out with others because of the instruction and exhortation of Scripture and the blight of alcohol and drug addiction in our culture (Proverbs 23:29-35; Proverbs 25:28; Romans 14:13-21; 1 Corinthians 7:24-27; Galatians 5:21: Ephesians 5:18; 1 Peter 4:1-6).

- Although health-care drugs are used, our conviction is that illegal or illicit drugs have no place in our home.

- Prayer forms one of the primary threads in the fabric of a healthy spiritual life.

  (Observed: Prayer is practiced in times of family worship, when facing difficulties or decisions, at times of travel, at bedtimes, and at other meaningful times of discussion.)

- Television offers little benefit to our home. We seldom have the television on during weekdays. It serves us at times with news, sports, and some entertainment. Theater movies are chosen based on theme, content, language, sexual context, kind of humor, general quality, and rating (Philippians 4:8-9; Ephesians 6).

- We believe in generous, first-fruits giving (2 Corinthians 8-9), in response to the wonderful gift of Christ on the cross for us. We are committed to giving 10 percent of our income to the local church in which we serve. We work to develop a giving heart and practice in our children as they give of themselves to serve others and give a portion of their money to support God's work through the church.

- We believe financial responsibility is motivated by our desire to be good stewards of God's material blessings to us. It is our value not to be in debt and to manage finances and debt without putting our family at risk.

  (Observed: We make an effort to adopt a standard of living that enables us to live off of 80 percent of our income, leaving 10 percent for giving and 10 percent for investing. We use credit cards but avoid any interest expense by paying the balance at the end of each month. We do not buy items with credit except our home or possibly a vehicle.)

- We place a high priority on being a contributing and growing part of the body of Christ in our church through worship, growth, community, and service (Hebrews 10:25).

- We believe that our speech should be pure, encouraging to others, and free of profanity and crass slang (Psalm 39:1; Ephesians 4:29-30), that it should be kind and not critical (Psalm 19:14; Proverbs 13:3; Galatians 5:19-20;

Ephesians 5:19; Colossians 3:16-17; James 3:10), timely (Proverbs 15:1, 23; Proverbs 25:11), and that our speech is a reflection of the thoughts of our hearts (Matthew 12:34—"You brood of vipers, how can you, being evil, speak what is good? For the mouth speaks out of that which fills the heart." Matthew 15:18—"But the things that proceed out of the mouth come from the heart, and those defile the man." Luke 6:45—"The good man out of the good treasure of his heart brings forth what is good; and the evil man out of the evil treasure brings forth what is evil; for his mouth speaks from that which fills his heart" (Philippians 4:8).

Marriage Values

We believe biblical marriage is fundamental to a healthy society.
It provides a stable, nurturing environment for children.
It should provide for a man and a woman's need for respect,
love and companionship, and sexual fulfillment.

1) We believe the purpose of marriage is to complete a man and a woman (Genesis 2:18). We believe the biblical responsibility of marriage and family protects a man from becoming selfish and a sexual predator. It allows a woman to fulfill her procreative and nurturing roles protected from destitution and loneliness. For both a man and a woman, it provides emotional security and confidence.

2) We believe marriage is a permanent mystical union, not a legal agreement (Matthew 5:31-32, Matthew 19:3-9). On a regular basis in our home, we look for opportunities to *affirm* verbally to our children our commitment to never divorce and our commitment to love and cherish each other as long as we live. At an appropriate age, we *explain* to each of our children our commitment to the permanency of marriage, the importance of marriage to sex, and the importance of sex in marriage.

3) We believe the pattern of a biblical marriage always contains the following elements (Ephesians 5:33; 1 Peter 3:7; Ephesians 5:31; 1 Corinthians 7:2):

   - Love and respect
   - Dedication to a united life direction
   - Intimacy (physically and emotionally)
   - Commitment to sexual faithfulness

4) We believe the husband's role in marriage is to take responsibility for his wife emotionally, financially, and spiritually. He is an initiator, leading and loving his wife. His role as provider goes beyond the financial, as he responds to her needs, strengths, and weaknesses, and encourages her spiritual growth and development. He knows how to appreciate and enjoy his wife (Genesis 2; Ephesians 5-6; 1 Timothy 5:8).

5) We believe the wife's role in marriage is to be a completer, supporter, and helper to her husband. She provides focused care and attention to his needs, supplementing him with her strengths, insights, and perspectives. She establishes a home environment that ensures emotional security for her husband, characterized by respect, love, trustworthiness, and availability. She follows the leadership of her husband as she manages the daily workings of her household (Genesis 2:18; Titus 2:5; Proverbs 10-27; 1 Peter 3:1-2).

Parenting Values

We believe children are a gift from God. They bring joy, but also a great responsibility. To abort, neglect, abandon, or fail to provide physically or emotionally for a child God has given is to be disobedient to God (Psalm 127:3-5).

1) We believe that the Christian parent is responsible to (1 Timothy 5:8; Ephesians 6:4; Deuteronomy 6:6-7; 1 Timothy 4:16; Proverbs 22:6):

- Provide for the children's physical needs.

- Provide a safe haven of unconditional love and affection.
- Provide guidance, boundaries, affirmation, and correction.
- Teach knowledge of God and character values by model and instruction.
- Understand the children and seek to help them develop their spiritual gifts and personality.

2) We believe the mother uniquely provides focused care and attention to the needs of her children. She establishes a home environment characterized by love, discipline, and kindness in partnership with her husband. She provides a strong sense of security and stability through the "awesome power of being there" (Proverbs 31:1-26; Titus 2:5).

3) We believe the father's role in parenting is to love and lead his family. He accepts the responsibility and takes initiative to provide for his family and to chart a course for their emotional, mental, and spiritual development. He is primarily responsible for teaching truth and values to his children (Deuteronomy 6:6-7; Proverbs 22:6).

Home Values

1) We believe the Christian family is the primary environment for spiritual growth and for experiencing God through (Deuteronomy 11:19; Psalm 119:9,11; Hebrews 10:24-25):

- Family prayer and worship

- Commitment to a local church
- Learning and applying scripture
- Reviewing our daily lives in light of spiritual truth

2) We believe the Christian family should have standards of moral purity in the areas of (Proverbs 20:11; 1 John 2:16; Romans 12:1-9; 1 Timothy 2:9-10; Mark 10:19; Acts 20:34-35; Ephesians 4:29):

- Language (truthful, courteous, encouraging)
- Entertainment (prudent)
- Substance abuse (self-control)
- Dress (modest, not pretentious)
- Money (honesty, giving a fair value)
- Work ethic (not lazy)
- Discrimination (value people and their life station)

3) We believe the Christian family is responsible to contribute to the good of others in the church, as well as the community, by (Matthew 25:35-45; 2 Corinthians. 9:7):

- Giving financially
- Participating in service
- Supporting missions
- Being a contributor

4) We believe the Christian family should be a model of mutual kindness, respect, love, and harmony; with family members learning to consider others, offering encouragement and help (1 Peter 3:8-10).

∾

Conclusion

Let me again encourage each of you reading this book to take the challenge of formalizing your family values as the two couples who have shared their family values above have done. Be creative but get specific! Let your family document serve you and your children the way a *coat of arms* served families of generations past.

ONE FINAL COMMENT: For those of you who do accept this Real Family Values assignment and complete it, would you allow me the opportunity of seeing and reading it? What a privilege! If I can respond to you at the time, I will. Send your documents to:

Robert Lewis, 12601 Hinson Road, Little Rock, AR 72212.

One couple who took me up on this challenge and agreed to let me see their finished document, later wrote me the following letter:

Dear Dr. Lewis:

What an impacting exercise the family values project was for my wife and me. Thank you for the challenge to spend the time to work through this process. The work and time to process these issues as a couple with four children was well worth the effort. It has enriched our understanding of our roles and helped us communicate to each other at a new level how we feel about our needs and abilities in fulfilling these roles.

Our family values document is already a great resource for us. We look forward to communicating it to our children and passing these values on to the next generation.

Thanks again for challenging us to document our profession of Real Family Values.

The Quest for Authentic Manhood

Robert Lewis has teamed with Dad the Family Shepherd to produce a conference for men titled "The Quest for Authentic Manhood." Dr. Lewis has done extensive research on the subject of manhood and has a powerful message to share with men.

The new conference helps men define their real identities and come to a better understanding of the nature of true manhood. "The Quest for Authentic Manhood" explores the barriers to manhood, examines the challenges men face today and, most importantly, helps men develop a personal vision for authentic manhood.

This conference presents dynamic material in a Friday night and Saturday format, then points men toward a process for change through small group accountability.

For more information on
"The Quest for Authentic Manhood" or the original
"Dad the Family Shepherd" conference,
please call 1-800-234-DADS.